Maya Achi Marimba Music  ..cmala

In the series

Studies in Latin American and Caribbean Music

edited by Peter Manuel

Peter Manuel, *East Indian Music in the West Indies: Tân-Singing, Chutney, and the Making of Indo-Caribbean Culture*

María Teresa Vélez, *Drumming for the Gods: The Life and Times of Felipe García Villamil, santero, palero, and abakuá*

Maya Achi Marimba Music in Guatemala

SERGIO NAVARRETE PELLICER

TEMPLE UNIVERSITY PRESS
Philadelphia

Temple University Press
1601 North Broad Street
Philadelphia PA 19122
www.temple.edu/tempress

⊛ The paper used in this publication meets the requirements of the American
National Standard for Information Sciences—Permanence of Paper for Printed
Library Materials, ANSI Z39.48-1992

Library of Congress Cataloging-in-Publication Data

Navarrete Pellicer, Sergio.
  Maya Achi marimba music in Guatemala / Sergio Navarrete Pellicer.
    p.   cm.
  Contents: A history of the Achi people of Rabinal – The belief in the dead –
Concepts and classifications of music – The marimba and the son – Good and
evil : music, alcohol, and women – Musical occasions – Cognition, values, and
the aesthetics of music – The economy of the son and the pieza – Music
within social interaction – Conclusion : "Who am I to know better than the
ancestors?"
  ISBN 1-59213-291-X (cloth : alk. paper) — ISBN 1-59213-292-8
(pbk. : alk. paper)
  1. Achi Indians—Music—History and criticism.   2. Folk music—
Guatemala—Rabinal—History and criticism.   3. Achi Indians—Social life and
customs.   4. Marimba—Guatemala—Rabinal.   5. Ethnomusicology—
Guatemala.   I. Title.

ML3572.G9N38 2005
781.62'9742—dc22   2004062128

2 4 6 8 9 7 5 3 1

Contents

Acknowledgments

IT IS NOT POSSIBLE to thank individually the many people who have supported this project directly or indirectly, in ways large and small. I am indebted to them all but want to mention some in particular.

My most profound debt is to those Rabinalenses who supported and collaborated in my research and who made our stay in Rabinal a pleasant experience, in particular Francisco Mendoza and his family, Jose León Coloch, Celestino and Bernabé Cajbon, Magdaleno Xitumul, Victor Tum, Pedro Morales, Vicenta Manuel Sesam, Julian Ordoñez, and Tono Lopez. Esteban Uanché died during the completion of my doctoral dissertation. He is among those to whom I owe my greatest thanks. His music and his reflections on it inspired this work; moreover, he became a valued friend. He is among Rabinal's greatest musicians and my only solace is that his music lives on and that he will be among the ancestors who continue to make community in Rabinal. Other Rabinalense musicians and friends not only taught me their music and their way of life but also the joys of a social world in which they welcomed my participation despite their understandable fears of dangerous outsiders.

This book is an extensively revised and reworked version of my Ph.D. dissertation, submitted to the University of London in 1999. Financial support was provided by CONACYT and CIESAS in Mexico, two institutions to which I remain indebted. CIESAS has continued to provide me with the opportunity to develop and expand my research as a social anthropologist and ethnomusicologist. For support, encouragement, and critical comments and suggestions, I would like to thank in particular Edward Schieffelin and John Gledhill, who have followed the development of this work since its initial conception as a doctoral thesis. I am thankful to Linda O'Brien, who kindly read the doctoral thesis and contributed important commentary for this book. Francisca Cooper has been a central contributor; her editorial work generated many exciting discussions about anthropology and history; Olivia Harris and Peter Wade made cogent criticisms about the strengths and weaknesses of the main arguments of the thesis that eventually became this book.

Technical support from Roberto Castelarín and Rubén Luengas has been essential for the musical transcriptions and the copying and editing of the music scores presented here.

I am indebted to the late Marcia Herndon and to Thomas Stanford, Carol Robertson, and Henrietta Yurchenco, who were my first mentors in the field of ethnomusicology. I would also like to thank friends and colleagues at my research center in Mexico, CIESAS, for their encouragement and support. Thanks are owed in particular to my friend and colleague Teresa Rojas. I would also like to thank Marina Alonso for her collaboration and enthusiasm during my first period of fieldwork in Rabinal.

I am grateful to my sister, Gabriela Navarrete, who helped with the translation of some sections into English.

My wife, Judith Zur, has been a true colleague throughout the stages of this research, and I am thankful most of all for the sharing of her skills as a clinical psychologist. Her experience allowed me to enter into the intimate thoughts of the people I interviewed. Her capacity to deconstruct people's discourses on the spot and to ask the right questions has earned my lasting admiration. I dedicate this book to Judith, and to my daughters, Sofia and Olivia.

Maya Achi Marimba Music in Guatemala

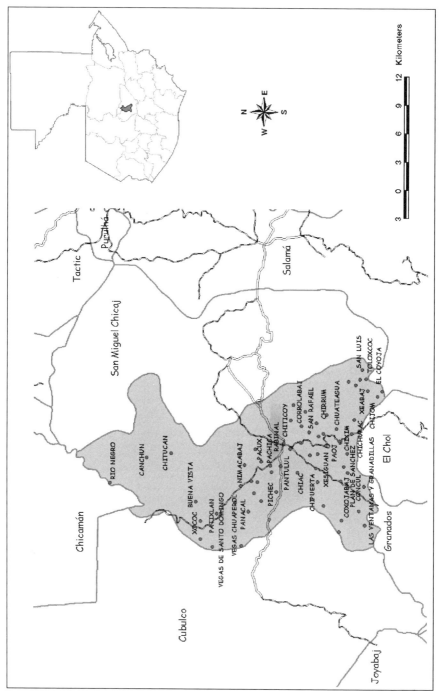

Map of Rabinal.

Introduction

THIS BOOK EXAMINES the marimba musical tradition of the Maya Achi of Rabinal, Baja Verapaz, Guatemala. The *son*[1] marimba is a long (7.08-foot) wooden keyboard instrument with large resonators played by three musicians (treble/melody, center/harmony, bass/rhythm), who perform on most musical occasions, secular and religious, to bring people together.

My original aim was to focus on the ways this unwritten musical tradition is transmitted from one generation to another. In the process of documenting what I had thought was a fairly straightforward musicological process, I was overwhelmed by the social experience of being in the field and by a growing awareness of the social nature of music. My attention soon moved from music as an objectified subject to the social relations, values, and interests of musicians and audience in relation to music making. It became apparent that musical meaning arises from the social and cultural contexts in which musical production occurs and that the conditions of its production are also the conditions of the reproduction of the Achi society.

The main theoretical thrust of this study is that musical meaning is a cultural construct based on memories of social and cultural experience. This thesis is elaborated in two main arguments. The first focuses on agency and competence within sociality and musical performance as a process of communication. I maintain that the meaning of music is constructed in the flow of social interaction during musical performance and in the social performance between musicians and their audience in everyday social relations. The second argument is closely related to the first and is framed in the context of social and cultural continuity and change. Here I argue that while the material and social conditions of music making and music itself are continuously changing over time, discourses about music and music making rework previous meanings; these, in turn, legitimize social practices as continuous with the past.

The study provides insight into deep structural aspects of Achi thought and allows the reader to understand the relationship between the myths, ritual practice, and behavior related to musical production. It illustrates the way socioeconomic and political conditions relate to musical strategies and discourses about music and musicians, and how these reproduce structural patterns of Achi thought. The way people make sense of their

FIGURE I.1. Marimba la reina Rabinalense. From left to right: Esteban Uanché, Celestino Cajbón, and Mincho Uanché. Photo by Sergio Navarrete Pellicer.

musical experience is framed within a cognitive structure, but this structure may only reveal itself as a moral challenge between needs, desires, feelings, intentions, and individual will (understood as the individual's social disposition to satisfy the demands of the community).

ANTHROPOLOGICAL WORK ON THE MUSIC OF GUATEMALA

With a few exceptions (e.g., O'Brien 1975; McArthur 1977), anthropological research into the music and dance-drama of Guatemala has not transcended the descriptive level (see Paret-Limardo 1962; Chenoweth 1964; Castillo 1977; Horspool 1982; Arrivillaga 1990, 1993). The main emphasis of these works lies in discovery, documentation, classification, and preservation, though the influence of certain theories and research methods can be detected in some of these works. Earlier ethnographies appear to be inspired by the works of Hornbostel and the Berlin School (Schneider 1991); definitions of the cultural roots of music are based on melodic typologies (Castillo 1977).

More recent ethnographers have taken a functionalist and culturally relativist approach. They describe the economic and technical production of instruments (Camposeco 1992), their repertoires and occasions in terms of functions (Horspool 1982; Arrivillaga 1990, 1993) with educational purposes (Paret-Limardo 1962).

The literature on dance-dramas is more abundant and focuses primarily on historical and philological analyses of written texts or libretti (Correa and Cannon 1958, Bode 1961; Mace 1966; Montoya 1970; Acuña 1975; Breton 1994), although there are a few examples of musical form analysis (Horspool 1982; Sacor, Alvarez, and Anleu 1991; Navarrete Pellicer 1994). Most research has a theme and a lot of musicological description but little or no analysis, or outdated arguments with few data to support them. The study of Guatemalan music reveals little about the society that produces it, let alone how the music is interpreted by or what it means to Guatemalan society. This book builds on the few exceptions to this general rule, such as Chenoweth (1964), O'Brien (1975), and McArthur (1977). Chenoweth's descriptive study of the Guatemalan marimba also provides a thorough organological analysis of the evolution of the marimba, with scattered insights concerning musical knowledge and performance practice that have been useful in my analysis of musical cognition.

McArthur's (1977) investigation into the motivations of dancers and dance organizers in Aguacatán, Guatemala, reveals a deep relationship between dance-drama performances and belief in ancestors. His findings indicate that dance-drama performance is a means of communication between the living and the dead. The purpose of dance-dramas is to please the ancestors for fear of retribution and to liberate them from their suffering. Although McArthur's cognitive approach reveals the motivation behind and meanings of dance-dramas and agrees with my own findings, it does not explain why the relationship with the dead is so important. In other words, it lacks an analysis of the Guatemalan worldview.

O'Brien's (1975) study of the "ancestor songs" of the Tzutuhil-Maya of Santiago Atitlán, Guatemala, does incorporate local worldviews and is, in my view, the most important contribution to date in the field of modern ethnomusicology on Guatemala. O'Brien's work refutes the widespread notion that the Maya had no songs. O'Brien has discovered a rich ancient repertoire of religious songs, accompanied by contemporary *ranchero*-style guitar music. These songs are deeply bound up with traditional concepts of time and space, and her analysis relates them to creation myths. O'Brien concludes that these songs are petitions to the ancestral spirits and the saints that help preserve the order of the world.

It would have been helpful if O'Brien had reflected upon the syncretic process that resulted in a combination of foreign music with ancestral song texts. This book sheds light on the issue of musical change and the preservation of meaning.

La marimba guatemalteca by Lester Godinez (2002) is an important recent source of information on the marimba of Guatemala, but it does not address the role of marimba tradition in social relationships and therefore does not take an anthropological approach to music. As a musicological work it nevertheless sheds light on the origins of the marimba and the history of the chromatic marimba, and on its musicians and repertoire, which are discussed in Chapter 4.

FIELDWORK METHOD

My interest in the music of Rabinal developed from my investigation of the annual performance of the "Rabinal Achi" dance-drama, which is also known to Maya scholars as the *baile del Tum* (Yurchenco 1980; Breton 1993) and to Achi speakers as Xajoj Tum. This short period of fieldwork (December 1993–January 1994), which formed the basis of my master's thesis (Navarrete Pellicer 1994),[2] left me with the desire to know the object of my study in greater depth.

My first visit to Rabinal took place under the auspices of the Center for Investigations and Superior Studies in Social Anthropology (CIESAS) in Mexico. My project involved videotaping preparations for and the performance of the Rabinal Achi dance-drama and recording its music during the fiesta celebrating the town's patron, San Pablo, 20–25 January 1994. My prior knowledge of the dance-drama enabled me to devise a very precise work plan, and I knew whom to approach in order to achieve the aims of my study. The relationships I established with the prestigious representatives of the dance-drama gave me privileged and direct entrance to the Rabinal's music and dance world. I taped as much as I could of the diverse events taking place during the main celebration, and people came to know me as the man with the "big eye" into their religious tradition. People were surprisingly kind and apparently did not mind my intrusive behavior. I was unaware at the time of the new understandings in Achi culture of social etiquette, especially toward strangers and non-Indians, that had developed during and after the height of the political violence between 1981 and 1983. I suffered no obvious repercussions from my ignorance, though I may have left some people feeling aggrieved.

During the festivities, marimbas were played virtually nonstop, from early in the morning till late at night, all over town. Marimbas attracted the largest audiences of children and adults, creating and expanding the festive environment well beyond the house where the event (*alegría*) was taking place. The omnipresence of the marimba sound reflected the importance people gave to it in their conversations about *marimbistas* and their musical performances.

I soon realized that Rabinal's numerous marimba ensembles varied in type and repertoire. During my short stay in the town I was able to observe and listen to many kinds of music on different musical occasions. I concluded that the best way to study the social nature of music in Rabinal was to study its marimba tradition. I had also noticed that in all types of marimba ensemble, the musicians were always male, ranging in age from ten to seventy or eighty. Furthermore, some adult musicians were obviously beginners, which gave me hope that I could learn to play the marimba.

I returned briefly to Rabinal in June and July 1994 and for a longer period between February and December 1995 with my wife, Judith Zur, to conduct fieldwork for the present book. Judith had conducted work on the exhumation of one of Rabinal's large clandestine graves during the previous year and had decided to respond to a local need by setting up workshops on mental health with rural health workers.

Our first move was to introduce ourselves to Rabinal's political and religious authorities and especially to the town's military commissioner and his civil commissioner assistants. Among the latter I recognized two marimbistas with whom I was already acquainted. I explained my interests to the group, and the presence of these musicians seemed to help forge an immediate response. We also visited the town's Dominican priests. During a conversation with one of them, I requested access to the parish historical records to search for musical information. The priest was pleasantly surprised by my interest and joked that I was the first person he'd encountered who was not interested in "searching for bones."

Guatemala's thirty-six years of low-intensity war had officially ended the year before, in 1994. The United Nations Mission in Guatemala (MINUGUA) was supporting and supervising negotiations between the guerrilla Unidad Revolucionaria Nacional Guatemalteca and the Guatemalan government. In Rabinal two major exhumations had been undertaken in 1994 and a third, which proved to be the largest yet found in Latin America, began in March 1995, within a month of our arrival. MINUGUA and the Catholic Church were investigating the atrocities and massacres that had taken place in Rabinal in 1981–82, which left 5,000 people dead or "disappeared."

For the first time, the political situation in Guatemala allowed an opening for people to give their testimonies about what had happened during the political violence. This opportunity was not without its price. Wounds were reopened and people again experienced pain and fear. The situation was tense, given that local perpetrators were still at large; the fear in the streets was palpable. Malicious gossip, a normal method of disseminating information, proliferated at an alarming rate; many of the dangerous rumors about future retaliation against anyone providing "foreigners" (i.e., MINUGUA) with information probably emanated from the army and their *Ladino*[3] supporters. Nevertheless, the successful exhumation of clandestine graves in the Rabinal villages of Chichupac, Rio Negro, and Plan de Sanchez encouraged other grieving villagers to petition for more exhumations; about thirty were requested of the forensic teams.

The grief that comes of reopening wounds was contained during the celebration of Rabinal's traditional anniversaries of the dead. We could hear and see these celebrations taking place all over town and in every village almost daily. The expression of mourning coupled with the new threats, especially toward widows who were organizing collective events to celebrate the anniversaries of their dead relatives for the first time since the violence, created an overwhelming feeling of dread in Rabinal.

The presence of foreigners had been rare until the exhumations began, and Judith and I therefore tried to dissociate ourselves from the UN mission in order to lessen the likelihood of evoking fear in others and bringing danger to ourselves (cf. Nordstrom and Robben 1995). I wondered if I was being paranoid when I felt that men fixing a bus across the street from our house were really spying on us. And perhaps it is coincidental that during the festivities of Holy Week (when local Ladinos, doubtless including assassins, return home from other parts of Guatemala), an apparently bloodthirsty motorcyclist tried to run me down. Our Guatemalan and foreign friends in the capital (who were involved in the restitution process) told us we were very brave to live in the quagmire that was Rabinal. Judith's work, which was providing us with many horrendous testimonies of persecution, torture, and murder, did nothing to quell our fear or the feeling that people were suspicious of us and avoided us. At the same time, however, Judith's work and her friendship with several health promoters in the villages allowed me access to places such as Xococ, which was implicated in the violence like no other village. Xococ had become a dangerous place, a fact confirmed by a Guatemalan friend who had been held and left tied up for hours during a recent visit. Yet Xococ is a relatively wealthy village with a vibrant musical tradition, and I was able through Judith's contacts to conduct research there with people who would otherwise have been inaccessible. My previous attempts to make contact through the municipal agents had failed because people did not trust the local government representatives, and musicians thought that they were being called to register their musical instruments for taxation purposes.

Because of the general unrest resulting from the investigations of the peace process, I decided to follow the advice of an old teacher of mine, the Guatemalan linguist Otto Schuman. He told me to work with those people with whom I felt most comfortable; bonds of trust would be created with relative ease with a few people, which in turn would increase the confidence of others. This is precisely what happened; the strategy worked to my advantage in the long run. My collaboration with the young musician Celestino Cajbón, whom I had met casually during a *cofradía* fiesta during my first visit to Rabinal in 1993, gave me access to his sixty-two-year-old maternal uncle, Esteban Uanché. Esteban was considered by most Rabinalenses to be the best and also the most *delicado* (grumpy) marimbista in town. Knowing his reputation, I had visited him five times to ask him for marimba lessons (for which I offered to pay); he refused to consider the matter. I had to wait until he came to me, which he did, once I began taking lessons from Celestino; his curiosity had been aroused and he decided to investigate. Once I had established a relationship with a member of his extended family, he gladly accepted the task of teaching me, without pay. I finally ended up taking marimba lessons twice a week, once with the young Celestino and once with Esteban.

My status as a foreigner, a man, a musician, a Mexican, and a Ladino (non-Indian and therefore untrustworthy, from the Achi Indian point of view), played an important role in my relationship with people in general. Being a foreigner, especially given the situation in Rabinal at that time, was initially a handicap. Only a few people were prepared to open the door to friendship, but, once I got inside, others began to collaborate with me and were willing to be associated with my work.

Being a *Mestizo* (Ladino) and a Mexican had several connotations. Being a Spanish-speaking Ladino with physical features similar to those of most middle-class (and hence powerful) Guatemalan Ladinos (who normally treat Achi people with disdain and as minors), did not help very much. In some instances Judith was also considered a Ladina, although she is more easily recognizable as a non-Guatemalan; her distant link with their Guatemalan Ladino oppressors led some Achi to have greater confidence in her. Once people knew I was Mexican, they began to react quite favorably toward me, because, historically, Guatemalans in general view Mexico as an "older brother." Indeed, being Mexican gave me the added advantage of a cultural background similar to that of Guatemalan Indian and Ladino society.

As a man and a musician in a social world dominated by men, I was given the same status as other musicians (who are exclusively male), which meant that musicians were open to exchanging ideas about their concepts of music making and especially about the relationship between music and women. My interest in learning to play the marimba helped musicians feel comfortable with me and be enthusiastic, cooperative, and patient. Musicians have always had a privileged and respected position in Rabinal society, a fact recognized by both Achi and Ladino audiences. But to reflect upon their (rarely discussed) personal skill and knowledge, which is the basis of their respectability, and to share it with me led to a pleasant relationship between us.

My attempts to learn to play the marimba (by no means an easy task) made it easier for me to gain an understanding of musicians' techniques and methods of musical practice and an active insight into their concepts of music. This process was mediated in both positive and negative ways by my training as a classical musician. Western concepts gave me a point of reference from which to observe and raise detailed questions about sound, technique, musical form, and style. Yet sometimes my approach to what they were doing and saying did not make sense. It was hard to let go of my musicological baggage and biases and start as the true apprentice I was. For example, my use of video to record special musical sessions in order to register techniques and generate musicians' comments on musical style (cf. Stone and Stone 1981) did not work as I intended. When I played the videotapes for the musicians, they were captivated by the images of themselves on the screen, and it was often hard to get beyond this.

A discussion of emic versus etic views (Alvarez-Pereyre and Arom 1993; Bauman 1993; Herndon 1993) is relevant here. I discovered that my understanding of listening to music was different from the musicians' understanding. I found that communication about making music was far more successful when I played side by side with them, memorizing positions and imitating their movements, which I could then use to illustrate a question or idea. Only when musicians referred to musical concepts themselves was I able to delve into them, sometimes requesting an example or stimulating further discussion.

Inspired by the ideal of bi-musicality proposed by Mantle Hood (1971), it was not only easy but necessary to become emotionally engaged and to observe through participation if I wanted to have any success in playing, let alone in understanding musical knowledge and practice (Tedlock 1991). As with language, the more I could play their music, the deeper my understanding of their musical tradition became.

Most interviews were conducted in Spanish, as all male adults and many women are bilingual. In a few cases, such as interviews with older women, another family member translated for me. I took Achi language lessons with Tono Lopez, a local linguist and a member of the Academy of Mayan Languages, who gave me important insights into the Achi worldview. He also translated and interpreted prayers that I had recorded in context.

I interviewed a wide variety of people in the field. My attempts to interview musicians resulted in a variety of responses, from those who refused to talk with me to those who encouraged my visits to their homes. My interviews were not restricted to musicians. Including musicians' wives in discussions brought to light interesting family dynamics, such as the conflict between a musician's domestic and public obligations. The views of nonmusicians—children, women, and men—on musicians and musical performance were also of interest. I also interviewed other ritual specialists such as *abogados*, who lead local Catholic rituals, and dance-drama directors.

I recorded interviews and musical performances with the participants' permission and was therefore not disruptive. These tapes were the best source of information for planning further interviews while in the field; during the writing phase, my tapes proved invaluable for organizing my data and for providing details that expanded on my written notes.

Formal interviews with guided questions were mostly conducted with musicians who enjoyed conversation and who felt constrained by a detailed questionnaire. I used questionnaires to get a sense of the types and uses of music and the number and distribution of instrumental ensembles and of musicians who were active in the municipality, and to obtain perceptions of musicians by young audiences.

I always explained that I would use my tape recordings of marimba music only to facilitate my study. Musicians did not object, so long as I gave them a copy of the tape, which I was always happy to do. Audiences in Rabinal record musicians' performances in order to relive the occasion at home; some people have even set up small businesses, reproducing and selling cassettes of music recorded at social occasions. Musicians disapproved of this common practice but were powerless to prevent it. The current debate among ethnomusicologists about the copyright of music recorded in the field (Seeger 1992) has no meaning to the Rabinalense, who are unaware that recordings of "world music" have become one of the most profitable sectors of the music industry in the United States and Europe.

In Mexico, as in other Latin American countries, governments have institutionally supported anthropology as a means of channelling cultural and social policies. This situation has strongly influenced anthropological practice, which is mainly concerned with popular organization, advising and supporting cultural and economic projects, and generally voicing people's needs and demands (Béhague 1991). I think that, whenever possible, the music researcher should promote the music and the musicians with whom he or she is working and help find funding for music projects that could have economic and cultural benefit.

The writing of this book has made me realize that the material I have collected and the testimonies I have edited convey only a partial truth about Rabinalense musical culture; the whole enterprise of research and analysis entails an enormous responsibility, which I alone must bear (Clifford and Marcus 1986).

The recent compilation of essays on fieldwork in ethnomusicology by Barz and Cooley (1997) resonates with several issues regarding fieldwork discussed in this work. For instance, a reflexive attitude may help us understand the role of subjectivity in the interactive experience with people in the field. Moreover, most of the material selected for analysis and writing up is determined by the quality of human relationships between the people collaborating during fieldwork. An awareness of our own cultural and social background in the light of postcolonial relations may help us understand people's intentions, attitudes, and behavior toward the researcher and vice versa, particularly if the researcher is an outsider. If we want to understand music as culture, we must reflect upon the social, political, and cultural roles of all participants during the field experience and beyond.

OUTLINE OF THE BOOK

The work is divided into two major sections. The first section (Chapters 1–5) is mainly historical but includes a discussion of the basic concepts of music and its place in the Achi worldview. The second section (Chapters 6–9) concentrates on the social and cultural settings of musical practice and on musical change.

Chapter 1 sketches the social and political history of the Achi people from early colonial times to the present. It addresses the historical role of the cofradías, the process of Ladinoization, the systems of exploitation, and the recent political and religious conflicts in the context of a counterinsurgency war lasting more than thirty-six years.

The next two chapters describe the basic Achi worldview. The concepts addressed here provide the ideological framework for understanding Achi views of music and musical practice. Chapter 2 focuses on the heart of local Catholicism, which is the belief in the dead. An analysis of the people's creation myths and their ritual discourses shows the relationship between the living and the ancestors and the role of music and prayers in the annual re-creation of the world. Chapter 3 presents an analysis of the general Achi concepts and principles of order applied to music, musical instruments, and musical practice.

The history of music is the subject of the next two chapters. Chapter 4 is divided into two main sections, the first dedicated to the history and development of the marimba in Central America and Guatemala in general and Rabinal in particular, the second to a historical and ethnomusicological analysis of the marimba son and its structural relationship to ritual. Chapter 5 presents an analysis of Achi ideologies concerning music, alcohol, and women, which are rooted in colonial history.

Chapter 6 focuses on the most important musical occasions in Rabinal, which are the anniversaries of the dead. It demonstrates the growing role of music during the fourteen-year process of ritual mourning. It also presents a personal experience during one of these family celebrations.

Chapters 7 and 8 address the subject of social and musical change and adaptation. Chapter 7 deals with the changes in the marimba teaching/learning tradition and the generational challenges that follow from this. It also includes an analysis of Achi aesthetic perceptions of style. Chapter 8 looks into economic aspects of musical change and the musical strategies adopted by musicians to cope with poverty.

Chapter 9 gives an analysis of daily social interaction as part of the process of musical communication. Chapter 10 presents the conclusions of the book.

1   A History of the Achi People
of Rabinal

THE END OF THE FIFTEENTH CENTURY saw the Achi[1] tri-
umphant over their neighbors and rivals, the K'iche' and the Pokomchis,
whom they had expelled from the Rabinal basin in Verapaz, toward the
more mountainous areas to the north. The Achi still celebrate this victory as part of the annual Christian festival of the patron San Pablo.

The Rabinal basin is located in the modern province of Baja Verapaz,
which is cut from west to east by the Sierra del Chuacus, which rises more
than 8,202 feet above sea level. The Rabinal valley, which lies to the
north of the Chuacus range, is 3,189 feet above sea level (the lowest point
in the modern municipality is at 1,312 feet). Several streams and rivers
descend these mountains and irrigate some of the numerous valleys before
joining either the Motagua River to the south or, as the Rabinal River
does, the Negro River system to the north. The area is cut from south to
north by two small tributaries of the Negro River that today have been
diverted to flow into the Chixoy dam on the northern border of the
municipality. The main Rio Negro continues to flow east and then north
under a variety of different names, serving as the national border with
Mexico before eventually debouching in the Gulf of Mexico. The climate
is relatively dry, with a mean temperature of 68–71° Fahrenheit and rainfall averaging only 29.5 inches a year (although this varies dramatically
between the lower subtropical dry forest and the subtropical humid forest of the higher land).

The Rabinal basin has been eroding for centuries. The Achi persisted
with their slash-and-burn method of agriculture as their new Spanish
masters felled trees both for the timber industry and to create extensive
cattle pastures. These practices damaged the thin topsoil, squeezed the
land available for subsistence farming, and prompted inadequate fallow-
ing, all of which contributed to the rapid destruction of the forest and
accentuated the process of desertification, the erratic and decreasing rainfall, and associated problems.

COLONIAL RABINAL

The K'iche' empire, in the heart of the western highlands, was con-
quered decisively in 1524 by Pedro de Alvarado. This defeat allowed

the Spanish military campaign to proceed to the east into the region inhabited by the Achi, Pokomchis, and Q'eqchi. The Rabinal basin, home of the Achi, was soon under military occupation and placed temporarily under the *encomienda* regime.[2] The area became an outpost for further military campaigns into the vast territory to the north (Bertrand 1987, 51), which was still considered *tierra de guerra* (war area) more than a decade later. The army was removed from the area in 1537, when, following an agreement signed by Bartolomé de las Casas, Bishop Marroquin, and Maldonado, the governor of Guatemala, the encomiendas were cancelled and the Dominican order was granted exclusive tutelage of the area baptized as the Verapaz (true peace), which comprised the modern provinces (*departamentos*) of Alta (upper) Verapaz and Baja (lower) Verapaz. The Dominicans controlled Verapaz for the next 300 years.

Bartolomé de las Casas (of the Dominican Order), together with the friars Rodrigo de Landa and Pedro Angulo, began to penetrate K'iche' territory and the area around Verapaz in 1537. They composed songs about the life of Christ in K'iché and taught them to four Indian merchants who became *cantores de trovas* (troubadours) (Friso 1981). These merchants took the Christian message to Indian villages, where the songs were accompanied by the <u>tum</u> (slit drum) and rattle. Soon thereafter, in 1540, King Charles V of Spain ordered the Franciscan provincial authorities of Mexico to send Indian musicians and singers trained in monasteries to help Las Casas with Guatemala's missionary work (Lehnhoff 1986, 77–78). These missionaries arrived in 1542, most probably from the Franciscan convent of Tlatelolco, and probably accompanied Father Luis de Cancer in his missionary entrance to Verapaz (ibid., 69–71).[3]

Faced with the language barrier, the most suitable Christian educational tools were music, dance, and theater. *Tocotines* (*villancicos*, poems set to *son* music) were composed for the *autosacramentales* (a type of religious comedy) to the Virgin. Comedies, nativity scenes, *loas* or *alabanzas* (short dramatic poems and encomia with musical interludes), dance-dramas such the Dance of the Conquest and the Dance of the Conversion, and the processional music for the *cofradías* were composed for performance during the fiestas of the Catholic annual calendar. The discovery of late sixteenth-century musical codices in Huehuetenango in northwestern Guatemala illustrates the rich repertoire of polyphonic music sung and played in remote Indian towns during that time. The codices include diverse musical genres, from plainsong, antiphons, masses, and villancicos to instrumental dances composed by renowned European maestros. Sixteenth-century Indian chapel masters, such as Thomas Pascual and Francisco de León, also composed, copied, and compiled similar musical

collections. Many of these compositions were also found in the Archivo Histórico Arquidiocesano (Archdiocesan Historial Archive) in Guatemala City, which suggests the performance of a common repertoire in both the cathedral and its smaller parishes (Lehnhoff 1986, 78–82).

While introducing European music for religious services to the Indian population, the friars discovered a rich vernacular musical and dramatic tradition[4] and adapted it to the needs of evangelization. The theater of evangelization[5] created a rich cultural legacy that is still enjoyed today. Verapaz, and especially Rabinal, has a rich repertoire of music and dance-drama owing to the control and isolation imposed on the region by the Dominicans (Mace 1966, 1967).[6]

Pragmatism led the Dominicans to turn to the indigenous authorities (*caciques*) who were heads of noble Indian lineages, using them as their local representatives in the Catholic Church's spiritual, civil, and economic enterprises (Piel 1989, 34). Thanks to an initiative instigated by de las Casas in 1543, the Spanish Crown recognized, protected, and compensated Rabinal's caciques, restoring their power (Percheron 1981, 19). Evangelization and the political and economic reorganization of the indigenous settlements in Verapaz under Dominican tutelage were possible only because of the active participation of the caciques.

The caciques were placed under the control of the provincial civil authorities—the Spanish *alcaldes mayores* (principal mayors) and *corregidores* (magistrates), who were in turn responsible to the Spanish Crown—and took responsibility for collecting royal tribute every six months; they were also the principal organizers of labor for the *repartimiento* system (Sherman 1979).[7] Rabinalense Achi constructed local roads and convents; they were occasionally taken to the colonial capital, Antigua, to help build the city. Later they were forced to work on local Dominican *haciendas* (estates) as well as their tropical plantations (Piel 1989, 126).

The cofradías enabled caciques to retain their authority after the abolition of their traditional base. These religious sodalities, dedicated to the devotion of a particular incarnation of Christ, the Virgin Mary, or popular saint, were introduced by the Dominicans, probably soon after they assumed control of the Verapaz. There were only three Indian cofradías in Rabinal before the mid-seventeenth century: the Virgen del Rosario, Divino or Santísimo Sacramento, and Santa Cruz (Percheron 1979, 61–62), all of which still exist.

Cofradías were part of a medieval sense of life as drama (Acroyd 1998), and their fiestas assisted in the diffusion of Christianity by attracting people to the new Indian towns, where they participated in the celebrations of the Catholic calendar.[8] The cofradía became the medium through which Indians were introduced to the mercantile economy. Royal donations of

land to raise cattle and crops were intended to generate sufficient income
to meet the costs of the local church, its priest, saints' festivities, and
community tribute taxes. The last indicates the link between religious
and civil authority that has been an integral part of the institution since
its inception. This was achieved through linking cofradía positions of
authority (*cargos*) with membership of the *cabildo* (town council). The
main beneficiaries were the elite Indian families, who controlled both in
combination with the Dominicans, who were responsible for administration and accounts (Percheron 1979, 81–86). But the exploitation and
abuse of the labor force and the draining of community resources were
not solely a Spanish affair. The caciques, who benefited from the control
of the town's labor force, the sale of community land to Spanish ranch-
ers, and their manipulation of cofradía resources, became private entrepreneurs. They also transformed themselves from heads of local lineages
into an elite group of families that ruled Rabinal under the Dominican
protection.

Thus the cabildo and the cofradías provided the institutional support
for the caciques' continued political, religious, and economic dominance
(Bertrand 1987, 111–13). Caciques preserved their power as *gober-*
nadores (governors) in the sixteenth and seventeenth centuries within the
new Spanish municipal organization of the Indian towns, even though
governors had to be elected by cabildo members and their election rati-
fied by Church and Crown (Percheron 1981, 20–21). The cacique gob-
ernadores and other civil authorities were members of the same group of
elite families who held cofradía cargos (ibid., 68–69).

Under the administration of Dominican priests, Rabinal's cofradías
became important economic enterprises. The cofradías' wealth and entre-
preneurial success peaked between 1776 and 1796, by which time there
were twenty Indian cofradías[9] and two Ladino *hermandades*[10] (brotherhoods), despite the religious authorities' efforts to reduce their number
in order to retain control of their wealth (Percheron 1979, 66–67). During this period the cofradías supported a rich and luxurious cult in the
parish church and could afford to pay for its music and other expenses.
A music school was established in 1783. The cofradías paid for the
teacher, who taught sol-fa, directed the choir, and played organ; the permanent orchestra, with various instruments such as violins, basses, clar-
inets, flutes, oboes, and trumpets; the church's small organ and a large
double-bellow organ; and a collection of musical scores imported from
Mexico (cofradía books, in the parish archive of Rabinal).[11] During the
nineteenth century the church orchestra developed into an ensemble of
string and brass instruments, remnants of which persisted into the first
half of the twentieth century. The marimba is conspicuous by its absence
from Rabinal's cofradía records; unlike other parts of Guatemala and

even other parts of Verapaz, the marimba entered Rabinal by a secular route (see Chapter 4).

In sum, the Dominican Order's businesslike character influenced the economic life of Verapaz profoundly. If it is true that the Dominican haciendas were among the most exploitive of Indian labor, it is also true that they brought the Indian economy into the modern era and served as a model for the wealthy cofradías, which functioned as solid businesses capable of maintaining the sumptuous religious cult and sustaining a privileged Indian class. This, combined with the Dominicans' exclusive control over Verapaz, prevented the advance of Ladino settlers until the eighteenth century.

THE PROCESS OF LADINOIZATION

The concept of ladinoizing indigenous communities developed from Enlightenment ideas prevalent at the end of the eighteenth century.[12] These gave impetus to the colonial government's liberal social policies, directed at transforming Indians into Spanish-speaking, westernized Guatemalans. The ladinoization of Indian towns that took place between 1775 and 1850 was not only an ideological posture; it also included policies that were deliberately destructive to Indian cultures and ways of life. For example, the colonial government insisted on the establishment of schools in Indian towns in order to encourage literacy in Spanish.[13] The only education the indigenous population had received previously was instruction in Christian doctrine and liturgy from the Dominicans in their native languages (Bertrand 1987, 145–46). In 1824 the newly independent Guatemalan state signaled its support for this policy by passing a law recommending that municipal and parish authorities implement measures to extinguish Indian languages, thus dissolving their cultures (Piel 1989, 294). However, this and later attempts to eradicate Indian languages were rendered ineffective through cash constraints coupled with local indifference to the education of Indian children.

The secular ideas of the Enlightenment also had a negative effect on the power of the Catholic Church. After independence in 1821, anticlerical politics led to the suppression of religious houses and the confiscation of the real estate they controlled. The Dominicans lost their last property in Verapaz in 1829 and the parishes were left abandoned (Bertrand 1987, 231). What was left of the cofradías' property (capital, land, cattle), which had been under their administration, reverted to state control, although it remained the legal property of Indian communities (Piel 1989, 246). Rabinal was unaffected by this, for the simple reason that its community lands had already been sold and its cofradías' property plundered by its municipal authorities, working in collusion with the

Dominicans, thus accelerating the transfer of land into private hands (Archivo Histórico Arquidiocesano, Visitas pastorales, vol. 41; Bertrand 1987, 132–94). This occurred between 1786 and 1809, when the bishop's pastoral visits to the towns were suspended.

The loss of land and property impoverished the cofradías and undermined the position of the indigenous elite, who had manipulated their assets to bolster their own authority. As a last-ditch attempt to hold on to their power, the indigenous elite transformed voluntary offerings to the cofradías into obligatory contributions; they also attempted to forcibly recruit the population into serving this institution, augmenting the number of cargos and thus increasing the cost of fiestas. This situation provoked rebellion among the indigenous population, who in the early 1800s denounced their own Indians' authorities (AGCA: A1, file 183, record 3747; Percheron 1979, 93–94). The contemporary cofradías and their numerous cargos, studied by anthropologists, are not the product of colonial cofradías but of the necessity to replenish funds and reorganize themselves during the early nineteenth century (Chance and Taylor 1985, 1–26).

More damaging to the indigenous way of life was the idea that Ladinos would be a civilizing influence on Indians. This was intended to help them integrate into Western society and, as the humanist liberals of the first half of the nineteenth century put it, "restore their dignity."[14] Ladinos were encouraged to settle in Indian towns[15] through the free transfer of Crown property (including cofradía lands) and Indian community lands. Land records show that a considerable proportion of the growing Indian population was pushed northward into the mountains, while incoming Ladinos controlled the best agricultural land on the valley floor (Bertrand 1987, 179–82). The resulting spatial separation undermined the ideologues' justification for the Ladino influx. Nevertheless, this means of ladinoization, which gained legal status through the *composiciones de tierras* (land re-registrations),[16] intensified following the Liberal decrees of 1825 (Piel 1989, 225, 309).

At the same time, the threatening dynamism of Rabinal's small Ladino population—which had increased from 128 to 451 between 1769 and 1816 (Bertrand 1987, 274, table 7)[17]—resulted in the Ladinos' acquisition of municipal power, gradually replacing the Indian cabildo with Ladino authorities (ibid., 232). This is the origin of bi-ethnic local government by a Ladino mayor and judge, with minor indigenous authorities beneath them. Until the twentieth century, participation in the cofradías remained the means of acquiring (extremely localized) authority in the indigenous community: Only those men who had held one of the lower six cargos in the cofradías could serve as *regidores* (magistrates) and *alcaldes segundos* (deputy mayors) in the cabildo, and they could only become cofradía *principales* once they had served the municipality (Percheron 1979, 68).[18] In ideological terms, the basic race conflict between Indian and Ladino stems from this period and intensified as the nineteenth century progressed.

With the emerging local power of Ladinos and the lack of Church interest once dispossessed of their wealth, cofradías became the stronghold of indigenous power and the bulwark of identity and indigenous separatism (Warren 1992, 48–64; McCreery 1994, 137, 288). One manifestation of this was local cofradías' efforts to preserve their musical tradition. The high turnover of parish priests following the Church's political and economic defeat, and the consequent deterioration of church property, was halted during the ten-year incumbency of Father Pedro Avella (1842–52) (Archivo Histórico Arquidiocesano, Vicaría de Verapaz, 1844–54, 68, vol. 7).[19] Major church organ repairs are recorded, as are frequent adjustments and changes of strings and reeds of the orchestral instruments.

But to reduce local political conflicts to an opposition between Indians and Ladinos (see Warren 1992) is simplistic, as this ignores the local political dynamics that gave birth to the new configuration of civil and religious hierarchy within the cargo system. Although the political power of the Indian elite was subordinated to the emerging power of Ladinos, an interethnic alliance was formed to exercise control over the rest of the population. The persistence of this arrangement today is seen in the alliance between Rabinal municipality's most conservative groups, such as the *cofrades* of the village of Xococ and the Ladinos of Rabinal town. From this perspective one can understand the role played by the cofradías in sustaining Ladino power, and the reactionary attitudes of some of the representatives of local Catholicism during the period known as *la violencia* (1981–83).

LAND AND LABOR

The creation of enormous private properties in Alta Verapaz and along the Pacific Coast dedicated to export cash crops dates to the beginning of Barrios's dictatorship in 1873. In 1877 Barrios decreed that all Indian communities' remaining *ejidal* land[20] be "liberated" and sold. Next, uncultivated lands were offered free of charge to national and international investors, provided that they were used (Piel 1989, 317–19). This is the origin of the large *fincas* (plantations) that still benefit from the seasonal labor and permanent migration of *colonos* (settlers) from Indian communities. Indian labor was obtained through the *mandamiento* (state-controlled forced labor) system (McCreery 1994, 220–23). By this time, government attitudes toward Indians had changed: According to neo-liberals, who had emerged as a political force following the coffee boom of the 1880s, Indians were an inferior race destined for work (ibid., 172–75).

As the Rabinal area lacked large tracts of national land suitable for export agriculture, the cultivation of commercial crops was small-scale and secondary to subsistence agriculture (Bertrand 1987, 247). Although Rabinal was only marginally integrated into the new national economic model, its Indian population was obliged by the *habilitación* system (which replaced the mandamiento system and reached its peak between 1915 and 1925) to provide the essential labor force on plantations in other regions.

The local Ladino population profited from the habilitación system: Indians were contracted by force, given part of their wages in advance, and then taken to the fincas to work off their debt over several weeks. The system was usually combined with the alcohol business. Large amounts of the wages earned or advanced to Indians ended up in the hands of Ladinos, who opened alcohol shops in the main towns where Indians were contracted (Bunzel 1952; Guiteras 1986; Hernández 1974; Pozas 1977; Taylor 1979; Navarrete Pellicer 1988; McCreery 1994). Most of the working population was reduced to debt servitude. The system also generated new patterns of drinking, serious alcohol dependency, and related problems in the Indian population. The state, however, benefited. Income from alcohol taxes during the 1890s was "the second highest source of revenue after import–export duties" (McCreery 1994, 177).

Owing to the coffee boom, Indians had both money and work at the beginning of the twentieth century, but the work was still obligatory and the proliferation of alcohol shops in Indian towns soon separated workers from their earnings. This situation, coupled with the scarcity of land in Indian hands, resulted in the systematic expulsion of younger generations to the plantations, either temporarily, as seasonal work, or permanently, as colonos.

Debt servitude was abolished in the 1930s by the dictator Ubico and replaced by new labor laws that applied to all working-class people, both Indian and Ladino. Under Ubico's 1934 Vagrancy Law, all male peasants who produced "inadequate" amounts of food for subsistence were liable to work for 150 days a year (McCreery 1994, 317). Peasants between the ages of eighteen and fifty-five were obliged to carry an identity card and a booklet (*libreta*) in which employers marked the number of days served. The system guaranteed the labor force for the plantations and the national road-building program. To enforce the law, police and military were given the power to control and draft any peasant who had not fulfilled his obligation.[21] Rabinalenses recall how military commissioners[22] hunted men across the fields and into the mountains, regardless of whether or not their libretas showed that they had worked the obligatory number of days, to force them into road gangs.

This was the state of affairs prior to the "revolutionary" period of Arévalo and Arbenz (1944–54). The rule of these democratically elected presidents marked the emergence of a social and political movement that agitated for better life conditions for all Guatemalans.

POLITICAL AND RELIGIOUS CONFLICT SINCE 1954

When Dominican fathers returned to Rabinal parish in 1972, the municipal mayor, an indigenous leader of local Catholicism, and the town's cofradías principales welcomed them with the warning that the priests were "servants of the town" and that under no circumstances were they to get involved in "political matters."[23] The warning stemmed from Rabinalense costumbristas' (traditional local Catholics) awareness of Catholic Action catechists' community organization work in neighboring El Quiché, which they saw as a threat to their own power and authority. They also felt threatened by catechists' campaigns against the cofradías, their fiestas and alcohol consumption (Arias 1990).

The Catholic Action movement attempted to reform the hierarchical power structures based on subordinated participation in the cofradía cargo system (see Chapter 2). They fought for more direct and egalitarian forms of participation in the community for the younger generation of landless semi-proletarian peasants. These peasants had virtually no hope of bettering their economic situation and therefore little chance of gaining access to the cargos that carried the possibility of achieving prestige and influential political positions. In Rabinal, Catholic Action grew exponentially between 1972 and 1981; Dominicans in Rabinal today calculate that at the beginning of the 1980s there were around 200 catechists and delegates of "the Word" working in Rabinal's villages.

The admonition of the Dominicans upon their arrival in Rabinal indicates the continuing political influence of the old costumbrista principales and their domination of local government decisions at the beginning of the 1970s. But, in contrast to El Quiché (Falla 1980; Diocesis del Quiché 1994), the struggles between local Catholics and Catholic Action had not resulted in irreconcilable antagonism in Rabinal. Under the respected and moderate guidance of Father Melchor Fraj, both Dominicans and Catholic Action catechists promoted the values and customs of traditional Maya culture, remaining on the margins and giving room to the cofradía organizations and their fiestas. Father Fernando Suazo reintroduced the liturgy and songs of praise in Achi, accompanied by choirs and a marimba ensemble. This development upset the town's Ladinos.

Protestants and the ultra-right-wing Apostolic Catholics[24] were the most aggressive force in the struggle against the power of Rabinal's costumbristas and cofradía fiestas. As in other parts of Guatemala, in Rabinal Protestants had flourished in the aftermath of the 1976 earthquake, when they offered programs to help the civilian population in the wake of the devastation. Local Catholics and evangelicals (both Catholic and Protestant), by contrast, interpret both natural disaster and political violence as God's punishment for lack of faith.[25] However, so far as evangelicals are concerned, local Catholicism is part of the problem because its pagan practices are remote from biblical texts. For evangelicals, denouncing the idolatrous cofradía cult is a sign of faith.

The number of Protestant converts increased exponentially during the political violence (1981–83) because it was believed that Protestants had a friendlier relationship with the army. There was some truth in this, particularly after the coup that brought General Efraín Rios Montt to the presidency in 1982.[26] Rios Montt's conversion to evangelical Protestantism gave a messianic character to military repression. Using the Dominican Order's radio and television stations to broadcast his message and expressing his ideology through the religious morality familiar to the masses, Rios Montt launched his campaign of moral reform, which he promised would end the problems of poverty and civil insurrection (Stoll 1990, 180–217). In the process, Rios Montt turned the evangelical churches into the army's allies and accomplices. His evangelism unleashed a process of massive conversion, as a desperate population sought to evade identification with the guerrilla by seeking refuge in the evangelical churches associated with the military.[27] In Rabinal, even local Catholic ritual specialists joined the stampede. Many musicians abandoned their instruments (and their income) to demonstrate the authenticity of their conversion.

Yet Rios Montt has a positive reputation in Rabinal: In a neat exercise in ideological manipulation, he purged the municipality's paramilitaries. These predominantly Ladino groups, charged with the selective elimination of community leaders, had taken to terrorizing the community by committing random killings in the street. Rios Montt's continuing popularity never ceases to amaze those who know of the atrocities committed by his underlings, including the massacres in Rabinal municipality and elsewhere in 1982–83 (EAFG 1995). Yet, despite its brutality, Rios Montt's government had an appearance of "justice or authority for all," an idea with strong symbolic meaning for both Indians and Ladinos.

The most important of Rabinal's five evangelical churches is the Church of the Nazareno, which is also the most powerful Protestant sect in the provinces of Alta and Baja Verapaz. Next in importance are the Assembly of God and the Bethesda Church; the congregation of the latter includes both Indians and Ladinos and has chapels in both Rabinal town and its more populous villages. Most congregants are women, which is apparently typical of most religions; in some cases, the congregation is 80 percent female. In response to this phenomenon and to avoid domestic conflicts, some churches only accept married couples, excluding the many women widowed by the violence, who are already excluded by their widowhood from the costumbrista cargo system.

POLITICIZATION AND COMMUNITY ORGANIZATION

The legal bases for workers' basic rights and organizations were established during the democratic governments of Arévalo (1945–50) and Arbenz (1950–54). The Code of Work was promulgated in 1947; the Law of Agrarian Reform was instituted in 1952. Two years later, with U.S. support engineered by the CIA, Castillo Armas ousted the democratic regime in a coup d'etat. Armas revoked the Agrarian Reform and began persecuting peasant leaders who had established local committees to implement land reform. Some Rabinalenses told me that Ladino employers promptly resumed their authoritarian low-wage regime with a vengeance.

Although Rabinal was largely unaffected by attempts at land reform, the hopes of its landless peasants had been focused on the coastal fincas, where large amounts of cultivable land were left idle (Barry 1987). There was no significant change in working-class employment conditions between 1950 and 1980, even though the national economy, with its heavy dependence on agro-exports, maintained a growth rate of 5 percent per annum (EAFG 1995, 51–56, 58).[28] Peasants' social and economic experiences on the fincas led to the creation of the *liga campesina* (Peasants' League) in the early to mid-1960s.

The exploited peasantry was not the only social sector unhappy with the dictatorship. Dissident young officers, who objected to increasing U.S. intervention in the army, formed the Armed Rebel Forces (FAR) in December 1962, mainly by recruiting poor Ladino workers. The participation of some indigenous Rabinalenses resulted in the army's brutal repression of the town in 1963; I was told there was a big massacre there in 1965. Several musicians told me that they had lost *marimbista* relatives at this time. Community organizations faltered with the loss of their leadership.

Rabinal experienced a brief social effervescence between 1976 and 1980. Various events had led to a rapid process of community organization. These included the arrival of international funds channelled through both Catholic and Protestant churches, support from various NGOs (non-governmental organizations) for the formation of cooperatives, and the presence of organizations such as AID (Agencia de Desarrollo Internacional) and CIF (Centro de Integración Familiar).[29] CIF, which had an enormous budget and a large infrastructure, inaugurated development projects, especially in education and agricultural techniques. Agency support notwithstanding, these projects depended on the ability of local leaders to channel funds to their communities. Hamlets that achieved the right combination, such as Chichupac, flourished rapidly, while neighboring villages were completely ignored. The NGOs' lack of planning and inequitable distribution of endemically scarce funds resulted in divisions and conflicts between local communities. The army, which had established a post in Pichec in 1976 and another in Rabinal town shortly afterward, took advantage of these new enmities, exacerbating them further as part of their effort to divide and crush the population.[30] In order to justify its intervention in Rabinal in 1980, the army spread rumors that all members of both external organizations and local cooperatives were also members of the Peasant Union Committee (CUC) and thus guerrilla sympathizers.[31]

La Violencia

The period of intense political violence in Rabinal (1981–83), which was just one small part of the massive military repression of Guatemala's civilian population, is remembered as la violencia (the violence), "the time of silence," of "danger," and of "rape." It has had devastating repercussions, both short- and long-term, for Rabinal society.

Army repression in Rabinal began in 1980. The first massacre occurred on 4 March in Rio Negro (EAFG 1995, 139). For most Rabinalenses, however, the period of extreme violence began in 1981 with the army's scorched-earth policy, which was intended to eliminate the insurgents' voluntary and involuntary support base. The army destroyed crops and livestock and burned homes, obliterating communities' physical base and social organization. Popular destinations for internal refugees from Rabinal were the provinces of Alta Verapaz to the north and Escuintla to the south, both characterized by plantation economies and familiar to Rabinalenses through seasonal work there. Thousands of landless Rabinalenses chose to settle permanently in the small towns near the plantations.[32]

More destructive was the introduction, in 1981, of the Civil Patrols (PAC)[33] which incorporated all men aged eighteen to fifty-five into paramilitary units under the indirect control of the army.[34] By forcing men to patrol the town block or village section in which they lived in twenty-four-hour shifts at least once a week, the army gained direct control over the male population. The system prevented men from leaving their homes, whether to flee or to obtain work, while simultaneously turning them into sitting ducks: It was easy to "disappear" someone at any time during patrol duty. Violence soon became generalized. Patrols from Rabinal's two largest villages, Xococ and Pichec, together with patrols from Vegas Santo Domingo and Ladino paramilitary agents escorted by the army, carried out massacres throughout the municipality. Of the estimated 5,000 Rabinalenses who lost their lives during this period, 2,009 were killed in massacres (EAFG 1995, 127).[35]

The army's purpose in imposing this scheme was to make the population directly responsible for the surveillance and massacre of their neighbors. Traditional forms of conflict resolution were replaced by denouncements to the army; the problem was resolved "once and for all." Historical or ethnic disagreements between villages, groups, and individuals, and even small unresolved family conflicts, became enormously relevant, leaving everyone vulnerable to betrayal. Some people welcomed the opportunity to strike their enemies; simple terror led others to cooperate with the army, betraying their neighbors in order to stay alive.[36] In pitting people against one another, the army transformed them into the vehicle of their own destruction.

Musicians, and especially marimbistas, were particularly vulnerable both within the community and without. Many Rabinalenses, especially those who had converted to the newer religious sects, envied musicians' status in the community, which extended beyond the local Catholic sphere (see Chapter 9); they were even targeted by rival musicians. As far as the army was concerned, marimbistas were the most visible symbol of Catholic custom. The army was particularly incensed by anniversaries of the dead, as these celebrations honored people they had eliminated as suspected guerrillas. Belief in the dead, which is the core of local Catholicism, thus became a subversive ideology that (like Catholic Action's liberation theology) needed to be eradicated. All indigenous gatherings with music were banned in 1981; the murder of musicians reinforced the message.

The direct participation of local men in the annihilation of their kith and kin ripped the social fabric apart, fragmenting groups and creating suspicion between relatives, friends, and work companions. Survivors living in Rabinal have to cope with both their own losses and their own forced complicity. The consequences of this forced participation—the atmosphere of fear, mistrust, and guilt—still reverberate in Rabinal. Feelings were particularly intense in 1995–96, when survivors celebrated the fourteenth anniversary of their relatives' deaths (see Chapters 2 and 6).

CONTEMPORARY RABINAL

Rabinal is one of eight municipalities of the Guatemalan departamento of Baja Verapaz and has an area of 124,539 acres.[37] Rabinal town is only 178 km northeast of Guatemala City by road, yet the lack of paving, particularly between the provincial capital, Salamá, and Rabinal, means that it takes five hours to travel by bus from the town to the city.[38]

According to the 1981 census, taken just before the military violence peaked, Rabinal had a population of 22,733. Considering Guatemala's high rate of population growth,[39] a statistical projection based on this census estimated that by 1992 the population of Rabinal would be 39,741; but the 1994 census count was only 24,063. The large discrepancy between projection and census reflects the political violence of the early 1980s, which led to the death of a quarter of Rabinal's inhabitants and the relocation of several thousand more. The birth rate among survivors also plummeted.

The 1994 census registered 82 percent of Rabinal municipality's population (nearly 20,000 people) as Achi speakers who referred to themselves as Achi people;[40] around 90 percent of Achi live in the municipality's sixty rural villages and hamlets, most of which lack electricity and direct access to water. Some 2,000 Achi live in town. Most Ladinos, including the municipal authorities, are located in Rabinal town, which accounts for 23 percent of the municipality's population (more than 5,000 people). Ladinos are also to be found in the municipality's two largest and wealthiest villages, Nimacabaj and Pichec, and in the exclusively Ladino village of Chirrum and the Ladino hamlet of Conculito.

Relations between the communities can be gauged from the fact that Ladinos refer to Indians pejoratively as *inditos* (little Indians). The Achi, by contrast, refer to all non-Indians as Ladinos, the implication being that they are foreigners.

Rabinalense Achi are peasants with poor land and little access to it. Their principal economic activities are subsistence agriculture based on maize cultivation combined with agricultural wage work on the fincas. They have a myth to explain the origins of the landscape, the illicit appropriation and impoverishment of their agricultural land, and the need to seek work on the coastal fincas. The story is that the small volcanic cones of Saqacho' and Chikak' miloj, situated between Rabinal town and Pichec, were large volcanoes until the creator of the mountains, Zipacná, heaved up the rich volcanic soil and took it to the coast. This is why the coastal plains are fertile and why people go there to work. When the volcanoes were in Rabinal, the land was fertile and there was no need for the people to leave in search of work.

The thief Zipacná represents the foreign Ladino plantation owners and those Ladinos who appropriated Rabinal's scarce fertile lands. Rabinal's thin topsoil and limited irrigation restrict year-round cultivation. It is estimated that only about 494.2 acres are available for irrigation (including the river plains), and most are monopolized by a small number of Ladino and Achi families. The majority of the population cultivates indigenous maize varieties in forestry land that is not considered appropriate for agriculture and therefore does not appear in land-use statistics. The forest keeps the thin soil moist and protects the crops from frost, resulting in small but relatively reliable yields.

Twelve landowners own 15 percent of all Rabinal's registered land; about 300 proprietors own another 50 percent; the remaining 35 percent is shared among more than 2,700 owners (EAFG 1995, 22). Achi properties are divided into small plots of a few *cuerdas* (1 cuerda equals 28.3 square feet); 68 percent of all Achi-owned properties are smaller than 3.7 acres and only 10 percent are more than 8.6 acres, which confirms the general process of fragmentation in Indian land ownership.

Although the Achi family is a group of patrilineal descendants, the right to land is inherited bilaterally. In contrast to other Maya groups (see, e.g., Stoll 1993, 46–54; La Farge 1994, 45; Zur 1998, 127–29), Achi men and women have equal rights over the land, and both mothers and fathers maintain their land or their rights to it, which they pass on as separate properties. Women's access to land and the general scarcity of residential property means that residence, while preferably virilocal, is frequently uxorilocal (women's family residence) or neolocal (new residence). It is common for a landless man to live on his wife's family lands or, in the case of couples who are landless on both sides, to look for a new place to live, often in the town.

Rabinalense peasants produce mainly maize, which (together with beans) forms their basic diet. There are two local maize varieties: long-cycle and short-cycle. The former is cultivated in the mountains over an eight-month period and the latter is grown in the warmer valleys in around fifteen weeks. Some well-off peasants who have irrigated valley land invest in mountain land so that they can grow both kinds of maize and thus avoid having to buy maize for their families over the year; they also sell part of their maize crop on the local market. Peasants with small plots of land, whether in the mountains or in the valley, also sell part of their maize crop to afford other essentials, buying the maize they need later in the year from their plantation earnings (EAFG 1995, 24). All peasants with land are self-sufficient in beans; they also cultivate chili, fruit trees, and vegetables in the gardens around their houses, mainly for domestic consumption.

Maize yields increased notably as a result of the "green revolution" of the 1960s. This was a combined package of "improved" hybrid strains of maize, fertilizers, and pesticides into which most Indians initially bought piecemeal, starting with fertilizer. Among Chimaltecos the introduction of fertilizer tripled productivity between 1964 and 1979, reduced by half the amount of land needed to feed a family, and solved the land shortage problem (Watanabe 1994, 131–35). Yet Chimaltecos still go to the plantations, as do Rabinalenses. In fact, the introduction of fertilizers made dependence on wage work an ineluctable reality, especially as "the price of imported fertilisers jumped five fold during the 1970s" (SIECA 1984, in Barry 1987, 40). Several Rabinalenses grumbled to me about the ever-increasing cost of fertiliser and its apparently decreasing effectiveness.

"Improved" hybrid strains of maize, designed for immediate consumption, also increased yields. For those who adopted the new agro-technology—i.e., most peasants—production became oriented largely toward sale at harvest time because, unlike local maize (*maiz criollo*), the new hybrid maize is floury and decays rapidly; it is unsuitable for storage and useless as seed corn. Increased yields depend on the annual expenditure of hard-earned cash for new imported seed stocks.

Pesticides have also become a popular farming aid among plantation owners and subsistence farmers alike. For the latter, this too has to be paid for from wage work. All in all, the green revolution "has not improved the lot of the peasantry [because] the technical package of seeds, fertiliser, and pesticides is too expensive" for most small farmers (Barry 1987, 169). By 1984 60 percent of Guatemalans were unable to meet minimum nutritional requirements and the average calorific deficiency for the poorest half of the population was 39 percent (ibid., 16, table 7).

Baja Verapaz is one of Guatemala's poorest provinces and occupies fourth place on the index of extreme poverty—80 percent of its population live in extreme poverty (SEGEPLAN 1994, 122); the expulsion rate of its workforce is therefore very high. Watanabe (1994, 40) calculates that around two-thirds of Chimalteco families send one or more members to work on the fincas. The situation seems similar in Rabinal, although I lack concrete data. Direct observation and local testimony confirm that most men aged eighteen to fifty-five (and frequently women and children as well) work on the fincas for one to four months between the end of October and the end of March. Many return to celebrate the fiesta of the town's patron saint in January, and then go back to the fincas.[41] A common destination is the cotton- and sugar-growing area around Gomera, Escuintla province in the south Pacific Coast, and the coffee plantations of Alta Verapaz.

In the first four decades of the twentieth century, the labor recruitment for the fincas was, with some variation, as obligatory and compulsive as the work systems of previous centuries. Older forced-labor systems had cynically depended on peasants' ability to feed themselves in their communities; the plantation economy depends on the survival of subsistence agriculture to sustain the labor force when it is not required on the fincas. As a government agronomist remarked, it is "a system made in the *cielo* (the heavens). The *indios* can grow corn in the mountains and then pick coffee and cotton during the other parts of the year. It is a system ordained by God" (Barry 1987, 10). This idea is so entrenched that questioning its validity is almost seditious. The reality is that the removal of Indian towns' community lands and the subsequent concentration of land in fewer hands, together with increasing soil infertility and the consequent reliance on ever more expensive fertilizers, have all accentuated peasants' reliance on paid work.[42] This is now vital for the survival of the subsistence sector rather than just one strand in peasants' survival strategy. Their dependence on finca work is such that any international movement in the price of Guatemalan agricultural products has immediate repercussions for their domestic economies. The Rabinalense subsistence economy is completely integrated into an agro-export economy dependent on the international market and controlled by just a handful of transnational companies.

In Rabinal one can broadly identify three socioeconomic strata according to access to the means of production. In the top stratum are the principal merchants and transport owners, all of whom are Ladinos who are also large landowners and control most of Rabinal's irrigated land and orchards. They produce cash crops and raise livestock for sale.

The common denominator in the middle stratum, which comprises both Ladinos and Achi, is the ability to generate sufficient income to avoid working on the plantations. It is made up of small-scale merchants, teachers, and professionals (who are predominantly Ladinos), Achi and Ladino peasants with some irrigated lands and orchards who cultivate cash crops on a small scale, and Achi artisans who supplement their subsistence activities through crafts such as pottery and weaving. One large family of artisan potters in the town, who are also hereditary musicians (the Ordoñez family), used some of their earnings to buy better musical instruments and form a *conjunto* marimba (an ensemble consisting of marimba, bass, and drum set) with loudspeakers. With other Achi artisans and Ladino teachers, the Ordoñez family also invests in Rabinal's dance-drama culture.

The situation in Rabinal is very different from that of El Quiché (Falla 1980) and Huehuetenango (Brintnall 1979), where the children of indigenous small-scale merchants became agricultural entrepreneurs and merchants who broke the Ladino business monopoly, diminishing Ladinos' power and to some extent replacing them. The indigenous entrepreneurs, who joined evangelical cults, also mounted a direct assault on the gerontocratic stronghold of local Catholicism (Arias 1990). When this movement reached Rabinal in the 1970s, confrontation failed to materialize, partly because the most traditional elements within local Catholicism have allied themselves with the municipality's Ladinos. They in turn have good social and economic connections with the Ladino communities of the neighboring municipalities of Cubulco and Salamá; they also receive unconditional support from the army, which still has a base on the outskirts of town.

While the top two social strata live mainly in the municipal town or the large villages of Pichec, Xococ, and Nimacabaj, the bottom stratum, which comprises the majority of the population, lives predominantly in the hamlets and consists almost exclusively of Achi families with little or no land (fewer than 3.7 acres). These families depend on paid work on the fincas or for wealthier Rabinalense peasants, for whom they sometimes work in exchange for a small plot on which they can produce some maize for domestic consumption.

Within the bottom stratum is a subgroup distinguishable by its extreme poverty. These families are direct victims of the violence; among them are survivors of the massacres in Rio Negro and Plan de Sanchez, who now live in Pacux[43] and in the Municipal Colony on the outskirts of Rabinal town. One of the survivors of the Rio Negro massacre, who lost every single relative and all his possessions and was forced to move to Pacux, told me that "violence has left us behind in this life." To him, the human and material losses he suffered are irreparable. This man and a considerable number of others in the same position remain in terrible misery.

The majority of Rabinal's musicians fall into the lowest and largest socioeconomic category of poor peasants. Their music gains them status and prestige as carriers of tradition and custom, rather than a regular income that could substitute for labor migration. Like most other peasants, musicians are agriculturists who work periodically on the coastal fincas year after year.

Health conditions in Rabinal municipality are deplorable. The town has a state health center with a doctor and a few nurses who are able to attend to only about 20 percent of the municipality's population; it barely covers the urban area itself.[44] The state is also responsible for organizing health technicians (who are generally community leaders) and voluntary health workers (including midwives). These workers, who receive minimal training, take health campaigns concerning such things as hygiene and the inoculation of children to rural areas, especially during epidemics; outbreaks of dengue fever and cholera occur at least once a year. Cholera is the most dreaded disease and one of the main causes of death through dehydration. The incidence of respiratory diseases, such as tuberculosis, and gastrointestinal illnesses caused by parasites is also high. The number of cases of measles is also significant (SEGEPLAN 1994, 125). Malnutrition plays a significant role in death rates, especially of children: In 1986 in Baja Verapaz, 53 percent of children aged six to nine suffered from malnutrition (ibid., 123), which is well above the average for this age group in Guatemala (37.4 percent).

The ineffable psychosocial consequences of the brutal repression experienced by many Rabinalenses are excluded from local health surveys. One of the town's former parish priests told me of his preoccupation with the marked increase in the number of suicides in recent years, which he attributed to the trauma left by the violence. By Rabinalense Christian standards, to take one's own life is equivalent to homicide because it goes against God's will. Collective desperation has shaken the ideological basis that gives coherence and meaning to life. The social demoralization of Rabinal's population, the high incidence of illness, and reduced access to health and hygiene education are all reflected in the frequent references to witchcraft and malicious envy as causes of illness (Chapter 9). People believe that they are exposed to malicious envy and witchcraft at the numerous celebrations for the dead and at cofradía festivities. This source of infection notwithstanding, most incidents of witchcraft-induced illness seem to be acute gastritis, amoebic dysentery, and, in one case, diphtheria, spread through the contaminated water used in the *atole* (maize-based beverage), and poisoning from home-brewed and distilled *cuxa* (a crudely distilled sugarcane alcohol) served at these events.

WHILE POOR, THEN, the Achi are not all the same but are differentiated in various aspects, including economically. Their recent history has meant that some of this differentiation is permeated with trauma (e.g., religious conversion, moral behavior such as betrayal, roles played during the violence). The tension between Indians and Ladinos is the product of a complex national and local history.

The history of the Achi of Rabinal reflects the belief, commonly held by Guatemala's ruling class and Ladinos generally, that one cannot be a genuine Guatemalan without becoming ladinoized. Admittedly, Article 3 of the Peace Accords, signed in 1996, goes some way to addressing this popular misconception, but it will be some time before attitudes change, if they ever do.

The situation in which the Achi now find themselves also reflects the contradictions inherent in the agribusinesses on which Guatemala depends for more than 50 percent of its export trade. On the one hand, these industries rely on a labor force that can feed itself outside harvest time.

On the other, these companies' insatiable hunger for land in which to expand their businesses make it increasingly difficult, and in some cases impossible, for their seasonal workers to support themselves for the rest of the year. Despite their contempt for "inditos," the last thing plantation owners want is a literate, ladinoized workforce. Thus the Achi, like other Maya ethnic groups, find themselves excoriated for what they are, while simultaneously being denied any genuine opportunity for personal or community advancement.

2   The Belief in the Dead

LOCAL CATHOLICISM (*Costumbre*) is commonly associated with the cult of the saints and the hierarchical *cargo* (office-holding) system of the *cofradía* (religious sodality). It is the cofradía that gives substance to Costumbre, and at the heart of this institution, and compelling its practice, is the pre-Hispanic Maya belief in the continuing life of the dead, who in time become ancestors.

Striking cultural similarity and continuity persist between the beliefs of today's Maya Achi and the practices of the early sixteenth-century highland Nahua.[1] For example, the Nahua categorized their dead by cause of death, attributing each category to a particular god; the dead person became part of that god's entourage, and his or her death was then celebrated at the annual festivities associated with that deity. People who died of natural causes were celebrated on the great feast of the dead; they went to the underworld and were mainly associated with Mictlantecutli, the lord of the underworld and God of the Dead. People whose death was connected with water were generally commemorated at the beginning of the rainy season, in the month known as Tepeilhuitl (month of the mountains when clouds accumulate and the first rains come), and were associated with Tlaloc, the God of Rain. As his servants or members of his court, they were considered good intermediaries between the living and the God of Rain, whose goodwill was essential for the success of the subsistence crops on which the living depended for survival. This belief survives among the Achi, as does the practice of calling the dead by type of death in a precise, fixed sequence. Today the Achi no longer celebrate water-related deaths during Tepeilhuitl; they have, however, continued to celebrate the start of the rainy season under the guise of the Catholic festival of Corpus Christi, which falls between 23 May and 25 June.

Another similarity between ancient Nahua[2] and modern Achi practice is the celebration of individual deaths for a fixed period of time, after which the deceased is celebrated only in community with the rest of the souls on 1 and 2 November, All Saints' and All Souls' Day in the Christian calendar. Admittedly, the time spans are different, but the principle is the same. The Achi say that after the series of celebrations are concluded, they have fulfilled their obligations to that particular spirit. Some anthropologists (e.g., Barbara Tedlock 1990; Farriss 1984; Hill and Monaghan 1987; Carlsen and Prechtel 1991) have identified a long list of examples of cultural continuity, and this chapter will also illustrate the continuity of certain cultural patterns and structures.

It is important not to underestimate the ongoing influence of Catholic evangelization on the ways Achi people think and interpret daily life experiences. Many of the narratives I heard concerning the persecution and death of relatives during the height of the political violence (1981–83) were expressed in terms of the last days of Christ's life, his betrayal, capture, scourging, and cruel death. The "emphasis on Christ as both victim and saviour of the world" was "part of the broad tradition of late medieval piety" (Acroyd 1998, 98). As the rest of Europe was confronting the challenges of Lutheranism, Spain was imposing Catholic orthodoxy. This orthodoxy was pre-Reformation Catholicism, complete with saint and holy day celebrations with processions, pageants, religious comedies, music, and the organizations to stage them (cofradías), which also functioned as a mechanism of social and political control. These customs, which survived intact in Spain a century beyond their disappearance in the rest of Europe (Woolf 1972), were therefore part of the cultural baggage brought to the New World. What did not survive in Europe (including Spain) was the cult of the dead that had been "so prominent in late medieval worship" (Acroyd 1998, 211). The assimilation of Christian practice is an important reality that should not be overlooked (Brading 1990, 184–204).

The aim of this chapter, then, is to demonstrate how the patterns and structures of pre-Hispanic concepts are presented both in contemporary myths about the ancestors and in the ritual practice of the Achi people as they re-create the ancestors' primordial actions and provide themselves with a sense of order based on repetition and feelings of stability, belonging, and continuity. To this end, I will analyze Achi creation myths such as the World of Light (i.e., the coming of Christianity) as explanatory paradigms of local history through which the superimposed Catholic cult undergoes a process of "rajawalization." That is, in order to provide sequence, continuity, and a sense of historicity to the cult of the ancestors, Jesus is incorporated as an authoritative ancestor (rajawal).[3] The power of Jesus as man and God is similar to that of the rajawales, and, according to the elderly musician Eligio Gonzales, Jesus is a rajawal because he is considered a Maya ancestor. The concept of rajawales links the living to the first ancestors and Jesus in a direct time line; the link is maintained by each generation's inviting the ánimas to participate in a continuous procession of life-crisis rituals loosely tied to the endless cycle of calendar rituals. The linear concept of time in the Christian paradigm, which establishes a beginning and a continuity of life until the final judgment, has been invoked to support the Maya status quo. The main paradigm imposed by Catholicism—the biblical account of Jesus' life and sacrifice—is incorporated, transformed, and interpreted as a myth of origin and creation that conforms to preexisting concepts of cyclical time and hence requires the ritual reenactment of the first ancestors' mythical deeds in order for life to continue.[4] The body of Christ is identified with the sun (ajaw), which has to be "lifted" every year for life to continue.

Rajawales[5] are not just the powerful ancient ancestors, the mythic heroes of the creation, the first Maya, and the lords of the world;[6] they are also the Christian saints, angels, incarnations of the Virgin, and, of course, Jesus himself. The spirits of the dead (ánimas) and living elders who have gained knowledge and experience through participation in the cofradías have power similar to that of the first ancestors; they too are deemed rajawales. Unlike living rajawales (cofradía elders), however, ánimas are part of the communion of souls that influences the destiny of the world and its human inhabitants. What they have in common is their knowledge and authority over succeeding generations.

The dead are invited individually and collectively to both life-crisis rituals and cofradía fiestas. Common to both types of celebration is the abogado (ritual prayer-maker),[7] who summons the dead in a ritual invocation.

THE ORIGIN OF THE "WORLD OF LIGHT" AND THE COFRADÍAS

The first men were the Wise Maya, who lived in a remote time in a dark world and possessed extraordinary powers: People say "they could see into the distance (future)," that they grew old but never died, and that they knew everything.[8] These men were the Achi ancestors who attained definitive victories over the K'iche' and Poq'omchis at the end of the fifteenth century and who constructed the forts and temples of Chwitna-mit and Kajyup fort in Rabinal.[9]

The "peaceful" conquest of colonial Verapaz, achieved through the Dominican Order's exclusive control of the province (Bertrand 1987; Saint-Lu 1968), has left its mark on Rabinalense myths that refer to the conflict between the ancient Maya and Christ and to the whereabouts of the Wise Men. These are myths about conversion, death, and rebirth, in that the sacrifice and death of Jesus set the example for others to follow: The rajawales lost their physical immortality, and the sun (ajaw) was allowed to rise. The first evangelization is remembered as the "coming of the Light," the time when ajaw rose, when Jesus was born, and when the Wise Maya disappeared or were converted into "people" (Christians).

There are several interrelated versions of this myth. For example, when I enquired about the origins of music, violinist Magdaleno Xitumul told me a story about the creation of musical instruments that is related to the life of Jesus, the envy of the first people, and the sufferings he went through on earth:

> People say that the ancestors were Wise Men, they know what is going to happen tomorrow and after tomorrow, they know everything, they know the law of our eternal Father because they are *sajorines* (Wise Men; soothsayers).[10] When these first sons of our Father went before the altar, they say they did not have anything to offer Him; because they were Wise Men (i.e., pagans) they did not use candles, they made their holy images but out of materials unbeknown to us. They were worshippers, but they did not use candles.
>
> Then Jesus Christ knew everything since an early age and the Wise Men did not like that; the first people were upset. The elders said, "What does He know? How could He be a Wise Man if he is so young?"[11] They were feeling very uncomfortable with Him. Whatever they spoke with little Jesus, they went to check in their books, but nothing of that was in them.
>
> Then they became very angry with Jesus. Then they said, "Where is He going to put us? If other people are going to be His sons, then we are nothing." That is why they accused Jesus of being a thief and a killer. The ancestors thought of giving a poison to Jesus, something to drink so that He would die. They all agreed to give Jesus a poisonous [alcoholic] beverage. First they tested it on one of themselves to see if it worked. Once all the little animals were inside the body of the man who drank it, he felt heartburn; he was very ill and was about to die. So what did they do? They searched for a remedy. They made the marimba, they made the *adufe* (square drum); they made the drum to cure him. They thought these instruments were good as a remedy, so they began to play the marimba, the violin, the drum, and so on. Then the little animals inside said, "What is that noise outside?" So they came out to see. The people saw the little animals; there was a male and a female. Later on, when the day came, they prepared the beverage for Jesus, but they say that Jesus never drank it, and so that is why alcohol remained with us.

The myth demonstrates the ancient Maya knowledge and their dual power of giving and taking life. They created both musical instruments and alcohol, which can cause illness and death or effect cures and give life. The first Maya, the Wise Men, were ajq' mes (healers);[12] they were ajq' iij (diviners) (Nash 1970; Wilson 1995); they were ajq' itz (evil sorcerers, witches); they possessed the dual forces of good and evil.

The power conflict is explained in terms of a generational opposition that threatens one of the main principles of order, that of seniority (see Chapter 3). By recounting the historical-mythical confrontation between the two religions and cosmic heroes, the Achi address the ongoing conflict between old life resisting death and the emergence of new life and a new order. The aspirations and ideas of the younger generation conflict with the status quo and the authority of the older generation, which is legitimized by the dead. The contemporary conflict between *Costumbristas* and Protestants is an extreme example of an age-old contest.

Generational conflict extends beyond life; it also exists between the living and the dead. The symbolic role of music, according to the myth, is central to this relationship. Music is a call and an offering of sustenance from the living to the dead. People say music helps the souls by temporarily releasing them from suffering; it also reestablishes a relationship of goodwill between the living and the dead. The way life continues depends on how this conflict is continually negotiated and resolved. This generational challenge to seniority applies to all aspects of social life and it is one of the important social forces of change in music (see Chapters 7 and 8).

Victor Tum, a well-known abogado, musician, and former kajawxel (head) of the cofradía de San Pedro Apostol, told me a different version of the conversion of the Wise Men:

> When Jesus was born the three Wise Men, the Black Men,[13] came to see. These three wise Kings are the Maya, they are people just like us, but they have a lot of money; they have their work, they are rich, they have land, horses, mules, bulls, and so on. In those times, there was no sun, nothing, no light, no stars, but when Jesus was born, all of a sudden the sun was lit, the moon too, and they have stayed that way ever since. The ancient Maya were people of the darkness, there was no sun so they never saw the sun. The Maya did not know anything, but they were the first people. Then, when Jesus came, they heard the sun was coming, the morning star was coming, and the dawn was coming, so they stopped working and went to see. They took the *tabor* [drum] with them, they made it to play for the child Jesus. The kings worked on the tabor to play with happiness; they made it, they created it to bring happiness to the place where Jesus of Nazareth was to be born, when the sun rose, when the morning star emerged. They looked for the yellow flowers in the mountain and brought them on horses, they went to see the child that was going to be born, they brought roses, incense, and white Madonna lilies. They left the work, the Kings, the Maya left it, and they became like saints because they made their offering. They went to see Jesus and Jesus blessed us as Maya people; we became people [Christians] because Jesus arranged it.

For their *cumplimiento* (act of devotion) in making a musical offering to the child, God turned the Wise Maya into saints and they became Christians. Following this logic, the saints and virgins (initially the Wise Men's wives rather than the various incarnations of the Virgin Mary celebrated by the cofradías dedicated to them today) are the first Maya ancestors who converted to Christianity and followed Jesus' path. They are the "first mothers and fathers" (ka nabe chu ka kaw) of the men and women who left Rabinal, the center of the world (uxmut kaj uxmut ulew),[14] in order to populate the earth. The first founding ancestors are particularly identified with the Virgin of the Sacrament (ixoc ajaw, literally, female lord) and the Holy Sacrament of the Altar, the body of Christ (achi ajaw, literally, male lord); the Achi terms express the duality of ajaw in its male and female manifestations.[15]

In another myth concerning the end of the world of darkness (the remote, pre-Hispanic times) and the emergence of the sun (the beginning of Catholicism in Rabinal), the Wise Men appear as Pharisees who fought against Jesus' wisdom and succeeded in killing him. The first ancestors used their extraordinary powers to bring masonry from the ruins of Kajyup (their temple in the "dark ages") through the air to construct the church, which they equipped with staffs, a lectern, censer, processional candlesticks, and cross—all made of silver.[16] They also bequeathed incense, candles, and the organization of the cofradías to serve God, thus giving light to the world. They then buried themselves under the arches of the church walls. Since then all generations have carried out the Costumbre (local Catholic custom), becoming the "dead who participated in the service of God" mentioned in every abogado's prayers (see below). The living remember and pay respect to the living spirits of the dead because their experience and knowledge permit them to communicate with God about people's needs on earth. According to the myth,

> The patzka (humble elders)[17] came from Jerusalem, journeying by land. Arriving here [Rabinal], they encountered the divine [sacrament] that was sitting, immobile, in front of the church. Everything was in darkness . . . . Although no one had succeeded in raising up the divine [sacrament] onto the altar, the patzka, exerting so much force that they became ill and grew goitres,[18] managed to lift the divine [sacrament] and fulfilled the request. This is how the first dawn of the world arrived and how the sun rose. When the patzka saw the day had broken, they buried themselves under the church. (Breton 1987, 5)

Thus the first ancestors raised the sun and buried themselves. As birth requires death, so the ancestors "planted" themselves under the church.[19]

The myth and ritual of lifting the Holy Sacrament, which identifies the body of Christ with the sun (ajaw), is reenacted every year at the festival of Corpus Christi, which coincides with the start of the rainy season and the planting phase of the annual agricultural cycle. Corpus Christi also marks the beginning of the ritual year and is the most important festival in the Achi ritual calendar.[20]

The Holy Sacrament is brought out in procession and the patzka dance-drama is performed. Participants dance in front of the ajaw (Divine Sacrament) to the music of the flute and tum (slit drum),[21] wearing masks with goitres and carrying planting rods in the form of serpents (which symbolize rain and lightning). The Achi say that the dancers are asking for rain and that their performance and paraphernalia symbolize earthquake, who announces the change in the weather, the lightning, thunder, and rain necessary for the fertilization of the land (Breton 1979, 181). The dancers' symbolic actions evoke the act of sowing and the fertilization of the land and are the vital forces that produce the rising of the sun (ajaw) and its movement along its annual path. The annual performance of the <u>patzka</u> dance-drama not only marks the arrival of the rains and the start of the planting cycle, understood as a rebirth and the beginning of a new cycle, but makes it happen.

The act of creation, when the world was lit, was the birth of Christ, and his sacrifice created the new world order. The ancestors who constructed the church and sacrificed themselves echoed Christ's deeds; the annual ritual repetition of these acts re-create and maintain the world. In other words, the Christian paradigm has been transformed and reinterpreted in a cyclical time frame that requires reenactment to maintain cosmic order and the continuity of life in the World of Light. It is a "plausible structure" (Berger 1967) that allows continuity and justification of the cult to the ancestors, accommodating itself in a discourse compatible with the dominant Christian religious structures.

Breton (1987) maintains that the structure and dynamics of myths of creation and maintenance of the world are homologous to the sequence of life-crisis rituals. He explains that the terms used to designate the status and roles of men and women in the different stages of their lives are projected into the religious dimension of ritual and myth as categories of the order and movement of the universe.[22] In Berger's terms (1967, 25–51), "cosmisation" takes place where the social construction and establishment of a divine order in the cosmos guarantees and legitimizes the social order.

The role of the ancestors operates in both cyclical and linear notions of time. The former requires the sacrifice and burdening of the first ancestors, the <u>rajawales</u> (including Jesus), and of the following generations to maintain the order of the cosmos and the continued movement of the sun on its path throughout the year. Simultaneously, a local concept of historical time is at work, in that the Achi trace their origins in a linear succession of generations,[23] starting with the first ancestors in the World of Darkness in the following sequence:

- Wise Men of the Dark World
- Jesus, or <u>ajaw</u>, the sun; Jesus' birth was the origin of the World of Light
- Saints and Virgins
- Illustrious ancestors: <u>kajawxeles</u>; musicians; everyone who served in the cofradías
- Ancestors in general (<u>q'ati q'amam</u>, literally, grandmothers and grandfathers)
- Recent dead
- Living Achi

All the dead who in life served in the cofradías, whether by founding them or maintaining them through cargos, are illustrious ancestors and form part of the <u>rajawales</u>. They are invoked first, each one by name, in the abogado's prayers. But the dead are also an indivisible collectivity known as ánimas q'ati q'<u>amam</u> (the souls of our grandmothers and grandfathers); hence to call one is to call all. The abogado nevertheless calls all the spirits of the ancestors with or without authority, whether or not their names or whereabouts are known, to join the living when they are called, so that no one is left out.[24] Forgotten ánimas are dangerous to the living.

Local interpretations of the Christian paradigm and of Catholic institutions—such as the cofradías—are based on older mythical models and profound cognitive structures (Breton 1987). The body of Christ in the consecrated offering is the sun (<u>ajaw</u>) itself. If the concept of primordial exchange, of sacrifice in order to permit the sun to rise and life to begin, is framed in the context of Christian discourse, then the story of the rising of the sun and the awakening of the world has also been used in Maya texts of the early colonial era as a metaphor of settlement, of the construction of their forts and temples and of Rabinalenses' control and power over the region (Breton 1994). The same metaphor was used to describe the settlement of both the K'iche' and the Achi people, as can be seen in the *Popul Vuh* (Tedlock 1986, 181–86) and in the *Annals of the K'aqchiqueles* (Recinos et al. 1967, 83).

In relation to the concept of space, the metaphor of raising the sun and the new dawn of the world refers to the inauguration of the political power of the government that cares for and protects both land and people. The birth of light and the raising of the body of Christ (<u>ajaw</u>) by the old and humble <u>patzka</u> ancestors are founding events analogous to the foundation and inauguration of Achi political and military power over the territory of Rabinal at the turn of the sixteenth century. This in turn is overlapped by the foundation of the town of Rabinal, with its church under Dominican dominion after 1537. The elision of these two political events is celebrated through the performance of the Rabinal Achi (<u>Xajoj Tum</u>) dance-drama during the festivities celebrating the Conversion of San Pablo, the patron saint of Rabinal, in January. This dance-drama is a reenactment of the establishment of the Rabinalense territory following their victory over the K'iche' (Breton 1994).

The Cofradías

The cofradías are religious groups organized in a hierarchical system of annual positions of religious responsibility called cargos (literally, burdens) that serve and care for the saints.[25] After marriage, when they become complete persons, men and women in the towns, villages, and

hamlets are not only encouraged to participate in the cofradía throughout their lives but also to adopt cargos of increasingly greater prestige and
social and economic responsibility in the service of the saints. The aim is
to attain, if possible, the seven cargos in one or more cofradía.

The seven grades in the cargo hierarchy are divided into two groups.
The secondary group contains the lower grades (4–7) who are known as
mayordomos (servants of the saints)[26] or achi (men); their main function
is to clean and decorate the different sites where ritual action takes place.[27]
Their wives are known simply as ixok (woman). The primary group contains grades 1–3 and the first is known as kajawxel (father/owner/lord);
his wife is known as the chuchuxel (mother/mother superior/female head).
This husband and wife are the "father and mother" of the cofradía and
bear the main responsibility for all aspects of the festivities for one saint
over the course of one year. Their "arms," the second and third achi and
their wives, assist them in this. The kajawxel is responsible for the organization and costs of the saint's fiestas. The chuchuxel controls the labor
of all female cargo holders and is responsible for organizing, calculating,
and preparing the food for all the festivities of the saint; in addition, she
has to prepare the meals for the *cargueros* when they visit other cofradías.
Upon completion of these tasks, they reach the position of *principales
pasados* (past principals) who integrate into *la asamblea del pueblo* (the
people's assembly or council of elders, which has only an advisory role).
As they no longer hold a cargo, they are diminished (*menores*) and subject to the new authorities in turn. It is thought that some principales pasados do not take kindly to this demotion and put their knowledge to evil
use (see Chapter 9).

The authority of principales pasados works horizontally rather than
vertically. They are also known as rajawales (town lords);[28] they may
become ritual specialists known as abogados, *tenientes*,[29] or *padrinos*
(names for prayer makers according to occasion). Abogado is the general
term for the ritual specialists who address appeals and prayers to God
and the ancestors on behalf of the living; they are known as tenientes
when praying in cofradías and as padrinos when praying during life-
crisis rituals. This is only an option for those former kajawxeles who
excel in memorizing all the prayers that constitute "the tradition of the
Lord" and can improvise within the structure of these prayers. Active
kajawxeles who have this skill are likely to have served as abogados
before becoming cofradía principales.

Within the cofradía, each group of cargueros has an abogado teniente
who has specific ritual duties and must be able to perform his work effec-
tively. One abogado teniente leads the prayers of the kajawxel and his second and third achi, and another abogado teniente leads the prayers of the
mayordomos. For the three cofradías that have them—San Pablo, San

Pedro Apostol, San Sebastián—another abogado teniente leads the prayers of the men who are in charge of decorating the processional altar with feathers (*plumeros*).

From the participants' perspective, service in the cofradías is both a right and an obligation. In the tradition of local Catholicism, assuming a cargo is seen as a sacrifice for the community's well-being that brings prestige to the carguero. Prestige accumulates as he progresses through his career, assuming greater responsibility as he occupies increasingly important cargos; he is remembered for his patronage in every prayer said in the local Catholic community. Participation in cargos, then, is an investment that brings social capital (Bourdieu 1986, 171–83), which translates into authority and influence. Until recently the acquisition of social capital, which is proportionate to the ranking of the cargo held, was available only to wealthier peasants; only they could afford the most prestigious and expensive cargos and accordingly candidates were selected from this small group.[30]

Most local Catholics can afford to participate only in minor cargos in minor cofradías and do not pursue higher positions; they are satisfied with fulfilling the basic moral obligation to serve. I did encounter some exceptions, however. One wealthy kajawxel participated in the cargo system in order to make his way out of poverty. As he related his continuous efforts to save and buy land, he seemed to be justifying his accumulated wealth as a reward for serving God. Yet this kajawxel also explained that, excepting a few traditional villages such as Xococ and Pichec, it is the poorest people who are most disposed to assume cargos because those with the most resources (whether Ladino or Indian) have a more commercial vision and refuse to invest their savings in the "service of God." Thus he placed himself on the side of the righteous and distanced himself from people who accumulated wealth while disregarding their religious obligations.

There are sixteen Indian cofradías in Rabinal (see Appendix 2), plus two Ladino ones.[31] Following the dualistic principle of order that structures Indian notions of the world, most cofradía images are organized in pairs and celebrated twice—on their own and their partner's saint's day. Those images that are not paired—San Sebastián, Santo Domingo, San Pedro Martires, San Francisco, and San Miguel[32]—are accompanied during their festivities with a minor, or junior, image of the same saint. Cofradías are also divided into a group of "big" cofradías and a group of "small" ones, as can be seen in Appendix 2.

Rabinal municipality is divided into four quarters, with the church in Rabinal town as the center. Two quarters fall in the higher part of Rabinal to the east (San Pedro Apostol quarter to the southeast is the most important of the quarters on the upper land), and the other two fall in the lower part of the territory to the west (San Sebastian quarter to the northwest is the most important quarter on the lowland). Most of the villages and hamlets of the municipality belong to San Pedro Apostol quarter or to San Sebastian quarter. Apart from those cofradías, which are dedicated to the saint of each quarter, the cofradía of the patron San Pablo—which is imagined at the center of the town, in the church—rotates annually from one quarter to the next (in a counter-clockwise direction) and its cargueros should be chosen from the quarter that has "possession" for the year. Most of the kajawxeles of the five largest cofradías, together with their second and third achi, are chosen from the most traditional villages in the lower, western half of the municipality, namely, Xococ and Pichec. This has enormous relevance for political and religious conflict in Rabinal because the main opposition to Catholic catechists during *la violencia* came from these villages, as did the civil patrols that participated directly in the biggest massacres in Rabinal (see Chapter 1). Since then the people of Rabinal town, the municipality's primary bastion of Catholicism, have not been welcome in Xococ, *Costumbrismo's* second stronghold, because of the latter's continuing support for the army.

Abogados and Their Prayers

Abogados and musicians[33] are the most important ritual figures in all local Catholic celebrations because they are the intermediaries between the living and all the dead ancestors and God. As intermediaries, abogados participate in all ritual activities that seek the intervention of God and the ancestors for the benefit of the living; they lead the ritual activity and, with prayers and music, request permission to enter the sacred world, opening the path of communication with the spirits.

Abogados are also commissioned to perform "devotions" composed of prayers that either aid the repose of the ánima of a client's deceased relative or solicit protection for the client from the ánimas or other powerful spirits.[34] Abogados perform similar rituals of permission and protection every Monday.[35] Early Monday morning, one can see most of Rabinal's abogados laying their candles before the saints in the town's principal church or on their way down to the Calvary Chapel, where they pray and carry out petitions of protection for the ánimas. As healers (ajq' mes), abogados perform *promesas* (pledges) which are prayers promising further *devociónes* (offerings) to a certain spirit or saint in exchange for helping someone to recover health; they also bless the construction of new houses or chapels, request that businesses do well, and so on.

The ritual activity during cofradía celebrations is structured around the "entry discourses" (permission to enter the altar) of abogados and the music that accompanies these prayers (big drum and flute and a marimba ensemble). These discourses are repeated each time any group of cargo holders requests permission to enter the sanctuary of the house where the celebration is being held (listen to the soundscape of cofradía, with music and prayers, on track 1 of the CD).

Once all preparations are completed, the abogado begins chanting in archaic Achi[36] to the accompaniment of both musical ensembles, who play independently of each other throughout the ritual. He begins his *parlamento* (literally, speech) with a prayer of thanks to God and the saints for a new dawn over the world's four corners. This first part of the proceedings refers to the dawning of the sky and to the four cardinal points of the earth, commencing in the east, then the west, then north, and finally south. This progress follows the course of the sun in a horizontal terrestrial plane, so that north is identified with the zenith and south with the nadir and night.[37]

When referring to the four corners of the world, the abogado gives examples from each direction—that is, the temple of the Lord of Esquipulas, where the sun rises, Cobán City church to the north, and so on. Each abogado makes his own particular selection. Then the abogado mentions the awakening of Rabinal, from the summit of the surrounding hills to the church in the center of town. He proceeds to awaken the four quarters of Rabinal, describing a circle that begins in the upper part of town

FIGURE 2.1. Achi woman at grave site on the day of the death. Photo by Sergio Navarrete Pellicer.

to the east and north (San Pedro Martir), proceeds to the lower part of town to the northwest (San Sebastián) and then to the southwest (Santo Domingo), and finally to the southeast in the upper part of town (San Pedro Apostol).

Next, the abogado mentions the dawning in the realm of the dead. The discourse follows an order based on the "underworld" (nighttime) course of the sun, which passes through Rabinal's cemeteries from the western, lower part of the valley, through the south, to those in the eastern upper land. The journey begins at the Calvary Chapel at Rabinal's oldest cemetery, on the western margins of town. Next is the second and more recent town cemetery, the Tamarindo, which is in the same direction. Then the abogado mentions the awakening in all the cemeteries in the low-lying land to the west: the cemeteries of Chitucán, Pajales, and Raxuj above Xococ village; Xococ's own cemetery; those of Patzun, Patzité; and the cemetery of Chiatzum, close to the village of Pachicá. After the dawning in the western cemeteries, the speech journey moves to the southeastern and upper lands of Rabinal, to the cemeteries of Chuatioxché, close to Concul, and to Palo Hueco, close to Chuategua.

The dawn in each of these places is described in metaphorical language that refers to the natural environment—to the birds that sing in thanks to God, for example. The speech of dawn, that is, of the creation of the World of Light, ends with the mention of the crucifixion of Christ and tells how his death represents the death of the first ancestor in the new World of Light.

The second phase of the ritual is the "roll call"[38] of the spirits. The spirits are called in hierarchical order, beginning with God the Father and his child, then the saints and virgins, then the Maya Wise Men who founded the church and left the silver staffs in service of the cofradías, as is related in the myths of the beginning of the World of Light. In family life-crisis rituals, family ancestors are slotted in here, beginning with anniversaries of the dead. For cofradía festivities, the abogado emphasizes all the dead rajawales (deceased cargueros), calling them in order according to their town quarter, in a counter-clockwise direction: northeast—northwest–southwest–southeast. This is followed by the names of all the deceased abogados and the musicians who accompanied them, the kajawxeles[39] and their wives (chuchuxeles), and the fourth to seventh mayordomos and their wives. Then a general call is made to those ánimas of the dead who did not hold a cargo and all the souls of the whole municipality.

Special mention is made of the "truant souls" whose misery is considered to have a negative impact on the living (cf. Zur 1998). This category of ánima is particularly important in Rabinal because of the thousands of deaths that occurred during la violencia, when it was impossible to perform remembrance rituals even for those who died of natural causes. Gatherings with music were banned for three years, beginning in 1981.

Truant souls fall within one or more of three categories: people who are not buried "properly" (in Rabinal's cemeteries), which means that no one holds vigil for them; people who died in common accidents; and people who died at the hands of others. Deaths resulting from human action are considered unnatural, as God did not decree them. "All these are the blessed souls," says the abogado, who then lists the souls by their type of death in time-honored fashion:

> The poor ánimas of those massacred in the time of violence; those who were tortured, hanged, poisoned, or murdered by machete, knife, or bullet; those whose remains were dumped in the hills, thrown in ravines, or buried in clandestine graves.
>
> Those who died on a journey (*ánimas caminantes*), whether on a *romeria* (pilgrimage), in hospital, on the coastal plantations, away on business, or doing military service. This category includes people who lost their way, such as Protestants.
>
> Those taken by the waters of the rivers and the sea, those who fell from trees, or into ravines.
>
> People who are not "complete" (unmarried and/or childless) are also called, as are single mothers, "all those who have no family [children] and no-one to remember them."
>
> The blind, the crippled, lepers, the children who died during that "evil time" and still-born ánimas—"the small innocent angels who did not know the world and hence are also ánimas in pain."

The invocation concludes with a summons to all ánimas "wherever they are"; the abogado commands each and every one to come because the offering is for all of them, rich and poor, Indian and Ladino, because everyone is equal in the afterlife. I was told that "even though their blood drenched other places, their soul knows where their town is and they will come."

The abogado's discourse, which has the same structure and content whether the event is a betrothal ceremony, wedding, cofradía fiesta, or anniversary of the dead,[40] is simultaneously a restatement of the origin myth and a recounting of genealogical testimony that defines the group and its territory (Breton 1980, 210). More broadly, this type of rite is a re-creation of the cosmos as related in the myths of origin of the World of Light (see Eliade 1987). Recounting the generations from first ancestors to the present day orders the world in time; it confirms the social order, which is portrayed as unchanging since ancient times. In other words, it is a discourse of empowerment that accumulates all previous authority and legitimizes the status quo.

This is never more the case than in cofradía fiestas, where the second part of the *parlamento* (roll call) is repeated each time different groups of cargueros arrive with their abogado. The entrance rite begins when the cargueros' abogado leads the way to the patio of the house where the cofradía celebrations are being held. Reaching the center of the patio at the front of the house, the cargueros' abogado begins the blessings of the four cardinal points (cumplimientos). During a second set of blessings, the group proceeds to the porch. Finally, during the third blessing, they arrive at the door to the entrance of the sanctuary. In each blessing, the abogado mentions that the blessings are being made in the same way as in the past.

Once at the sanctuary entrance, the visiting groups greet one another and then their abogado hails the host kajawxel and his abogado, who are situated just inside the door to the sanctuary; they come out to greet their visitors one by one and then go in again. The visitors' abogado requests permission to enter to give their offerings and contributions and to pray the *misterio* (a set of Catholic liturgical prayers, recited in Spanish) and then launches into the parlamento as given above. He then performs three more blessings and gives thanks to God and the ancestors. From inside the sanctuary, the host's abogado signs his approval by making gestures and an *aaaaaa* sound. This gesture is known as *chineando*, which means, "Yes, everything you are saying is true, it is right." He then responds with a similar long speech (to which the visiting abogado starts to *chinear*), after which he gives permission for the visiting abogado and his group of cargueros to enter. During these prayers, alcohol is poured on the ground as an offering to the sacred earth; then the abogados offer drinks to the visiting group to the right and left of the door. This entrance rite takes about two hours. Once inside the sanctuary, the visiting cargueros and their abogado fall on their knees before the main altar and pray a misterio, thus concluding the entrance rite; the order of the world is confirmed, as is the men's place in it. This is emphasized by the change in the music played on the marimba outside on the patio: each time a group of cargueros arrives to perform this entrance rite, they interrupt the cycle of *sones* to play a *son de entrada* (entrance son) (see Chapters 4 and 6).

THE LIVING AND THE ÁNIMAS OF THE DEAD

These invisible entities from the actual, historical, and mythical past are omnipresent in the consciousness of the living; the relationship between them can be delineated in three important Achi concepts that not only place an individual's life in direct relation to the past but also link it to the future:

1. The justification for and legitimization of human survival is based on recognition of the experience, knowledge, and social practice of previous generations. "To follow custom as our ancestors did" is, as the

Achi boldly say, a "burden and responsibility" during their time on earth. Fulfillment of this obligation brings happiness to the dead and may aid the survival of the present generation.

2. The omnipresent idea that life is in God's hands, is transient, and that death can occur at any moment.
3. The notion that the living have a soul (ánima) that continues to exist after death, joining the congregation of ánimas. The ánimas hope that the living will remember[41] them by performing Costumbre, that is, by inviting the ánimas with son music and prayers to join and celebrate festivities with the living on earth. This is a requirement for the continuation of life.

Living humans have a body and a soul or spirit (ánima) which resides in the heart,[42] which is also the site of memory, emotion, and will; the heart, together with the mind (*mente*) is the center of knowledge. Among some Maya groups, such as the Mam of Santiago Chimaltenango (Watanabe 1994, 89–105), the ánima is seen as something that is acquired and develops during the socialization process: individuals internalize culture during social participation and interaction, forming criteria and values that guide and sanction behavior.[43]

In Rabinal it is said that in death, only the body dies. The deceased is remembered as an ánima that has passed to the other life, where it joins the communion of souls of the dead. Continuity of life after death is founded on the immortality of the soul. I frequently heard people say, "The dead are more alive than the living." Abogado Pedro Morales Kojom explained:

> What dies is the body but not the spirit. They continue walking. We are the dead ones because we cannot see them; they can see us. They are able to look at us but we are unable to look at them; we lack that power. Fortunate is the one who can see a deceased person. They walk in the air. They do not tread on the ground. The spirit never dies. It will be judged but not until the last day, until the world ends, when all the living and the dead will be judged.

According to ancient belief, ánimas reside within the sacred earth; it is only as a result of Catholic influence that the ground in which they live has become synonymous with Christian cemeteries. Catholic influence is also responsible for the idea that once the spirits have passed through the cemetery, they join God in the sky.[44] Like God, the ánimas are omnipresent and "see and hear everything we do and say and even know what we are thinking." Their omnipresence and their closeness to God make them both witnesses to and guardians of the moral order and divine law; their presence in all aspects of life is a reminder of behavioral ethics and moral values that serve as a reference for the living in both their actions and thoughts. These roles grant ánimas a moral weight over and above the respect they merit as ancestors.

Maintaining good relations with the ánimas is of vital importance; "forgotten" ancestors are believed to cause economic and (sometimes fatal) health problems for their living kin. To avoid this frightening prospect, people perform rituals of remembrance, calling them with music and prayers to have a moment of "relief and rest" in order to mitigate their suffering and to enjoy once more the various "flavors" of life–offerings of food, more music, *guaro* (locally distilled cane alcohol), *candelas* (candles), and incense.[45] All these offerings are seen as having been created by the ancestors to celebrate the World of Light. Son music is the most important offering, as it has been played since the first primordial events, both as an offering and a remedy, whether in celebration or as a plea for the preservation of life. Indeed, the son is a symbol of life. In exchange for these offerings, the living invoke the knowledge and experience of the ancestors in order to obtain their blessings so that their prayers may reach God. By willingly inviting the dead with music and prayers to participate in all religious celebrations, the living attempt to placate them and prevent retribution; they say that they can feel the ánimas' presence while listening to the music and that in these circumstances their presence is not frightening. Fulfilling one's obligations to the dead is, then, a form of self-protection, particularly against other people's envy and thirst for revenge (see Chapter 9).

Individual contacts between the ánimas and the living can be interpreted as a good sign or a bad one, depending on what is being communicated, how, and by whom. The dead communicate in several ways. They may appear in the form of butterflies, which have been seen as manifestations of the soul since pre-Hispanic times (Furst 1995, 28). The spirits may also make their presence felt during the night, producing noises in different parts of the house, making animals restless; people say that the white-clad[46] spirits are nearby, moving rapidly through the air just above the ground, prospecting for souls to collect during the midnight rounds. Such visits give rise to fears that there will soon be a death in the household. Several people told me that their parents or grandparents had had conversations with the spirits as they lay dying in their homes, receiving them as guests, and causing great worry to those who could not to see them. The most common time for spirits to appear to individuals is late at night on the streets and dirt tracks when people are on their way home from a fiesta, drunk and vulnerable. At night the streets, mountains, and roads are all dangerous places where evil-intentioned spirits may appear (Watanabe 1994).[47] Particularly dangerous are the ánimas of people who, for one reason or another, were not properly buried in the cemetery and wander in pain because they have no one to look after them (cf. Zur 1998).

Spirits commonly communicate through dreams, when the sleeper is unable to exercise conscience or will. *Marimbista* Julián Ordoñez pointed out that since dreams are beyond an individual's control, they provide an ideal context for visits from the ánimas:

> It is as if one were dead and not in control. Suppose that someone in your family had died thirty or forty years ago. You will see them in your dream like a portrait [painted] forty years ago. It is we who are lost, and not their spirits. Why do we still dream of them thirty or forty years later? We are the ones benefiting here on earth, not them. They are in another life and perhaps suffering there; but they know they have family, so they come and we dream and see them here after thirty or forty years.

The appearance of dead people in dreams is of particular relevance to Costumbristas and is frequently reflected upon and subjected to searching interpretation.[48] Although some people told me that the ánimas can simply give counsel, many others said that they appear in dreams to admonish the living for some fault or other. It is generally thought that the dead should not need to visit a person's dreams, especially if that person has fulfilled his or her obligations to that ánima. According to abogado Victor Tum, if the visiting soul speaks, the dreamer is in mortal danger; silence means that death is close to a relative or friend.

Regardless of this ambivalence, such dreams are valued for their premonitory and normative quality; their significance is a theme that often appears in conversations between parents and children, who learn to interpret them as omens or warnings of misfortune. Fears and anxieties about conflict, illness,[49] and death are released unwillfully through the presence of ánimas in dreams. These dream visits are invitations to make personal and family reflections about morality, social obligations, and responsibilities when conflicts occur. As the moral conscience of the collectivity, each time an ánima appears to an individual, it creates an instance of moral judgment about that person's wrongdoings and inappropriate thoughts.[50]

Within the contemporary religious context, with its religious divisions, where Protestantism has gained substantial ground and thrown belief in the dead into question, testimony about the ánimas' existence constitutes an act of faith. Testimonies serve both as self-reflection on behavior and morality and as an expression of loyalty to, and respect for, the ancestors.

The sudden appearance of an ánima in a dream can be frightening, however, especially if the visiting spirit was a victim of la violencia. These ánimas not only pass judgment on the living but also haunt them with tales of their own suffering; they are considered malicious. Research into mental health undertaken by Judith Zur with the assistance of local health workers and myself revealed that the appearance of the murdered and massacred in their relatives' dreams was one manifestation of survivors' guilt and fear of persecution. Zur's (1998) work on K'iche' war widows echoes Rabinalense ideas concerning the appearance of these souls in dreams: Their malice stems from the fact they have been denied entry to the afterlife. Their visits cause great fear. Widows turn to sajorines to interpret their dreams and their physical and emotional afflictions; according to local belief, these afflictions result from spirits' visits in dreams. One sajorin told a widow that her physical pain related to the grief in her deceased father's heart. She had been unable to "remember" him because his body had not been found; abandoned and suffering, his spirit became a vengeful presence, and not just to her—such wandering souls roam the places where they died, scaring passersby. The selective murders and disappearances in Rabinal and the massacres that followed in 1981–83 (EAFG 1995) transformed the municipality into a landscape of terror. Danger zones multiplied during this period. For example, the area close to the Pachalum elementary school was haunted by the soul of the teacher accused of owning communist literature and hanged from a tree. Other victims' souls haunted the Pantulul and Pachalum bridges, from which many people were thrown to their deaths, and so on. The fear generated by these sites, which are found all over town, in the cultivated fields, and in the bush beyond, is one of the motives for exhuming the inappropriately buried dead. Recent changes in Guatemala have opened up political space and allowed its people to speak for the first time about the atrocities they suffered for almost four decades; thirty exhumations have been requested in Rabinal alone, and the forensic anthropology teams working in Guatemala hope to be able to oblige them (Rolando Alecio, personal communication).

BELIEF IN THE IMMORTALITY OF THE ÁNIMA is perceived as fundamental to the continuity of existence from the time of darkness to the present: Carrying out the ancient customs assures that continuity in the present. Local Catholics are thus morally compelled to uphold the duty of maintaining the world through their demonstrations of faith and devotion to God; they do this by remembering and calling together their dead. In return, the dead remember the living by assisting with their appeals to God. But the ánimas are much more than a conduit to God. They are the carriers of society's moral values; they are the witnesses to the actions and thoughts of the living, the monitors of their descendants' behavioral ethics. They are the guardians of morality and of God's law, the collective memory of the living and a reminder of what people forget. In short, they are manifestations of the collective unconscious.

The reenactment in prayer and ritual of myths about the ancestors' deeds at the beginning of time creates and maintains a dynamic order of the world; the metaphor of dawning, of the lighting up of Rabinal, and the following of the sun's path throughout the day and throughout the year, sets the beginning of a new cycle and is simultaneously a genealogical account of the ancestors. These two spatial-temporal elements, the recognition and definition of the territory familiar to dead and living Rabinalenses and the hierarchical recounting of their descent, are the foundations on which local Catholics reconstruct their history as a discourse of identity, legitimization, and social continuity.

These cultural practices link all past generations with the living in the major and collective responsibility of maintaining the world and rendering it meaningful for past and future generations. A satisfactory and meaningful relationship with the dead is a goal and a point of departure for musicians and audiences to participate in religious musical and dance events. It is a goal because remembering the dead guarantees their good will toward the living, and a point of departure because it legitimizes musical and dance practices as they are performed and interpreted as a continuation of the ways of the ancestors.

3 Concepts and Classifications of Music

ACHI CONCEPTS OF MUSIC, music making, and musical instruments are organized and operate in the same paired categories used to explain the order of the natural and social worlds. That world is governed by the principle of dualism, which is manifest in an order of hierarchical (unequal) pairs with distinct characteristics. The elements of the pair are sometimes opposed but are intrinsically complementary (Lévi-Strauss 1995, 235–42; Tedlock 1986, 77–82). The principle of duality is applied to all categories of order: senior/junior, right/left, feminine/masculine, and so on.[1]

In this chapter I will look at the pairs of categories used in relation to the conceptualization of music and show how these categories are related to each other in such a way that they establish correspondences with the human and cosmic order. The sound images and shapes of music and musical instruments are heard and seen as manifestations of the dual quality of nature and human beings.

Classifying the spiritual, physical, and social world in hierarchical pairings predates the conquest and seems to be the aspect of Indian life least affected by 500 years of Christian proselytizing. It is a system of thought that has been virtually impervious to European concepts of oppositional pairings. This is most clearly indicated by an absence of that most basic of Christian oppositions, good and evil. While ideas of good and evil are common currency among the Achi, they are subsumed under traditional category pairings and are thus not antagonistic but complementary.

THE PRINCIPLE OF DUALITY

An analysis of the concept of twins as a principle of duality, unbalanced in the cosmos and in society, led Lévi-Strauss (1995) to the conclusion that duality is one of the philosophical principles ruling Amerindian societies. The explanation of the world is derived from this dual principle and is held in both permanent disequilibrium and hierarchy.

The structures of mythic characters are correlated with each other; they are not symmetrical or identical but complementary. The fundamental notion of duality in perpetual imbalance exists not only on an ideological plane but in some cases as an organizing principle for society itself. This principle is clearly manifest in Maya mythology in relation to the continuous succession of pairs of mythic heroes in *Popul Vuh* (Tedlock 1985): Creation proceeds from an ever-widening dialogue between the gods, in which the concept of duality is treated as the "very nature of the primordial world and of anything that might be created in that world" (Tedlock 1986, 81). In Mesoamerican thought, creation proceeds from opposed but complementary dualities and occasional quaternities. When a trinity occurs, it is complemented with an aspect or image of one of the other three; thus it is increased to four or reduced to two. For example, when I asked why all three kings in the biblical nativity story are black, I was told that one had an ash-blackened face because incense smoke blackened his face while he was contemplating the baby Jesus; another had his face blackened because he knelt on one knee rather than two; the remaining two fulfilled their obligations correctly: Another king was added in the explanation; two committed an error and two behaved correctly. Then in ritual they are reduced to two: In the dance-drama about the kings performed on Christmas Eve, two dancers represent the three kings.[2]

The physical world is also conceived in pairs: for example, sky and earth, mountains and plains. The creation of human beings occurs in fours: four men first, representing the four tribes of the world and the first mothers and fathers; their four women appear later in the story (Tedlock 1986).[3] All of them were created from food, from white corn and yellow corn.

Achi people conceive the order and qualities of the world and of all living things in the same way. Pairing is a cognitive strategy used to order the world and society; all categories of hierarchy, gender, and genre operate in dualities. This, then, is the underlying principle of Rabinal's division into four quarters. The municipality was first divided into higher land (to the east) and lowlands (to the west); these sections were then divided in two, creating the four quarters of the town, with the church as the center of the universe.

The saints are also conceived of in pairs (see Appendix 2) and dual principles of seniority (the older taking precedence) and gender determine their relationships. Most of the saints of Rabinal's sixteen *cofradías* are organized in pairs in such a way that whenever one is celebrated, its pair is also celebrated. For example, San Pedro Apostol is celebrated with his "younger" twin (San Pablo) on their shared saints' day (29 June) and again on the festival of the Conversion of San Pablo on 25 January. As Jesus sits at the right hand of God, so San Pedro Apostol occupies the right side and his younger brother occupies the left. The image of San José is paired with the image of the Virgen del Rosario, and so on.

Even children are thought of in pairs. Once, when Tono Cajbón's wife was telling me about the large number of children she had had, she counted them off in pairs, classifying them as "older" or "younger" as she went along. At one point she said, "Bernabé [her eldest son] isn't really the brother of Celestino [her second surviving son] because another son died after Bernabé. Celestino is the brother of Miguel Angel [her fourth son]."

Duality and Music

Everything in this world is dual, existing in complementary pairs. Of the many pairs of categories applied to music, the principal ones are:

q'ojom (percussion instrument) and su' (wind instrument)
Indian and Ladino
female and male
first and second
senior and junior
right and left

Su' and Q'ojom

The Achi classify their musical instruments by the way in which sound is produced. The classificatory system distinguishes two instrumental families: those on which sound is produced by striking the instruments (q'ojom), and those instruments that one has to blow (su').[4] Most of the instruments played in Rabinal fall into one of these two categories. (Stringed instruments such as the violin, the *violón* (double bass), and the guitar do not have names in the Achi language, even though the violin, accompanied by a square drum (*adufe* or tupe),[5] is used to accompany ritual prayers.) The q'ojom category includes all types of percussive instruments, such as drums, tumes (slit drums), and every kind of marimba; the su' category includes flutes, shawms, and trumpets.

Most instrumental ensembles are formed from a pair of instruments, a q'ojom and a su'. The ensembles for *son* music (the music of the ancestors) are shown in Appendix 3, together with ensembles for *pieza* music (nontraditional music).

All percussion instruments have primacy over wind instruments, as can be seen by the fact that all musicians are called ajq'ojom (workers of the drum). Furthermore, musical ensembles made up of a q'ojom and su' instrument pairing are named after the percussion instrument. The violin-and-adufe or tupe ensemble is called ajtupe mam (musicians of the tupe); the little flute-and-big drum ensemble is called ajnima q'ojom mam (musicians of the big drum), and the trumpets-and-tum ensemble is called the aj tum mam (musicians of the tum), and so on. Yet within the ojom-and-su' ensemble, the general rule is that the wind instrument is considered the first, or leader, of the two. The only exception to this is the big tum (slit drum) ensemble, in which the drum is considered the first or leader within its own musical ensemble.

This general primacy of percussion instruments may be explained by the fact that these instruments are more difficult to manufacture and are therefore considered more valuable than the su' instruments. Big drums and tumes are made from a single piece of hollowed tree trunk and are therefore more hardy and durable than wind instruments, which used to be made of cane but are nowadays made of copper or steel. Because of their durability, percussion instruments can be inherited down the generations—I saw drums dating back to the nineteenth century. Ancestor musicians had played them, and this gives them their greatest value. They are treated with more care than any other instrument. In fact, ancestor musicians' souls are said to reside in these old drums, and their knowledge, skill, and seniority helps to make the music sound good. Francisco Cortes, a drummer from Pichec, told me how he took care of his big drum: "We hang [up] the drum, and give it alcohol [pointing at the hole where the air comes out] because we are not the only ones who play it. Many others have passed [through life] playing it. When we die, others will play the drum. We have to remember those players who have died. We put the alcohol in it to remember them, because they are here inside."

FIGURE 3.1. Shawm-and-big-drum ensemble. Photo by Sergio Navarrete Pellicer.

FIGURE 3.2. Flute-and-big-drum ensemble. Photos this page by Sergio Navarrete Pellicer.

FIGURE 3.3. Flute-and-<u>tum</u> ensemble.

INDIAN AND LADINO

The basic distinction between Indians and Ladinos that characterizes Guatemala's social composition and organization has its origins in the country's colonial past (Warren 1992; Smith 1990; Adams 1994; McCreery 1994; Wilson 1995). From the early conquest period to the middle of the eighteenth century, settlements were divided into Indian towns and Spanish cities. In the latter lived Spaniards, their American-born descendants, Spanish-speaking Indians, Ladinos, African slaves, and mulattoes. Rabinal was established as an "Indian town"; today both Indians and Ladinos live there, albeit separately.

The Achi consider themselves descendants of the ancient Maya and thus the first inhabitants of the area;[6] they view Ladinos as foreigners because they arrived later with a distinct language and culture that emanated from the cities. The opposition between Indians and Ladinos contains a distinct ethnicity that is primarily expressed in the distinction between the rural culture of the majority Achi population, dispersed in settlements with no services, and the urban culture of Ladinos, who live in towns where all the services are concentrated. These differences are also applied to make distinctions between cities and Rabinal municipality as a rural area.

THE SON AND THE PIEZA

In terms of musical genre, the Achi establish a primary distinction between son and pieza music;[7] these are the musical categories used when referring to the distinction between Indians and Ladinos. The classification of sones and piezas has a historic and ethnic background that takes precedence over any other way of classifying music, and it is the most general distinction made by the people of Rabinal.[8] The classification, derived from empirical concepts used by Guatemalan society itself, is a clear and simple opposition between indigenous and Ladino culture.

Son music and the instruments used to play it are the musical heritage of the rajawales, the first Maya ancestors of the world of darkness, and that is why Rabinalenses consider it the musical genre of the "Indian race."[9] The musical repertoire of most of the musical ensembles in Rabinal are exclusively sones, which are played for the annual ritual cycle in cofradías, dance-dramas, life-crisis rituals, and on other occasions (listen to the son music example in track 2 on the CD).

By contrast, pieza music is generally considered, at least in classificatory terms, "foreign music"; so too are all newer musical genres, including popular radio music. Yet when I rephrased the question on separate occasions, I found that people did not find the pieza music they heard on the radio alien at all (see Chapter 4). The pieza repertoire includes waltzes, foxtrots, *cumbias*, *corridos* (polka style), *boleros*, *pasillos*, *merengues*, *guarachas*, and other popular rhythms. Piezas are Rabinalense Ladinos' favorite musical genre, but as Ladinos do not play music themselves, Indians play piezas for them at their festivities and ballroom dances. Piezas also attract the younger generation of Achi, who prefer to contract *conjunto* marimbas (pieza marimba, double bass, and drum set) for dancing at the groom's house at weddings. Ladinos say that pieza music is more *decente* and that Indians who hire conjunto marimba ensembles that play piezas are more "civilized" (listen to the pieza music example, track 3 on the CD).

Pieza music is also very popular in arrangements for both new dance-dramas and new versions of old ones. The same phenomenon occurred in the late nineteenth century, when what are now known as Ladinos introduced "old" piezas for the new dance-dramas of the time. That dance-dramas frequently portray Achi history may explain the acceptance of these piezas, which seem to have acquired the status of quasi-sones. Generally speaking, sones are equated with Indian history, while all musical

FIGURE 3.4. Son marimba at cemetery on the Day of the Dead. Photo by Sergio Navarrete Pellicer.

genres and styles introduced since the nineteenth century by Ladinos and "foreign" Indians are piezas and are equated with the foreign Ladino culture. Thus the classification contains other oppositions, such as rural (hamlet) : urban (town), uncivilized : civilized, and ancient : modern.

Son music is further classified according to context: there are sones *de baile* (sones for dance-dramas) and sones de cofradía. Sones de baile are only played for dance-dramas (which are performed at cofradía fiestas),[10] and cofradía sones are played for cofradías and on all other occasions, both religious and secular. Generally speaking, most musical ensembles participating in cofradía rituals, dance-dramas, or *zarabandas* use the same musical repertoire. For example, the sones played by the flute-and-big drum ensemble for each dancer in the Moros Tamorlán dance-drama are the same sones that the ensemble plays at cofradía rituals. The difference lies in the order in which the music is played. In the cofradía context, sones are grouped together by the number of mallets used by the center player, and the playing order within each category is unimportant, as the sones accompany neither dancers nor dancing order. It is the introductory formulae that are important here, as they act as markers for entrance rituals. In secular zarabandas as well as in the *surtido* sones (requests) played at the end of the ritual cycle, there is no order whatsoever. In short, the importance of order according to context changes music from one kind to another.

FEMALE AND MALE

Achi men and women are not considered complete unless they marry and have children. If people die before achieving these goals, it is believed that their souls will suffer because they left no family on earth to take care of them; they are therefore called especially to receive prayers.

Traditionally, wedding rituals bring a series of economic, social, and religious obligations and rights to the married couple and their parents (especially the groom's parents), as well as to the rest of the community through participation in the cofradías.[11] Tradition and modernity meet in wedding rituals, and their social value is reflected in the type of music chosen: son marimba in the bride's house, a conjunto marimba in the groom's.[12]

Some musicians explained that the difference in the music at the two parties was due to the fact that men are accustomed to hearing conjunto marimba music everywhere they work outside the community, while women, because they stay at home, are not. This explanation reflects general perceptions of the historical role Indian men and women have played in the capitalist system. While men have been extracted temporarily but periodically from their communities by Ladino authorities and contractors

FIGURE 3.5. Conjunto marimba at a wedding. Photo by Sergio Navarrete Pellicer.

to satisfy the labor needs of the plantation economy and to build the national infrastructure, women have remained in their communities, frequently taking on the entire responsibility for their family's needs. But this is an extremely stereotypical view. Women are not isolated from external cultural influences, though it is true that as children girls often spend more time working in the household than do boys. This results in intermittent school attendance and sometimes prevents girls from going to school altogether. But as they grow up, girls mix with others in Rabinal's weekly market and some also go to markets in nearby *municipios*; they are likely to be part of a work group preparing food when a relative organizes a fiesta; they listen to popular music on the radio. Women are being increasingly drawn into the labor market. Young single women go on their own to other urban areas including Guatemala City to work in *maquilas* (assembly plants) or as servants; young married women accompany their husbands to the plantations.

The difference between the musical genres played at the bride's and groom's fiestas is a way of reiterating and maintaining the ideal of traditional gender roles. The nurturing and domestic role of woman contrasts with the negotiating or political role of man, which implies greater exposure to the Ladino world. Women's nurturing and predominantly domestic role turns them into living symbols of Achi culture. This reification of women as the incarnation of local culture serves to maintain and preserve the cultural identity of Achi society; it also imposes limits and norms for correct female behavior that operate as a mechanism of male control over women, who are affected by this dynamic from an early age. At the same time, the pieza music played by the conjunto marimba at the groom's house symbolizes his wealth and higher social status because it identifies the groom with the popular culture emanating from the wealthier urban Ladino world. Ladino Mario Valdizón Ayala remarked, "In the weddings of *inditos* [literally, childlike Indians; a pejorative expression] who are more civilized, they use the pieza marimba at the groom's party because the young man already has had relations with Ladino people."

Among the tasks assigned to women and men within daily domestic life, the woman's role of daily nurturing and feeding the family is undoubtedly the most important. Through local Catholicism, this female role is extended to ritual activity, for it is women who prepare the food for all the guests. The preparation of food to be offered is a powerful symbolic act of sharing between family and community. Men are the negotiators, the *abogados* and musicians who make the symbolic offerings of food; but the offerings themselves, such as music, are generally symbolized as female.

Music is considered female because it is symbolic sustenance that is shared between the living and the dead. During fiestas its voice calls the people and the spirits of the dead to enjoy this and other offerings that have been specially prepared for them. Music is a food that nurtures sociality among the living and between the living and the dead. The violin and the tupe accompany the abogado's prayers to wake the souls of the dead to participate in anniversaries of the dead. Pipe and tabor music is a devotional or Marian call inviting people to contribute alms, maize, beans, candles, or money for the images of the Santos Reyes (Three Wise Kings), and the Virgins of La Natividad and Rosario (see the pipe-and-tabor ensemble in figure 3.6 and listen to its son music on track 4 of the CD). The big drum and flute call people's attention by announcing the arrival and departure of processions and entrances and exits to the cofradía altar (track 5 on CD). The marimba calls the people to the "four quarters of town" to participate in the festivities and to eat the tamales and other foods. When marimba music is played in zarabandas at cantinas, or when a festivity continues beyond the sones of farewell to the *ánimas* late at night, and surtido sones are being played, the instrument's female voice calls for dancing and drinking with women—in other words, to sexual interaction and evil.

The female spirit of the marimba has a dual character. It may take either a Marian and nurturing (motherly) role or the young female call of sexual pleasure (see Chapter 5). Among the Maya Atitecos, the wife of the youngest ancestral hero[13] is called Maria Castellana, a Ladino woman associated with all the delights of love. She is transformed into Maria Zarabanda, the many-breasted marimba woman (Tarn and Prechtel 1986, 177).

Calling the people is a female role, as pipe and tabor musician Eligio Gonzalez explains:

> This drum [tabor] is a woman because she is the one who calls everyone to the fiesta with a lot of love [devotion]. When the saints come [in procession or when visiting houses], people cross themselves when they hear the drum, waiting for the saint to pass, wondering which saint it might be. Then the people bow when the saint arrives. Even when people are in the middle of eating, they stop and go to see the drum coming . . . . The flute is the same—su' is its name—it is a woman because it calls the people; it accompanies the drum.

Music making is defined in terms of male and female complementarity: The female nature of the musical call, which is the offering itself, complements the exclusively male role of playing the music and delivering the

FIGURE 3.6. Pipe-and-tabor ensemble. Photo by Sergio Navarrete Pellicer.

offering. Complementarity can be further illustrated in the relationship between musicians and their instruments. For instance, the flute or pipe and tabor is the only ensemble in which both musical instruments are considered female. The apparent anomaly is resolved by the fact that it is the only ensemble in which one man plays two instruments. The female and male categories operating here refer to the complementary relationship between the male musician and his female instrumental ensemble. The opposite situation is found in the simple marimba ensembles, where three or four musicians play one single instrument that is considered female. Young musicians also make sexual commentaries on the interaction between themselves and the female voice and bodies of their instruments (see Chapter 5).[14]

Female and male duality is also used to describe the complementarity of instruments in musical ensembles of two instruments. Female and male attributes ascribed to instruments and parts of instruments follow the basic principle that female is to male as high is to low. The same principle is also used to describe the differences between the two sounds of double-headed drums. The skin of the head that is played is tightened for tuning purposes to a high pitch, which is considered the female side. The opposite side produces a lower pitch and is considered masculine. The female or high-pitched tone is preferred because musicians claim that it produces "more sound"; in other words, it can be more easily heard from afar.

Musicians also justify male and female qualities in other ways. In the pipe-and-tabor ensemble, for example, the reasons for assigning gender also relate to sound properties, but in a quite imaginative way. Both sides of the tabor are tightened together so that they are tuned to the same high pitch. The difference between them is a snaring sound produced by small pieces of wire attached to a string that extends across the drum skin on one side; this is the female side because it has a "necklace." The side played is the "male" side, but the characteristic sound of the drum is produced by the resonance of the female side. The layer of tripe applied to the holes of the marimba's resonators (which is what gives the instrument its unique buzzing sound) must come from a sow.

Female and male qualities are sometimes related to other pairs of categories (such as first and second, right and left), but musicians rarely make these associations explicit. For example, it is rare for musicians to mention female and male categories when talking about leading and following. Analyzed from different points of view, my data suggest that female instruments (or parts of instruments) play a leading role, but I was not able to develop this theory further. Stating the association between leadership and femaleness presents a contradiction with male dominance in daily life; it is not an issue that musicians feel comfortable with, and

FIGURE 3.7. Violin-and-adufe
ensemble at cemetery. Photo
by Sergio Navarrete Pellicer.

their silence speaks volumes. Nevertheless, the implications of giving not
only leadership to the female instrument, but also primacy through its
occupation of the right side—which is the sun side—are topics that require
further investigation.

The most important ensemble in terms of ritual practice is the violin-
and-adufe ensemble, as it accompanies the abogado's prayers to call the
souls to anniversaries of the dead (musical example on track 6 of the CD).
Before being replaced by the marimba about thirty years ago, this ensemble used to accompany abogados in cofradías and at weddings as well; a
generation before this it was also the musical ensemble played at zarabandas. In this ensemble, the violin is regarded as the female instrument.
This is the only ensemble about which musicians make the following
associations, which I am inclined to think are valid for most instrumental ensembles and their music: Female is to male as first is to second, as
high is to low, and as right is to left. The primacy of female over male is
also found in the order of naming their ancestors, q'ati q'amam (grandmothers and grandfathers). This primacy contrasts, at least at first glance,
with the generally subordinate position of women to men in everyday life.
Despite their central economic and educational role in the family, cultural
norms imply that women lack the requisite knowledge to negotiate with
both living outsiders (Ladinos) and dead insiders (ancestors). These roles,
and the authority accruing from them, are left to men.

The conceptualization of music cannot be seen simply as a direct reflection of social relationships. Cultural systems as moral and value systems are deep structures that do not interact in a mechanical way with social processes. "Female" may be associated with "first" in that certain social and religious values are derived from the central role of women as nurturers and providers of the sustenance. Their primacy in this realm is a reversal of male domination in daily life, which occurs during festivities where music is played, in changing moods, triggering memories, eliciting emotions, and changing perceptions.

FIRST AND SECOND

This pair of categories is used to define leadership. The local terms for leading and following are to "pull" and to "tail" behind. Leadership is a highly valued quality of people who have the courage to take on social responsibility for the benefit of the community. Cofradía *cargo* holders, abogados, musicians, civil authorities, and community leaders are all respected for the "burden" they assume in creating consensus, voicing the interests of the community, and organizing and conducting projects for the common good.

Leadership is essential to music making. All musical ensembles have a first or lead musician who "pulls" the other musician(s), and second musician(s) who *coleando* (follow) the leader. In son music ensembles, first and second voices correspond to the melodic part or instrument and to the rhythmic instrument or parts (including the harmonic part in the case of the marimba), respectively. The only important exception is the son music played by the big tum-and-two-trumpets ensemble for the Rabinal Achi dance-drama, where primacy is given to the percussion instrument. The big tum has primacy over the trumpets because each son is distinguished by a different rhythmic pattern played on the tum and because the tum starts and finishes each son with a particular musical formula called an *alto* (stop). José León Coloch, drummer and director of the Rabinal Achi dance-drama, defined the instruments' different roles: "The instruments that have music changes in the sones are the tum with different rhythms and the lower trumpet. The first trumpet is the same." The second (lower-pitch) tone trumpet has a rhythmic supportive role; the first (higher-pitch) tone trumpet plays the same fanfare *por puntos* to indicate specific points in the proceedings, such as the point at which the warrior dancers make their war cries four times in the direction of the four corners of the world, or to separate the dialogue of the two main characters (K'iche' Achi and Rabinal Achi). The musical parts of each instrument are relatively autonomous, coordinating at points—like altos and war cry puntos—where musical patterns change (example of tum and trumpets son on track 7 of the CD).[15] Both Jose León Coloch and the older, experienced first-trumpet player Victor Tum told me that the tum leads the music, but in practice Victor leads the ensemble by signaling to the tum player. This is because his usual tum partner, Jose León, is otherwise occupied in performing the most important role of the K'iche' Achi, and younger apprentices who take his place on the tum are "no good."

In the violin-and-adufe ensemble, the violin is considered female and first. Here the violin takes the lead because it carries a melody and begins and ends the sones, and when both change rhythmic pattern, the violin leads and the drum follows.

In music, leadership is defined according to the voice that changes first or more often. With this in mind and considering the musical repertoire of most ensembles and the instruments' positions within each ensemble, instruments with a predominantly melodic role that also produce higher-pitch tones are first, and are positioned to the right (from the musicians' perspective). These are the treble section of the marimba and all su' instruments (except trumpets, as explained above) and the violin. The second and "follower" parts and instruments, positioned to the left, are the q'ojom instruments. These are all percussion instruments: the harmonic and rhythmic sections in the marimba, drums, and tumes (except the big tum, as explained above).

The formula for consistent correspondences is that first is to second as su' is to q'ojom, as high is to low, and as right is to left. The first/second category pair is also applied to the subordinate role of music in relation to the dance-drama performers.

The different order between cofradía sones and sones de baile outlined above stems from the first and second relationship established between music and dance-drama or religious ritual. Music "follows" the ritual or dance-drama actions. When no ritual activity is performed or when music is played on nonreligious occasions, son music is played with no particular order and is known as surtido sones.

First and second are often related to senior and junior—for example, when apprentice musicians learn to play from older musicians. Traditionally, senior musicians play the leading, high-pitch tone instruments because their melodies are the most complicated and require the most experience (see Chapter 7). I have already suggested that despite the fact that q'ojom instruments are considered second, they have a kind of primacy at a general level that stems from their senior position as physically older instruments that have been played by ancestor musicians.

RIGHT AND LEFT

In music, right and left are important categories of order that are always used in association with "first and second" (above): The leading and high-pitch tone instruments are to the musicians' right; and it is the right hand that has the most work and changes to perform.

Christian ideology visualizes Jesus as sitting to the right of God the Father in heaven, thus giving primacy to the right side. According to Tono López, an Achi linguist and member of the Academy of Mayan Languages in Rabinal, the right side is also associated with east, north, and "up" orientations, which are believed to be the path taken by the sun during the day, while the left side is associated with the west, south and "down" orientations of the sun's path under the earth, closing the entire cosmic circle (see Chapter 2). The path of the sun is reproduced in ritual prayers and actions that are organized in hierarchical order, beginning from a conceptual right orientation.

HIGH AND LOW

In the dual description of the world, high and low represent sky and earth, mountains and plains, or east (sunrise) and west (sunset). In ritual these categories are associated with first and second, right and left. *Cargueros'* and abogados' ritual crossing to the four corners of the world in religious celebrations moves to the right and is performed first standing up facing the sky and then again kneeling facing the earth.

In music, high (alto) and low (bajo) refer to high-pitch tone and low-pitch tone respectively, although no direct associations are made with up and down directions. Rather, alto and bajo are associated with right and left, which are related to up and down directions as previously explained.

SENIOR AND JUNIOR

This is one of the most important category pairings to be applied to relations between living generations and between the living and the dead. Values and behavior are learned from older generations, whose knowledge and experience serve as a guide that younger generations are meant to respect and follow. Senior and junior are by nature an oppositional duality, and the authority of the elders is always contested ground as soon as the younger generation feel that they have gained enough knowledge from their own experiences to vie for position. Senior and junior categories are not related to a specific number of years, age differences between people being relative and always indicating a senior or junior position.

Learning music in the traditional way follows the principle of seniority in that teachers are older and more experienced musicians. For instance, in the learning tradition of the big drum and little flute, apprentices learn to play the drum first and then the flute. As drummers gain experience accompanying the flute, they eventually begin to play the flute, which is more difficult. When flautists are too old to fulfill their obligations as musicians, drummers start to look for someone who is willing to take up the drum and switch to the flute themselves. The senior/junior relationship between flautist and drummer guarantees the transmission of skills, knowledge, and style from one generation to the next.

A similar procedure is adopted for learning the marimba, although today it is often youngsters who teach their elders the new music (see Chapter 7). Achi find it conceptually difficult to separate experience from age or maturity, as can be seen by the myth built around the twelve-year-old Jesus confounding the elders in the Temple (Luke 2) cited in Chapter 2.

DUALITY IS THE MAIN PRINCIPLE OF ORDER under which all other categories operate. It is a cognitive strategy that orders the world (both natural and social) and explains its qualities in terms of relationships between binary symbolic categories. Every form has its complementary form, which may be related to other pairs of qualities. When musicians talked to me about music, musical instruments, and music making, they usually made only one association with a pair of categories. Reference to a second-category pairing was generally only made to explain further the properties defined by the first pair. They rarely made abstractions of all the possible associations simultaneously.

Those categories that directly address the social order (e.g., Indian/Ladino, female/male) receive more attention, for they explain how views about society (in this case, ethnicity and gender) give meaning to music. And in turn, musical sounds, musical instruments, and music making become symbols or images of the dual and complementary order of social relations.

4   The Marimba and the Son

MARIMBA MUSIC is part of the "soundscape" of all of Guatemala's hamlets, villages, towns, and cities. Its present repertoire includes dance *sones* from the seventeenth, eighteenth, and nineteenth centuries such as the *zarabanda*, the *contredanse* and dance, and a rich repertoire of sones; it also includes many other dance pieces of the nineteenth and twentieth centuries, mainly waltzes, known as "semi-classical pieces," and classical music of the piano repertoire. We may also hear pieces from the jazz band repertoire of the first half of the twentieth century. And because transistor radios have made *marimba* music accessible to all, the repertoire has further diversified with adaptations of Latin American and even international popular music. What is quite stunning is the musicians' ability to keep in vogue the many diverse kinds of music that are part of Guatemala's musical history.

In this chapter I will focus on the historical origins and development of the marimba and the musical genre known as *son*. The first section is a broad review of the social history of the marimba in Guatemala from its arrival in the sixteenth century to the present; this will be complemented with references to the presence of the marimba in other regions of Latin America. The African origins of the marimba and the European provenance of most of its repertoire suggest that the marimba music tradition developed during the colonial era in towns with multiethnic populations—Spanish, Ladino, mulatto, and Indian. It was therefore born as a *Mestizo* (mixed) tradition.

The second section examines the way people remember the introduction of the marimba in Rabinal, where it is played exclusively by Achi musicians. The marimba began to be incorporated into Achi ritual life some two generations after the Achi began playing for Ladino festivities at the turn of the twentieth century; I describe the types of marimba found in Rabinal. The third and fourth sections are dedicated to the historical and musicological analysis of son music; I will discuss the relationship between the musical structure of the son and the historical and social context in which it is played.

The final section takes a brief look at the introduction of radios and tape recorders, which have revolutionized marimba playing in Rabinal. This has been included here because nonindigenous music presents many of the same issues that Indians faced during the early colonial era and between 1750 and 1850, when the state promoted the settlement of Ladinos in Indian towns.

A BRIEF HISTORY OF THE MARIMBA IN GUATEMALA AND ITS PRESENCE IN LATIN AMERICA

The passionate nationalistic discourse that arose in Guatemala during the first half of the twentieth century and continues into the present provided the context for Guatemalan musicologists' interest in the origins of the marimba. Marimba music had been part of the daily life of all social groups and classes in Guatemala's bigger towns and cities for several generations, and it is therefore not surprising that intellectuals such as Jesus Castillo (1977), David Vela (1958), and especially Armas Lara (1970) claimed a pre-Hispanic origin for the marimba and glorified it as an ancient national treasure.[1] As such, the marimba has been employed as a symbol of the cultural identity of all Guatemalans.

That Guatemalans lack a common heritage was shown by the controversy that arose in the national press in 1977–78 concerning the poetic inscription selected for a national monument to the marimba in Quelzaltenango City.[2] One participant in the debate—Rafael Ixcot, an Indian intellectual who took the pre-Hispanic origins of the marimba for granted—pointed to Ladino society's attempts to legitimize and authenticate "national" culture through the ideological manipulation of Indian cultures. Ixcot remarked on the actual separation and conflict between Indian and Ladino societies in Guatemala and bitterly criticized the erection of monuments and the composition of poetry glorifying the indigenous race, which were designed merely as a façade for foreign tourists. According to Ixcot, the monument and its inscription also served another purpose: They were, he said, "cathartic expressions of the Ladino who needs exorcism to alleviate himself from their shameful feelings of their collective subconscious" (López Mayorical 1978, 334; Monsanto 1982, 61–72).[3]

Although the African origins of the marimba had been known to academics for several decades, the debate about the instrument's function as a national symbol (which simultaneously veiled the country's multiethnic nature) has erroneously promoted the idea among the wider public that it is an ancient Maya instrument. A recent book by musician and researcher Lester Godínez, *La marimba Guatemalteca* (2002), is an important contribution to the understanding of the origins and transformations of this remarkable instrument. This work very clearly and systematically summarizes our knowledge about the African origins of instruments of this type, characterized by the "consecutive grouping of wooden bars"—xylophones of diverse kinds—and the probable Southeast

Asian influence on the development of African instruments. This can be seen in the case of the *kilangay* of Madagascar, the *m'bila* and the *valimba* of Mozambique and Malawi, and the *balaphon* (a kind of marimba) of the Mandinga of Guinea and of western coastal Africa. According to Gerhard Kubik, the word "marimba" (or its variation "malimba") is a term of Bantu origin from the root *rimba* or *limba*, meaning "flat protruding object" with the prefix *ma-*, and thus designates an instrument with a succession of bars or flat keys.[4] The Bantuist Yves Monino relates the term to the kikongo Bantu language.[5] The arc marimba, with resonators of *tecomates* (gourds), used in Guatemala is built with surprising similarity to the Chopi Bantu *timbila* of Mozambique, and with the *balaphons* of the Mandinga of western Africa.[6]

Garfias's (1983) comparison of Central American marimbas with those found in Africa from Senegal to Mozambique supports Chenoweth's conclusion about the African origins of the Guatemalan marimba (1964). Garfias found strong similarities between African xylophones and the arc marimbas with gourd resonators of the Guatemalan highlands, Guanacaste, Costa Rica, and Masaya, Nicaragua. He suggests that the African marimba could have been introduced to the Americas along the Pacific coastal areas of Costa Rica and Nicaragua (ibid., 207). Garfias has no explanation for the diffusion of the marimba, which did not reach other regions of the Americas inhabited by Africans, yet extended to regions, such as the Guatemalan highlands, populated by indigenous peoples. Indirect evidence for his theory can be found in the colonial archives. Documents attached to a 1769 prohibition (Chaclán 1993) mention the marimba being played in Santiago de Apastepeque (now in El Salvador, Santiago de Apastepeque is in the Pacific hinterland and forms part of the cultural corridor through which, Garfias suggests, the marimba traveled to the Guatemalan highlands from the slave settlements on the coast between Costa Rica and Nicaragua).[7]

Today the marimba tradition can be found in virtually all Central American countries as well as in Ecuador and Colombia. Scruggs's (1998a, 1999b) detailed studies of the dance of the marimba in Monimbó, Masaya, and in the city of Masaya, in Nicaragua, gives details about the use of the twenty-two-key arc marimba accompanied on guitar or *guitarrilla* during the celebrations of the saints and especially of the dead.

The Nicaraguan arc marimba lacks the tecomates of the Guatemalan marimba. Its resonators were originally made from bamboo, but cedar was later substituted in the same cylindrical shapes. These resonators also have holes in their lower segments that are covered with a membrane made of pig's gut and stuck into place with bee's wax (Scruggs 1999b, 96–99). The music accompanies a dance called a marimba dance, a generic name for several dances with differing costumes that are performed during the processions of the saints. Scruggs documents the presence of the marimba in Izalco, El Salvador. Marroquín (1998, 709) states that in this country there are two kinds of marimba—arc and Creole—but does not describe them. These references testify to the continuity of the marimba tradition in El Salvador that dates to the eighteenth century if not earlier, according to information from Santiago Apastepeque. Godínez (2002, 148) affirms that the use of the diatonic marimba is almost extinct in this country but that there is a strong presence of the Guatemalan chromatic marimba. This is also the case in Honduras and Belize. Scruggs (1998a, 742) adds that in Tegucigalpa, the capital city of Honduras, as well as in the capitals of the other Central American countries, the double marimbas, accompanied by double bass, drums and other instruments, are frequently played in tourist hotels.

Carlos A. Fernández records the presence of the marimba in Costa Rica (1998a, 695). He describes a simple marimba with thirty to forty-two keys, introduced in the eighteenth century by Franciscan missionaries from Guatemala. In the nineteenth century it was a popular instrument in the area of Guanacaste and the central plateau of Costa Rica. The *son suelto* (single son) dance called "Mamachilinda" presented by Fernández is a song and dance that has characteristics of the *baile suelto* similar to that of the Guatemalan son (ibid., 699).

In Mexico the marimba has a very strong presence in the southern states of Oaxaca, Veracruz, Tabasco, and Chiapas. Here the Chiapas-style chromatic marimba built by Borráz from Venustiano Carranza is used. It has a keyboard layout similar to that of the piano and in this respect differs from the marimba Hurtado of Quetzaltenango, Guatemala, which has two rows of keys, one above the other. In Mexico the chromatic marimba is played on its own or accompanied with other instruments—generally the double bass or bass, drums, and a group of both brass and woodwind instruments. In the Isthmus region of Oaxaca the marimba has been incorporated into large orchestras, while in Chiapas there are many modern marimba groups that have been encouraged to use the "pure" marimba, a tradition described by Kaptain in his well-known book, *The Wood That Sings: The Marimba in Chiapas, Mexico* (1992). It is worth noting that even though Chiapas and Guatemala encompass the same ethnic cultural region, the diatonic marimba has almost completely disappeared from Chiapas. But the diatonic or simple marimba survives as a very vital tradition throughout Guatemala.

The marimba is played in other areas of the American continent, including the coastal regions of Colombia and Ecuador. App (1998, 400–412) mentions the use of the marimba within the Afro-Colombian musical tradition on the Pacific Coast. Liberated blacks initiated the construction of these marimbas during the sixteenth century using principles from the models of western Africa. The keys are made out of palm tree bark laid on two wooden planks with bamboo resonators. The number of keys varies from eighteen to twenty-eight. They are normally played by two musicians: the *bordonero* (bass) plays the melodic ostinato on the lower keys and the *tiplero* (treble) improvises a contrapuntal melody with ornaments on the higher register keys. The marimba is hung from the roof of a *palapa* (palm shelter). In the entertainment context, the *currulao* (courtship) is danced in the marimba house. It is believed that the currulao is a seventeenth-century dance that was dispersed along with the migration of slaves from the area of Cartagena toward the Pacific Coast with the migration of the slaves. The group that plays the currulao consists of two *cununeros* (people who play two conical drums, one large, one small), two *bomberos* (who play the drum or double drumhead *bombos*), two marimberos, a *guasa* (rattle), and a principal male singer, commentator, or *glosador*, with a female chorus forming the "answerers." The marimba and drums play complex syncopated rhythms accompanied by songs with comments and answers. There are at least thirty different bass currulao melodies combining nine different rhythms that include the *bambuco*, *agua larga*, fugue, *patacoré*, and others. The choreography of the dancing couple represents the courtship between a man and woman; the woman rejects the man until he gives up, whereupon she accosts him. Schechter (1998, 427–28) found this same marimba currulao dance tradition among the Afro-Ecuadorian tropical forest dwellers of Esmeraldas on the Pacific Coast. He compares it with the homophonic texture of the marimba music of Central America. This is essentially contrapuntal, incorporating overlapping rhythmic cycles (added rhythms) that create complex poly-rhythms related to the rhythmic organization and texture typical of western Africa. It observes in the singing an interplay between the glosador (commentator) and the soloist among those who respond.

In Guatemala the oldest existing references to the marimba are those of the western highlands, which state that the marimba has been played since 1680 by Indians from villages around the old capital city of Guatemala (now known as Antigua). The historian Juarros quotes Don Diego Félix de Carranza y Córdoba, priest of Jutiapa, who, in his description of the inaugural ceremonies and dedication of the new cathedral of Santiago de los Caballeros in Guatemala, mentions in the procession "a troop of militar drums, kettledrums, bugles, trumpets, marimbas and all the instruments used by the Indians" (Godínez 2002, 80–91; Chenoweth 1964, 74).

In a 1928 news article, Victor Miguel Diaz stated that the marimba was widely used among Guatemala's Indians by 1737: "in those days, some marimbas could be seen in various Indian communities as well as in the regions of San Gaspar and Jocotenango, each instrument is played

FIGURE 4.1. Arc marimba from Chichicastenango. Photo by Judith Zur.

by one individual."[8] Later the same year, when describing the Santa Cecilia procession, Diaz commented: "and here is added the noise made by players of *chirimias* (shawms), reed flutes, drum in confusion, *marimbas de tecomates* (gourd marimbas) and many other instruments which the natives played simultaneously, producing noise enough to be heard from a great distance" (Chenoweth 1964, 75).

THE MARIMBA AND THE ZARABANDA

It is my belief that the early adoption of the marimba by indigenous societies is a testimony to the early cultural and racial mixing of African, Spanish, and Indian populations. Evidence for this view can be found in the African origin of the instrument, the European repertoire, and the predominantly Indian musicians. Numerous decrees forbade the presence of mulattoes and Mestizos in Indian towns,[9] which suggests that it was common for these ethnic groups to live together in settlements. The record also suggests that the different ethnicities shared a musical culture and the ritual customs essential to their religious life. Zarabandas were common among Indian, Spanish, Mestizo, and mulatto populations in the Indian towns of Zapotitlán province (the contemporary provinces of Retalhuleu and Suchitepequez) in the early 1600s (Ordoñez 1989). One and a half centuries later, in 1769, Archbishop Cortés y Larras affirmed that the zarabandas were commonplace throughout the Guatemalan Archdiocese (Alejos 1992, 243).

The earliest references to zarabandas appear in a poem by Fernando Guzmán Mexía in a Panamanian manuscript of 1539[10] and in a composition "glossed in the divine manner" entitled "Zarabanda ven ventura, Zarabanda ven y dura" (Zarabanda come thine fortune, zarabanda come and stay), by Pedro de Trejo, a Spanish poet living in New Spain (López Mena, 1996, 80, 101, 102, 219, 220). Trejo's Christmas carols and chansonettes were sung during solemn religious ceremonies at the cathedral in Pátzcuaro, Mexico, in 1566–67. The title and first couplet and refrain of his famous zarabanda go like this:

El criador es ya criatura.	The Creator is now a child
Zarabanda ven y dura.	Zarabanda come and stay.
Tiene Dios hecha una ley	God has a law made
desde que Adán le ofendió,	for Adam offended him,
que al hijo, que es Dios y rei,	which the Son obliged to die
a la muerte le obligó	because He's God and King,
por salvar a la criatura.	thus were all God's children saved.
Zarabanda, ven y dura.	Zarabanda, come and stay.

Pedro de Trejo lived during the most violent period of the Inquisition and was tried and convicted; he died shortly after serving his sentence. His zarabanda and Christmas carol compositions reveal a folkloric vein, and, while he cultivated the major arts, these pieces place him in the tradition of the minor arts associated with songs and dances that were so hotly condemned by the Inquisition.

According to Cervantes and his contemporaries, the zarabanda and the *chaconne* were the most popular dances of sixteenth-century Spain. In his "Celoso Extremeño" (The Jealous Man from Extremadura) Cervantes talks about the "devilish son of the zarabanda," and the character Loaysa sings the lines of the zarabanda "in the divine manner." In the "Ilustre Fregona" (The Distinguished Washerwoman) it appears as a contemporary dance together with the *folias* and chaconnes (Salazar 1949, 347). What is striking in these frequent references is that we are told that these dances were performed to music played by guitars and other instruments, with songs characteristic of each dance. The *Diccionario de autoridades* (Dictionary of the Authorities) of 1737 (1990) states that the zarabanda is a "vivacious and jolly music and a dance of repetitious, immodest movements of the body." It adds that Covarrubias traces the origins of the word to the Hebrew "zara," meaning, among other things, "to move in circles." This source also says that the "dirty and indecent poem called zarabanda, is sung, played and danced at the same time." The popular enjoyment surrounding the zarabanda is also denigrated in the same sources, which use the same harsh adjectives used when the dance was banned in Guatemala and New Spain during colonial times.

Just as the marimba in America is connected to the black slave population, the word zarabanda is also tied to the central African Congolese and Nigerian Yoruba religions practiced in Cuba. This is where the *santería* (an Afro-Cuban religion) has a zarabanda god image—its equivalent is the Ogun of the Orisha, the god of metals, and of the forge—the archetype of the violent events that result from human frailty and lack of control. He is represented as a country fellow with straw hat and machete.[11] It is no surprise that characters such as this should be present in dances called zarabandas organized in the sugar cane fields, as is mentioned in the historical sources of this and the following chapters.

Historical sources give two meanings to zarabanda.[12] It is a social event, where people drink and dance to son music at *cofradía* fiestas, at children's wakes, peasant ranches, or in cantinas; it is also a particular dance in which both men and women participate, also performed during cofradía celebrations and, by extension, the music of that dance.[13] In other words, the colonial authorities' use of the term represents the denial or rejection of any religious element in what was being performed; it is in this sense—a nonreligious social event with music, dancing, and alcohol—that the word is used today in Rabinal. In the contemporary neighboring department of Alta Verapaz there are instrumental ensembles called zarabandas formed by a harp, a small guitar, and a *rabel* (a bowed string instrument). Saenz Poggio (1997, 81) identified them from 1877 as a sort of orchestra called zarabanda (listen to track 15 on the CD).[14]

Zarabandas originated as dances within Ladino cofradía celebrations in which other colonial castes participated. These became popular among the newly introduced Indian cofradía celebrations. Colonial religious and civil authorities issued prohibitions against musical and dance events such as zarabandas, where the mingling of the races and high alcohol consumption deviated from colonial civil and religious authorities' ideals of religious devotion.

The personal and financial interests of local Spanish authorities often led them not only to turn a blind eye to the presence of fellow Spaniards, mulattoes, and Mestizos but to open taverns in Indian towns[15] close to Ladino plantations, ranches, and unauthorized dispersed settlements (*pajuides*) (Alejos 1992, 252). In 1877 José Saenz Poggio (1997, 71) recommended that festive dances in the style of the rustic villagers be played and danced during the private gatherings of Guatemala's upper-class society in order to exercise and improve the health of ladies: "Hopefully may the rustic villagers be an example. They who in thatch roof shacks, with no more illumination than a burning pine torch happily gather and dance to the son music of the gay marimba, the much talked about *barreño*."[16] The chronicler undoubtedly refers to the pajuides of colonial times, when Ladinos, Indians, and mulattoes shared dance, music, and song during moments of rest and entertainment and on religious holidays. These conditions induced cross-cultural exchanges, and it was on this fertile ground that the development of the marimba began, later spreading to the whole country, including the important towns of the provinces of Huehuetenango, Totonicapán,[17] and above all the cities of Antigua and Quetzaltenango. The latter city is considered the capital of the marimba because it was there that the most illustrious Guatemalan families of marimba players appeared. The chromatic marimba was also invented in Quetzaltenango at the end of the nineteenth century.

Indigenous societies' adoption of the marimba guaranteed its survival and the development of local characteristics in terms of both the instrument and the music played on it. Similarly, the popular musical repertoire and other musical instruments introduced to Indian towns by the Spanish in the sixteenth century survive today, in this case mainly among Maya groups. In addition to the African marimba, new instruments included the *vihuela* (a sixteenth-century five-string Spanish guitar), the *rabel*, the viola, the harp, the shawm, and various kinds of drums.[18] The Indian villages adopted all these instruments and developed local repertoires that were soon identified as part of the Indian tradition.

While hardly unfamiliar with the revelry surrounding European Catholic festivals, the colonial authorities were appalled by the presence of what they considered secular music, profane dancing, and alcohol consumption within the ritual sphere. As far as they were concerned, these things demonstrated Indians' continuing faith in pagan cults, with their disorderly behavior and excesses, and indicated a lack of respect for God.[19] Hence the application of the word *zarabanda* to both these events and particularly abhorrent elements of it.

Priests complained about the practice of holding zarabandas at children's wakes. In 1769 Archbishop Cortés y Larras announced that anyone performing them would be excommunicated, although it seems that there was some tolerance of these events if they took place in daylight. The evidence collected for the archbishop by the deputy parish priest of Santiago de Apastepeque about children's wakes makes no mention of dancing.[20] It does, however, give direct information on the ethnicities of participants and the instruments they played (Chaclán 1993, 83–87). Guitarists included a free mulatto who played sones; a man from León, Nicaragua, and an Indian, each accompanied by an Indian playing the *caramba* (musical bow), and another mulatto accompanied by a stranger from a neighboring town playing violin. By 1769 some instruments—the marimba and caramba[21]—were already seen as being played solely by Indians.

Other records show that Indians' and poor mulattoes' use of music at children's wakes was also common practice in Verapaz. A royal provision sent on 18 April 1799 to the provincial mayor, then resident in Salamá (now the provincial capital of Baja Verapaz), asked him to persuade Indians and mulattoes to limit the number of festivals and zarabandas held to celebrate the saints and children's wakes.[22] Unfortunately, this document does not include information about the music. However, a manuscript dated 1847 from the Indian town of Cajbón, Alta Verapaz, reveals that six Indian musicians played the marimba at children's wakes and another three or four played violins; they also played the harp, which, through striking the resonating box, was also used as a percussive instrument (Morales 1983, 62).

Another possible reason for the relative scarcity of musical information in the colonial records concerning children's wakes is that music at these events was too commonplace to remark upon. Music was an integral part of children's wakes in Spain:

> Children's wakes are considerably different from adult wakes. According to Catholic dogma, children die without mortal sin, therefore proceeding directly to heaven without traversing through purgatory. Thus the death of an angel, not withstanding the pain and selfish grief of the parents, is a joyous event. Previously, friends and relatives, particularly the young, gathered with guitars and castanets to express their happiness by singing and dancing all night. This dance for the angels was particularly characteristic, at least in recent history, of the Mediterranean region, in the South from Castellon to Murcia; in Extremadura and the Canary Islands. (Foster 1985, 253)[23]

In sum, it is safe to say that the history of the marimba in Guatemala is closely related to the history of the zarabanda, especially the zarabanda as social event. Even as late as 1802, when the Catholic Church was rapidly losing its political grip on the country (see Chapter 1), the religious authorities were still railing against this music and these dances. An example of this is found in a document from Suchitepequez province that disapproves of the celebration of zarabandas among Indians and mulattoes, men and women, every Saturday and Sunday.[24] In effect, the diverse ethnicities appearing in contexts where the marimba is featured makes it an omnipresent tradition. Nevertheless, the marimba's role as a symbol of nationalism occurs later, during the first half of the twentieth century, coinciding with the Ladino elite's romantic and exotic vision of the Indian's cultural heritage. This has produced profound ideological messages and has encouraged the identification of the Guatemalan nation-state with the ancestral culture of Indian societies (see Anderson 1991; Bartok 1987; Turino 2003).

The Zarabanda and the Son

Stanford (1984a, 10–11) argues that in Mexico the term "son" has three aspects: musical, literary, and choreographic. From a musical point of view, the main characteristic is the 3:2 proportion in the rhythm called *sesquialtera* (from the Latin "sesqui," meaning addition of one half: 1 + 1/2 = 3/2). This term derives from a proportion of mensural notation (Apel 1961, 96–125), which means, in plain terms, the reduction of three pulsations into two pulsations in the same duration of time, and therefore the increase of the temporal value of each pulsation by one-half. This is represented by one dot in each pulsation. Rolando Pérez sees in this change the influence of African music in the south of Spain and Latin America (1990, 65–69).

This proportion also appears in contemporary writing as the alternating of simple triple meter 3/4 and compound duple meter 6/8. With respect to the literary form, it has a strophic structure, with a refrain. The instrumental introduction can be played between the *coplas* (stanzas), which are the basic component, usually consisting of four, five, or more octosyllabic verses or lines, with a love or picaresque theme. The choreographic aspect is a couple's dance with *zapateo* (foot tapping).

An analysis of the tunings, structures, and rhythms of the string instruments and music of the Zinacanteco Maya and Chamula Indians of Chiapas indicates that in sixteenth- and seventeenth-century Mexico, harps, guitars, and violins were very similar to the instruments, musical groups, tuning techniques, and rhythms common to Spain and other Western European regions (Harrison and Harrison 1968). The Harrisons reason that both the San Sebastian son and the bolonchon Zinacanteco and Chamula (secular-themed songs among the Chamulas, accompanied by string instruments) are chaconnes (a sixteenth-century dance originating in New Spain), and that their basic rhythms correspond to that of the zarabanda, with its characteristic sesquialtera proportion of 3:2. Stevenson (1986, 28) also argues that zarabanda and chacona dances appeared first in Mexico in the middle of the sixteenth century, later gaining popularity in Spain (cf. Van der Lee 1995, 216). And Stanford (1984a, 10–11) believes that the zarabanda, *jarabe*, *pavana*, and other dance pieces are variations of the son type.

During colonial times, the villages where Mestizos, mulattoes, and Spaniards lived together with the overwhelmingly Indian population celebrated their feast days with dances that alternated with the singing of stanzas in diverse metrics. One of these dances was the zarabanda. Later on the *seguidilla* gained popularity: "the *seguidilla* sidelined the zara-banda and others will come that will lead to its downfall and disappear-ance."[25] The seguidilla was the most widespread form throughout Spain and had a strong influence on some types of son in different parts of Mexico (e.g., the jarabe, *jarana*, and *huapango*). From a literary per-spective, Saldivar (1987, 246–50) traces elements of the contemporary Mexican son to Spanish *cancioneros* (songbooks) and believes that six-teenth-century popular Mexican love songs were sones.

This Spanish tradition was reinterpreted and transformed by African slaves into idiosyncratic dances that in turn inspired such church musi-cians as the Portuguese organist and chapel master of Guatemala Cathe-dral, Gaspar Fernández, to write four- and ten-part pieces used in church services. When living in Puebla, Mexico, Fernández compiled a cancionero between 1609 and 1616 (Tello 2001; Lehnoff 1986, 124–32).[26] The song-book includes Christmas carols called *guineos*, which are learned musi-cal interpretations of popular music with Spanish lyrics that imitate the pronunciation of Africans and mulattoes. One guineo is entitled "'Tururu farara con son," indicating an African-Spanish text accompanied by son music. The sentence "zarabanda tengue que tengue" appears in another guineo for five voices called "Eso rigo e repente" (Stevenson 1986, 29–34), in which the music presents a sesquialtera (3:2) proportion in the melody but not harmonically; the rhythmic patterns are long but not complex and keep varying.

The influence of the black and Indian cultures on the composers and chapel masters of the cathedrals are part of the rich exchange of musi-cal ideas among the so-called popular oral and the written traditions dur-ing the colonial period (see Burke 1997, 124–35). In his analysis of the work of the eighteenth-century Guatemalan composer Rafael Antonio Castellanos, the musicologist Lehnoff (1994, 112–15) traces the influ-ence of Indian and black Christmas carols. He notes musical and liter-ary elements in these songs that refer to the manners of speech among these social groups. The cases of other master chapels of the late eigh-teenth and early nineteenth centuries where popular *villancicos* were written include Esteban de León Garrido, Miguel Pontaza, and the Saenz family (Behague 1980).

THE MARIMBA AND DANCE-DRAMAS

Marimba music was also incorporated into Guatemala's rich repertoire of dance-dramas (Mace 1981, 83–136).[27] Some dance-dramas of pre-His-panic origin are accompanied by diatonic marimbas with wooden res-onators for one musician called *tenor*:[28] examples include the kiej (deer) dance-drama of the Ixil towns of San Pedro Necta, San Juan Ixcoy, and

San Francisco de Cotzal in the province of Quiche (Paret Limardo 1963, 18), and the famous *palo volador* (flying pole) dance-drama of the towns of Cubulco and Joyabaj (the municipalities to the west of Rabinal).[29] The music of other versions of these ancient *bailes* (dance-dramas) in other towns used to be and in some cases, still is—played on pre-Hispanic instruments or European string instruments (Paret Limardo 1963; Montoya 1970, 26). This suggests flexibility in the adaptation of bailes to local musical traditions.

Most of today's repertoire of Guatemalan dances are re-creations of colonial dances and dance-dramas, mainly from the literary form called *loa* (praise), written in Spanish by Ladino amateur writers during the nineteenth century, when the most important period of ladinoization or Ladino colonization of the Indian villages took place (see Chapter 1) (Mace 1981, 83, 111–13). The dances were choreographed for the celebrations of the cofradías and were based primarily on Indian oral tradition. Nowadays they also tackle contemporary concerns such as ecology.

Some of Rabinal's most popular dances today were actually written in the nineteenth century, among them the dance *los toritos* (bullocks) which is known as the *costeño*. This dance, which is represented by many different groups in Rabinal, is the one most people want to see performed.

For purposes of this discussion, the most important element of these nineteenth-century dance-dramas is the accompanying music: European dances adapted to the diatonic marimba. The main theme of the costeño is a *contradanza* (French contredanse).

The musical example of the contradanza shows the basic characteristics of the French contredanse, which is a 2/4 meter with four eighth notes on the bass, a local rhythmic variation on the melodic line that resembles the tango rhythm of the Cuban contradanza, also derived from the French version, and the same form consisting of two sections of eight measures, each repeated twice or in variation form (Fernández 1989, 116–34).

Costeño   Tango

The *animalitos* (little animals) dance includes another old dance, *danza de la muerte* (the dance of death) from the early nineteenth century. This is a slow piece with a simple triple meter. Here the sesquialtera is evident in the changes in accent and rhythm produced by the combination of simple triple meters written in eighths and triple meters written

CONTRADANZA

FIGURE 4.2. Score of the contradanza from the Costeño dance-drama.

(*Continued on next page*)

FIGURE 4.2. *Continued.*

DANZA DE LA MUERTE

FIGURE 4.3. Score of the *Danza de la muerte* from the Animalitos dance-drama.

in one quarter note, two eighth notes, and another quarter note, with an accent on the second eighth note. This rhythmic change gives the effect of a transformation into a 6/8 compound duple meter with a quarter note and an eighth in the first beat and an eighth with a quarter note in the second beat. At the same time, the accompanying voices have this 6/8 meter, thus producing a sesquialtera melodically and harmonically.

The conservation of the original choreographed steps of this dance is impressive. It is danced by a couple of animalitos who, arm in arm, shoulder to shoulder, make the rounds, walking very slowly. With each step a leg is crossed in the air and then a forward step made on the way down, which moves the dance along; in one step the left leg is crossed to the right and in the next the right is crossed to the left. The dances of the costeño and toritos are considered "old pieces" and are certainly priceless examples of late eighteenth-century or early nineteenth-century repertoire. (Listen to musical examples on tracks 8 and 9 on the CD.)

THE DEVELOPMENT OF THE MARIMBA

The earliest marimbas in Central America were arc marimbas with gourd resonators played by one musician. The instrument is either strapped to the neck of the player or rests on one leg, sustaining the trapezoid-shaped frame that holds together the keys, the arc, and the hanging resonators. The arc holds the keyboard against the player (the arc is also used to lean the instrument on the seat of the player). The keys are joined by a string that goes through the tuning pegs that are stuck to the frame; the ends of the latter are attached to the ends of the arc. Over time, in some cases, the gourd resonators were replaced with bamboo and the instrument acquired four legs, although it was still played by one man; bamboo marimbas, known as tenores, were 47.2 or 59 inches long and had twenty-two or thirty-two keys, giving one tone over three octaves or four tones over four octaves, respectively.[30] The sound quality of the diatonic marimbas progressively evolved as the material of their resonators was changed from bamboo to wood and the length of the keyboard was extended, finally reaching the five términos (octaves) plus five tones of the simple marimba used today. José Saenz Poggio (1997, 24) reveals that during the eighteenth century a perfected marimba was introduced in the cathedral's music chapel. Lester Godínez (2002, 113–15) attributes this technological innovation to the cleric Juan Joseph de Padilla. We suppose that he refers to the diatonic marimba with wooden resonators or sound boxes and of three-, five-, or seven-octave keyboard.[31] The introduction of the marimba in the chapel suggests that music scores for this "improved"

FIGURE 4.4. Diatonic son marimba from Xesiuan. Photo by Sergio Navarrete Pellicer.

marimba must have been located in the cathedral library; nevertheless they remain elusive.

The technological advancement of the diatonic marimba in the eighteenth century and its incorporation in the cathedral also suggests that the musical tradition of this instrument was only later taken up by urban Ladinos. This is so even if the instrument is played mostly by Indians throughout the country. The double-key or chromatic marimba created by Sebastián Hurtado[32] in Quetzaltenango and by Corazón Borráz in Chiapas, Mexico (Eyler 1993, 48; Kaptain 1992, 19) at the end of the nineteenth century is testimony to the existence of urban, marimba-playing Ladino families who thus perpetuated the folk tradition of marimba music.[33] The chromatic marimba is a modern phenomenon in the expanding urbanization of Quetzaltenango and Guatemala City, but the diatonic marimba was already popular in urban and rural settings.

It is known that Sebastián Hurtado perfected the chromatic marimba in 1894, and that he was encouraged in this by Julián Paniagua Martínez, the musical director of the Quetzaltenango Band, who gave him the idea of adding a second row of keys so that the tonalities could be switched easily without the need for wax.[34]

The improved chromatic keyboard meant that musicians could adopt the entire repertoire of both fashionable classical and semi-classical ballroom music. A short time later, at the turn of the twentieth century, the marimba became part of the repertoire of the orchestras that were Guatemala's version of North American jazz bands. The tradition of the son was simultaneously relegated to the diatonic marimba kept in Indian rural areas. Urban composers kept writing the typical son in 6/8, but now on chromatic marimbas and only as elements of nostalgia for an idealized world of Indians.[35]

The Hurtados had begun their career playing "native Indian music" (Eyler 1993, 48), that is, the son repertoire, but once they had constructed the chromatic keyboard (which is longer than that of the son marimba and requires four players), they turned to *piezas*—the "semi-classical" repertoire of popular European dance music, Latin dances, and "classical" works readily available in reduced score versions for the piano, all of which can be played on the chromatic marimba. The chromatic marimba, with its increasingly diverse repertoire, became an urban phenomenon. Chromatic marimba ensembles with drum set and double bass—and, soon after, the marimba orchestras, with a complete section of trumpets, saxophones, and trombones as well as drum set and double bass—were soon competing successfully with orchestras and bands for contracts in ballrooms, cafes, restaurants, nightclubs, and hotels, providing the cities— that is, the privileged classes and nascent tourist industry—with musical entertainment.[36]

The most popular rhythms over the past seventy years have been blues, boleros, foxtrots, six-by-eights (better known as *guarimbas*),[37] waltzes, *cumbias*, and swings, as well as *corridos*, and the sones "tipicos." Other, less common but equally popular, music includes ragtime, tango, rumba, polka, *danzón, merengue, pasillo, paso doble, chachachá, guaracha, marcha,* and some fusions such as the bolero-chachachá and the bolero-mambo. We also find hymns, *bossa novas, phantasies, bambucos, sambas, gaitas, porros,* and even rock and ska (Sánchez Castillo 2001, 3–106).

The chromatic marimba was first played in public in Guatemala by the Hurtados in 1899 (Kaptain 1992). The Hurtados were also responsible for the identification of the marimba with Guatemala as a nation. They introduced the instrument to the United States, as well. Starting in New Orleans in 1908, they toured the country, progressed to playing night-clubs, and made recordings of their music. The great success of the Hurtado family both within and outside Guatemala stems from a strong marimba tradition shared with several families from Quetzaltenango, such as the Bethancourts and Ovalle-Bethancourts. Other marimba groups and marimba orchestras that have been part of the modern history of the chromatic double marimba are "Marimba Antigua," initially directed by maestro Alberto Velázquez Collado in the city of Antigua, the "Kaibil Balam" marimba of Víctor Manuel Del Valle of Chiantla, Hue-huetenango, and the marimba orchestra "Maderas que cantan" of Marco

Tulio López, who used to liven up the Colonial Ball Room in Guatemala City (Sánchez Castillo 2001, 125–91; Godínez 2002, 223).

The diatonic son marimba continued to expand in Indian towns, where a wide range of marimbas were being played in various contexts in the 1920s and 1930s (Teletor 1945, 1955; La Farge 1994; Wagley 1949; Tax 1953; Schultze Jena 1954; Bunzel 1952). In the little town of Panajachel in Atitlán, Tax (1953, 97, 177) found only one gourd marimba, which was played at cofradías and in taverns during fiestas; its modest importance is indicated by the fact that it was cheaper to hire this marimba than a drum-and-flute ensemble.[38] In the same period, the marimba tradition was well established in the Q'anjob'al town of Santa Eulalia (La Farge 1994, 112, 114), where there were various marimba ensembles, including a one-man marimba and a drummer for the bull dance-drama, a "full" marimba for five players for the music of the cofradía celebrations, and a municipal marimba. A marimba was played in church in the Mam town of Chimaltenango (Wagley 1949, 86, 106) to accompany the prayers, responses, and litanies (some in Latin) chanted by the choir. Another, played by two musicians, was hired for the bull dance-drama at a cost of $30, a price that suggests that these were outside musicians, probably from Totonicapán.[39] "Marimba companies"—probably simple marimbas for two or more players—were hired to play in Ladino *estancos* (temporary booths for the sale of illegal *aguardiente*, or alcohol); these were the so-called zarabandas.

THE INTRODUCTION OF THE MARIMBA TO RABINAL

Indian traders from the western highlands introduced the tenor marimba to Rabinal, which had no previous marimba tradition, at the end of the nineteenth century—that is, at roughly the same time as the chromatic marimba was being introduced to the cities.

The one-musician tenor is no longer played in Rabinal town, although it can still be found in the more remote villages and hamlets. By the 1930s it had become a teaching aid; like other *marimbistas* in their sixties or older, Esteban Uanché learned to play on one. His father rented it for him from Chipuerta hamlet before apprenticing him to his own teachers, Cayetano Lajuj of Vegas Santo Domingo, Pichec, and José Leon Alvarado of Xococ; these men owned the bigger, five-octave, forty-key, contemporary son marimba, a three-man marimba made in Quetzaltenango and Totonicapán. Few families owned such instruments. Julián Ordoñez, who was sixty-seven when I interviewed him and lives in Rabinal town, still plays the simple marimba that José Leon Alvarado helped his father buy some seventy years ago in the mid-1930s. He remembers going to Totonicapán, where the merchant who sold it to them said, "You know lads, the mother of the marimba is Totonicapán," implying that the marimba originally came from that town and that his marimbas were the authentic instruments.

Paulino Jerónimo of Rabinal town, in his seventies, proudly told me that his great-grandfather, Mariano Jerónimo, had introduced the simple marimba to Rabinal in the 1890s:

> My grandfather, Cirilo, a marimba player himself who has just reached fourteen years,[40] died at ninety-eight years of age. When they were players, he and his brothers, Justo, Santiago, Goyo, and Daniel, could hardly be found in Rabinal. Since there were no marimbas in Salamá or Cobán[41] and only one here, they took it with them. They carried the marimba on their backs because there were no roads then. They were requested at Salamá; from there they would travel to Tactic, Cobán, and so on. And because then there were many German plantation owners, they went to play there. Sometimes they would be gone for a month at a time. They would finish a celebration somewhere and would then be taken somewhere else. But, as I mentioned, they had a simple marimba.

The ladinoized Jerónimos are the only Indian family I encountered to insist that there have been marimbas in Rabinal for at least a century—never mind that the collective memory of Rabinalense Achi dates marimba music to "the beginning of time." Esteban Uanché assured me emphatically that there was not a single marimba in Rabinal when he was a child in the 1930s. According to him, every cofradía festivity, anniversary of the dead, and wedding was celebrated with the violin and *adufe*, and the only marimbas in town belonged to contract musicians brought in by Ladinos to play pieza music at their festivities.

> In the past there were no marimbas in this town [Rabinal and its neighboring villages]; there was only the violin and adufe, that's all. There was nothing [more] for there was no money; you know very well that the only people that want [marimba] are the rich, not the poor. The poor have to work. They go to work without food, and many die of hunger. And the poor are working in their maize-field [milpa]; [military] commissioners come and take people to work on the roads, hitting, kicking, and whipping us. They have no pity on the poor.

The apparent contradiction between the old men's testimonies is resolved by the fact that, so far as Esteban was concerned, the Jerónimo family played "foreign" music for "foreigners" in "foreign" places, that is, piezas for Ladinos outside the Indian community. But there is more to this argument than a disagreement about the introduction of the marimba—namely, local rivalries and interethnic relationships. Esteban's contemporaries confirm that there were very few marimbas in the municipality in their youth and that these were located in Xococ and Pichec. The Jerónimos are seen as ladinoized Rabinalenses with close ties to the powerful Ladinos and the army, and not followers of the Achi tradition. As Paulino Jerónimo himself explained to me, "My family only played pieza music; they were the ones under the military commander's orders, they only played for the great [powerful, wealthy] men. The zarabanda is a separate thing for those who play sones. Those who play sones cannot play piezas."[42]

After buying their first chromatic or double marimba in the 1920s, the Jerónimo family—Paulino's father and uncles—expanded their repertoire with more complex pieces (which included sections in a minor tonality) in order to keep up with the tastes of their Ladino clientele; this marimba, which they named "La Predilecta" (the favorite) was acquired by the municipality for Sunday concerts held next to the parish church, festivals, Ladino ballroom dances, and other events for military officers stationed in Rabinal town. Oddly, Paulino never learned to play the chromatic marimba himself and continues to play the simple diatonic son marimba.

By 1935, according to Paulino, cantinas were hiring marimba music for zarabandas held during the major festivals. This indicates that despite the small number of son marimbistas at the time, their music had been accepted for certain occasions. During those years marimba music accompanied new Spanish versions of two nineteenth-century dance-dramas—the costeño and the caman chicop, which is known today as los animalitos (Teletor 1945, 52). Although Paulino says that the Indian population did not hire marimbas for their celebrations in his grandfather's day (i.e., the early 1900s), clearly the process of substituting the "little music" of the violin and adufe with sonorous marimba music in the communal, public aspects of Indian cofradía celebrations was getting under way in the 1930s. A rapid increase in the number of cantinas in Rabinal town in the early 1950s helped spread the marimba tradition. Paulino remembers that there were as many as twenty-four zarabandas in permanent locations and estancos (temporary booths selling alcohol),[43] each with its own marimba, during major fiestas. By the end of the decade, the marimba was the instrument of choice for most religious and life-crisis celebrations, and only the most diehard traditionalists still resisted the change. Magdaleno Xitumul, himself a violinist, still resents his parents' insistence on violin and adufe music at his wedding in the 1960s.

Zarabandas were held in Rabinal's cantinas during religious festivals until 1981, when, at the height of the political violence, the army imposed a curfew and banned all gatherings with music. The "great silence" began. Marimbista Tono Cajbón blamed the collapse of the zarabanda tradition on la violencia and its aftereffects:

> Before, well, in truth there was not such violence; all people were respected. But now it is no longer possible, because now in the cantinas you will always find someone carrying a gun or a knife, a machete; it is not possible, before it was happier. The zarabanda stayed [until] about fifteen years

ago, you see, there was no room, there was a state of siege, that's when the carrying on stopped, neither firecrackers nor fireworks, there is nothing. When things were like that, even to kill a hog or a chicken you needed a license. That's what they did to the zarabanda, you needed a license, but nobody needs it now because there is no more zarabanda. Now even in the cofradías there is freedom again, there are firecrackers and marimba music. Because there was a time when there was no marimba. That prohibition lasted about three years, without racket, without anything. Now it is rather merrier, but there is no zarabanda, definitely no more.

Mario Valdizon Ayala, the Ladino owner of Rabinal town's premier bar, El Motagua, which was located in a prime position just off the plaza, gave me strictly economic reasons for the demise of the zarabanda:

I used to be one who hired the marimba for dancing. It used to be set here in the cantina to attract people, to play music; hence people follow the music and there is the business. Later I did not continue because for the town celebrations they set cantinas on the street, right? Then the marimba is playing here, and as the son would end all the people would pour out to drink at the street cantinas, and they would come back to dance. So I said, "Why should I continue being such fool?" on the one hand, and on the other, the marimbistas kept rising the price. It is no longer possible.... I contracted for every major celebration but everything was inexpensive. The marimba player would earn three quetzales [then equivalent to $3] from six in the evening to six in the morning, the whole night. A quart of *guaro* [alcohol] would be provided by midnight and then a cup of coffee and bread and that was all. Today they charge twenty quetzales per hour.

I asked him, "Up to which year were there zarabandas?"

There still are sometimes, the custom is there, it exists, the will is there, but the cost is out! Here at that corner a young man contracted for one or two days of the celebration, but I wouldn't risk my profit. How much can he make? If he pays twenty quetzales per hour, it is 240 quetzales per night, and if he sells a whole box of guaro, he might have about thirty quetzales left for profit. No, it is no longer possible. The *inditos* complain to me, why don't I have marimba if it is so joyful? Yes, it used to be joyful when it was inexpensive, when it was possible to give it away, but now is no longer conceivable.

MODERN MARIMBAS

The diatonic simple marimba (also known as the marimba *sencilla* or marimba de sones) is the most common type of marimba both in Rabinal and within the Indian population as a whole. There are about forty simple marimbas, mostly son but also a few pieza marimbas, in the municipality. Rabinal town and the larger villages have a concentration of marimbas and the rest are scattered in the smaller villages. Some are not played publicly and others, like livestock, are kept solely to be sold in times of need. In addition, there are ten *conjunto* marimba ensembles (marimba de pieza, bass-and-drum set), all of them located in the town and larger villages.

THE SIMPLE MARIMBA

There are two types of simple marimba: the son marimba and the pieza marimba. They are structurally similar, being distinguished by the different ranges of their keyboards, the number of musicians required to play them, the type of music played on them, and the kind of events at which they are played.

The son marimba has forty keys or five and a half *términos* and is played by three musicians. As their name indicates, these marimbas are used to play the sones repertoire. The range of son marimba is:

The pieza marimba has forty-two keys and is played by a set of four musicians; the extra player, who embellishes the main melody on the highest keys, is known as a *requinto*. Although mainly used for playing piezas, the pieza marimba can also be used by three musicians to play sones. The pieza marimba range is:

The marimba de pieza is also known as a conjunto marimba because, on occasion, it may become part of a musical ensemble that includes a counter-bass and a drum set. An extensive repertoire of popular urban music can be played on the pieza marimba. Once the preserve of the Ladino population, this music is now also enjoyed by Rabinalense Indians, for whom it is the music of choice for weddings, dancing, and modern dance-dramas.

Simple marimbas are tuned in major keys, usually C major, but it is common to find them set to F Major and G major and occasionally to other major keys. Esteban's two son marimbas, for example, are tuned to E major and A-flat major, respectively. These diatonic marimbas may also be transposed to a neighboring tonality by applying small amounts of black wasp wax[44] to the keys occupying the seventh scale degree of the major scale with the purpose of lowering the tone by one half tone (semitone). For instance, if the marimba is tuned in G major and wax is applied to the F keys, the marimba will be transposed to C major. The change of tonality is only practiced for the four mallet sones (see below). The tones of the marimbas are not tempered in equidistant tones and semitones; the intervals vary between 1/4 to 3/4 of a tone, producing, as a result, unequal octaves of a peculiarly rich sound that is different from the tempered scale of the piano.

MARIMBA PRODUCTION, MAINTENANCE, AND REPAIR

Marimba production (both diatonic and chromatic) is almost exclusively an Indian craft. According to Camposeco (1992), workshops producing marimbas in Guatemala are chiefly found in San Juan Ostuncalco in Quetzaltenango province; San Marcos, San Marcos province; Santa Eulalia, San Miguel Acatan and Jacaltenango in Huehuetenango provinces; and in various places in other provinces such as Totonicapán, Chimaltenango, Tecpan, Villa Canales, Salamá, and Guatemala City. I visited two marimba workshops in Cobán and Carcha in Alta Verapaz that supply the whole region down to Baja Verapaz. Some Culbulco traders make a limited number of marimbas but were not producing when I visited them. I was unable to visit marimba workshops in the western highland towns.[45]

There are no marimba producers in Rabinal, though Esteban Uanché remembered that in his youth there was a carpenter, Julio Sis, who used to make them. Until his death, Esteban was the only person in town who repaired son marimbas; he could replace broken parts but not make or tune keyboards, which he had to contract out. Esteban frequently bought broken or abandoned marimbas, which he renovated for resale. He also received marimbas on consignment from merchants in San Miguel Acatan and Cubulco, which he calibrated, redecorated, and resold at 30 percent above cost; he was the only marimba trader in town. No one travels the markets selling marimbas anymore; Julián Ordoñez gave up the business following the outbreak of violence in neighboring El Quiché province in the 1970s. He explained, "We sold marimbas for about five years. It would take three days from here to Toto [Totonicapán] as we took them by foot. Nowadays you cannot trade, because if you carry money there is no way you can avoid the assaults on the road."

Watching Esteban work gave me detailed knowledge of the structure of the marimba. The keyboard of the simple son marimba rests on a trapezoid frame called a *mesa* (table), which measures 7.08 feet in length and 5.9 and 24.4 inches, respectively, on each side, and has four legs. The railing where the resonator's "ears" rest is held in its interior. The hanging resonators are trapezoid structures whose bottom end is an inverted pyramid. Throughout the length of the table there are several slots for pegs that sustain the keyboard: a cable runs through the holes in the pegs and the keys themselves.

Different types of wood are used for different parts of the marimba. The table and legs are generally made of pine. A better-quality, harder wood is used to make the keys and pegs; cypress, *hormigo* (*Platymiscium dimorphandrum* Donn), and *granadillo* (ebony; *Amerimon granadillo*) are ideal for the *puro acero* (pure-steel) sound when struck. The resonators must be constructed from mahogany because it allows the best resonance and does not break easily.

Calibrating and replacing the membranes of each resonator is the most important and specialized aspect of repair and maintenance work. Each resonator has a hole at the bottom surrounded by a ring covered in black wasp wax, which serves as an adhesive to attach a very fine membrane made from the interior layer of pig tripe. These waxed rings with thin membranes form the *mirlitones*[46] that produce the marimba's character-istic buzzing sound (*charleo*). The size of the rings varies according to the size of both resonators and keys. The malleability of the wax allows the calibration of the size of the holes, achieving the appropriate aperture for the required resonance. The resonators are arranged from largest—for lower bass keys—to smallest—for higher treble keys. Starting with the bass keys, the first thirty have resonators containing a hole; five of the remaining ten or twelve keys have resonators with no holes; the rest have no resonators. There are only five different calibers for the thirty res-onators bearing holes, resulting in five different groups of six resonators each with the same caliber.

Tripe membrane is so soft and fragile that it breaks after a few per-formances. To apply the membrane correctly, it is necessary to stick it with the ball of the little finger so that it adopts the curve of the fingertip and avoids stretching too much when it sticks to the wax. This allows it to vibrate without breaking when the air is pushed out of the resonator each time the key is struck. When the wax hardens, many musicians add more when replacing the tripe membrane, reducing the size of the holes. This results in the alteration of the correct diameter corresponding to the tone of the key on the top of each resonator. Consequently proper buzz is lost, and with it the magnitude of sound of the instrument. Esteban com-plained about musicians who do not replace membranes regularly or cal-ibrate the rings, which results in the muteness and poor appearance of their instruments. Sneering at the marimbas brought to him for calibrat-ing, he told me, "Look at the amount of wax, they resemble a child's ass, full of excrement."

The *bolillos* (mallets) used to play the marimba are made in different sizes of various materials. The heads of the mallets used for the lower register are the biggest and are relatively soft. Those used for the middle range are slightly smaller and harder. Both are made of local rubber. The heads of the treble player's mallets are the smallest and hardest; they are generally manufactured from pork tripe and are only available in the capital.

THE DOUBLE OR CHROMATIC MARIMBA

The double marimba is composed of two chromatic marimbas, a "big" marimba for four players and a tenor marimba for three. The leader of the group is the *tiplista* (treble) player of the "big" marimba and develops the main melody; the other three musicians are the requinto and embellish the main melody on the higher keys of the keyboard; and the bass and center players together are responsible for rhythm and harmony. The tenor marimba has one bass, one center, and one requinto player, who play in counterpoint with and *segundean* (follow in parallel motion) the "big" marimba melodic lines.[47] Like the conjunto ensemble (diatonic marimba de pieza), the chromatic double marimba ensemble includes a counter-bass and drum set, which add modern sounds and rhythms.

The keyboard on both marimbas is chromatic (by semitones). The "big" marimba has a range of six whole octaves and a variable number of extra semitones. The tenor marimba's range is three whole octaves and various numbers of semitones.[48] There have never been more than a very few double marimbas in Rabinal municipality, largely because chromatic keyboard playing techniques are vastly different from those practiced by local musicians. Only a few ladinoized Indians, essentially the Caballero and Jerónimo families plus one or two other individuals, have learned the necessary skills to play the chromatic or double marimba.[49] The popular pieza repertoire can be played in its original key and by modulating to minor and other keys if necessary, without having to adapt the pieces the way simple marimba players have to do.

As mentioned earlier, the double marimba repertoire is vast, and one can actually listen to the music of more than a century on today's marimba radio programs. The repertoire includes corridos, cumbias, guarachas, mambos, boleros, pasillos, fox trots, 6/8, blues, and especially waltzes such as the old "Carmela" or the famous "Flor del Café," composed by Herman Alcantara, and other waltzes inspired by the Rabinal landscape. I have chosen Julio Antonio Perez's waltz, "Naranjales de Rabinal" (Orange Groves of Rabinal) as an example of the repertoire, found on track 10 of the CD.

Musicians' precarious domestic economy limits the spread of double marimba ownership, as this ensemble is expensive, and it is difficult to keep such a large number of musicians together in a very limited and uncertain market. Today Rabinal's only double marimba belongs to the municipality and is played by members of the two families mentioned above at Ladino festivities such as weddings, fifteenth-birthday celebrations, baptisms, school events, and other weekend events financed by the municipality. Demand is low in Rabinal and it is generally necessary to look for contracts outside the municipality in places such as Salamá, San Jeronimo, Purulha, Granados, and El Chol. With the exception of Purulha, these are Ladino municipalities able to pay 1,000–1,500 quetzales (up to $250) for a night of double marimba music.

SON MUSIC

The literary works of Miguel de Cervantes indicate that from the end of the sixteenth century onward, the word "son" was used for any kind of popular music (Salazar 1949, 293–361); nevertheless the term is also used when referring to the playing of a musical instrument as defined by the *Diccionario de Autoridades* (1990). In the eighteenth century the term had the latter meaning, specifically in the case of the instrumental segment of popular music that separated it from literary and dance aspects (Saldívar 1987, 249, 252; Stanford 1984a, 7).

In contemporary literature on popular and traditional music there is a tendency to use and abuse the word "son" in a generic sense, that is, with reference to all popular and traditional music. In addition, the broad classification into two categories—the Indian and the Mestizo or *chapín* son, in the case of the Guatemalan marimba tradition (O'Brien 1980; Stanford 1984b)—applies essentialized ethnic criteria to distinguish the musical characteristics of diverse musical traditions. According to such a classification, all of the marimba son music appears as a part of the Mestizo tradition. Chenoweth (1964, 79–81), O'Brien (1980), and Stigberg in the *New Harvard Dictionary of Music* (Randel 1986) define the Guatemalan marimba son as having the following characteristics: homophonic texture, major tonality, diatonic melody, triadic harmony, a moderate to rapid tempo, and a combination of simple triple and compound duple meters.

THE SON IN GUATEMALA

In his classification of the Guatemalan son, Lester Godínez (2002, 206–8) distinguishes between two kinds of son: the son from the Indian context or environment and the son from the pseudo-Indian or Ladino context. According to this classification, the marimba sones may belong to either context, depending on who is playing them and where and how they are played. This differs from the previous definition, which considers all marimba sones part of a Mestizo or Ladino tradition. The son from the pseudo-indian or Ladino environment is composed and played by Ladinos, but it is inspired by the folk Indian tradition.

While this classification draws from a similar dual model of Indians and Ladinos, it does not transform musical characteristics into ethnic and cultural essences. The ethnic criteria in this case only point at the social and cultural environments in which the music is played and subordinate musical traits, influences, and musical changes to those contexts. The relevance of this classification is that marimba sones are composed and played in both social and cultural environments.

Godínez includes in the first type of indigenous son environment the traditional son and the cofradía son, which can be distinguished from each other only by the specific religious function of the cofradía son.[50] In both cases the son has one theme, and occasionally two or three; the meters used are mainly 3/4 in moderate tempos and 3/8 in fast ones, but 6/8 also occurs. Their structure doesn't always conform to eight measures; it can also be found in five and ten. Besides, it is a kind of son played by the Indians in their own villages on simple tecomate marimbas or other instruments.[51]

In the pseudo-Indian or Ladino environment we find the típico son, the barreño son, the Easter son, the chapín son, and the son with folklore projection. Again, these are all sones written by Ladinos and Mestizos based on Western musical structures, but with some Indian melodic and rhythmic elements.

Irrespective of the method of classification, there is a mutual influence between Indian and Mestizo traditions. One can hear influences of the cultivated versions that Godínez calls "pseudo-Indian." The son played by Rabinalenses on their simple marimbas and the sones derived from the romantic ideology of Ladinos draw constantly from the folk Indian musical tradition (see Turino 1991).

Stanford (1984a, 26–32) argues that one of the main musical traits of the son is the sesquialtera. It is indeed one of the most important features of the ancient son, and the Guatemalan son barreño is one of these, as I was told by indigenous musicians in Rabinal and as is confirmed by historical sources (Saenz Poggio 1997, 70–71).

The sesquialtera is found in other marimba sones and is particularly evident in the violin and adufe sones of Rabinal. Several musicians in Rabinal told me that the violin and adufe sones are the same ones found in the repertoire of marimba sones in Rabinal. However, the characteristic poly-rhythms and faster tempo of the marimba transforms them to such an extent that, to my ears, there is little resemblance between them. It is probable that in the repertoire of the violin and adufe sones we would find examples among ancient sones that gave rhythmic origin to marimba music. Listening to the violin and adufe son (tracks 6 and 14 on the CD), we can identify the following rhythmic sesquialtera pattern in the melody played on the violin and the adufe drum, which make the connection to the ancient or colonial son that spread through many regions of Latin America.

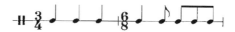

Until about thirty years ago, sones were danced individually in circles in a peculiar dancing-step style; people danced with a meditative attitude, gazing at the floor. This ancient Indian style differs considerably from today's Ladino mode of dancing in couples, swaying from side to side. This style may have been introduced to Rabinal at the same time that the marimba became popular among the Achi in their religious celebrations. The marimba sones often have texts, although few people actually remember them. In practice they are played like instrumental pieces.

Within the indigenous son tradition we find information about texts accompanying the sones such as the b'it (wake) songs of the Q'anjob'al people of Santa Eulalia (La Farge 1994, 69), the "Songs of the Face of the Earth" of the Tzutujil Maya of Santiago Atitlán (O'Brien 1975), and the welcome and farewell Achi songs, played by violin-and-adufe ensembles, to the souls of the Rabinalense Achi ancestors.[52] In all instances, the words are sung to the accompaniment of string instruments; in the latter two, the music may also be played on a marimba, in which case there is no singing (O'Brien 1975, 35–36). There are also traditional songs or nursery rhymes in Spanish that are popular in Rabinal, such as the mishito (little cat), which is a son.

Rabinalense Sones

Nowadays the Ladinos or Mestizos in Rabinal use the term "son" in a derogatory fashion when they speak about the music of the inditos (little Indians). The Achi deem all that they consider ancestral music sones.

The variety of sones in Rabinal depends on the type of musical ensemble that plays them and reveals different degrees of European tonal influence (listen to examples of these musical ensembles on tracks 2, 4, 5, 6, and 7 of the CD). For example, the Rabinal music of marimba sones has a greater affinity with the son music of the violin and the adufe than with that of the flute and *tamborón* (big drum) or that of the *pito* (cane flute) and *tamborcito* (small drum) ensembles or the shawm-and-tamborón ensemble. The violin and adufe share precedents with European folk dances that were reinterpreted in an interethnic colonial context. The melodies and the rhythms played on the flute-and-big-drum ensemble, shawm-and-big-drum ensemble, and flute and small drum, by contrast—even if derived from military and religious Spanish calls (a matter requiring further investigation)—do not obey general European concepts of tonality and form. At the same time, music played with groups of trumpets and the *tum* mainly during the Rabinal Achi dance has virtually no connection to European music. The ancient rhythmic formulas found at the beginning and end of the Rabinal Achi dance can be heard in the sones of many other Middle American Indian groups (Navarrete Pellicer 1994).

The repertoire of marimba sones in Rabinal is a rich musical heritage shared by many other traditions of Indian sones of Guatemala, which in turn are connected to Spanish folk music, like the zarabanda, dating back to colonial times. The marimba son in Rabinal has its own characteristics of performance style (see Chapter 7) but shares some rhythmic patterns, horizontal and vertical harmonic structures, and its general form with the marimba sones of many Guatemalan Indian towns. The rhythmic patterns in the melodies in figure 4.5 show the great variety of rhythms found in Rabinal.

The harmonies are open triads, and common progressions are I–V–I–V–I or I–IV–I–V–I.

The form of the son varies in the number of sections and themes. It may have two, three, or more sections and is always an open-ended structure; their length depends on the ritual context. Each section has eight to twelve measures with a theme that usually includes two melodic motives in tonic and dominant. Sometimes the theme is repeated with varying rhythms and sometimes it is alternated with other themes *ad libitum* until the treble cues, with a slight *rallentando*; a final cadence (*terminación*) is then played. For instance, the *entrada* son played at the beginning of celebrations and in rites of entrance to the main altar of the house where the event takes place has a short version of the following form: A–A2–B–A3–B2–C–C2–A4–final cadence or terminación (figure 4.6, track 11). This lasts a few minutes but may be extended up to fifteen minutes, alternating and repeating the theme with variations as well as adding others, depending on the particular time, during the development of the performance of the rite of entrance at the domestic altar.

At the commencement of the celebration, sones usually last only a few minutes; as the event develops, the themes are reiterated over and over and the sones become longer and longer. Along with this ever-increasing duration of the sones, the tempo is accelerated, ranging from 1/4 = 80 to 1/4 = 120.

The *costa chiquita* son that we show in the following score (fig. 4.7, track 12) has a shape similar to the previous one. It has an introductory

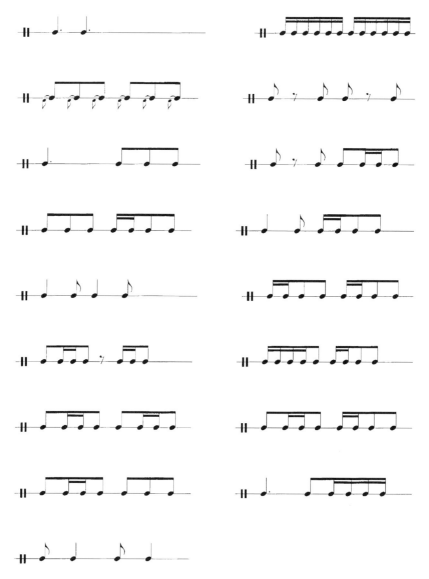

FIGURE 4.5. Examples of marimba rhythmic patterns.

ENTRADA

FIGURE 4.6. Score of entrada son.

FIGURE 4.6. *Continued.*

SON COSTA CHIQUITA

FIGURE 4.7. Score of Costa chiquita son.

FIGURE 4.7. *Continued.*

theme, which is repeated with variations, followed by three different sections and then a repetition of the third section with variations. In this case the marimba player performs a whole repetition of the sections played with variations and ends with a perfect cadence that is characteristic of most of the Rabinal sones. This example shows the common practice of repeating the whole son as many times as necessary: The harmonic accompaniment of the first theme is usually used as a bridging formula: A–A2–B–C–D–C2–repetition with variation and terminación.

In the following score of the San Pablo son (fig. 4.8, track 13), we again see the same structure of consecutive themes or sections some of which are repeated. In this case the introductory theme does not repeat, but the second and third do: A–B–B2–C–C2–D–C3–terminación.

The variation is one of the principal characteristics of the son, and the themes stand out more for their rhythmic diversity than for their melodic content. As in the case of the other examples, the first measure of the San Pablo son is played exclusively by the melody without accompaniment. This feature cues the rest of the players and the audience to identify the son.

PERFORMANCE ORDER

As with many folk traditions, performance practice depends on the development of the musical event. Analysis of the son repertoire and the sequence in which it is played confirms that social context—that is, the structure and process of ritual events at which music is played—determines the type, performance style, and general form of the son cycles.

In Rabinal marimba sones are categorized by the number of mallets used by the center player. In "four-mallet" sones (e.g., entrance sones),

SON SAN PABLO

FIGURE 4.8. Score of San Pablo son.

FIGURE 4.8. *Continued.*

the treble leader, center, and bass players hold two, four, and two mallets, respectively. In "three-mallet" sones (e.g., costa chiquita son), the most popular and thus most frequently played sones, all three players hold three mallets each; and in "two-mallet" sones (e.g., San Pablo son), while the treble may play with two or three mallets, the center and bass have two mallets each (musical examples 11, 12, and 13, on the CD: four, three, and two mallet sones, respectively). The main effect of these differences is only a fuller sound, because they play the same basic triadic chord at different octaves. This is significant, however, because the more sound there is in a celebration, the better and happier the occasion.

The performance of the son repertoire is arranged in a fixed order that forms a day cycle of sones beginning early in the morning and ending late at night. During celebrations lasting more than a day, such as cofradía festivities, each day has a whole musical cycle, with its own beginning, development, and end:

Entrance sones (four- and three-mallet sones)
First cycle of four-, then three-, then two-mallet sones
Second cycle of four-, three-, and two-mallet sones
Set of requests for dancing
Exit sones (four-mallet sones)

This sequence is interrupted by entrance-exit sones whenever the rite of entering and exiting the domestic altar is performed. It may also be interrupted by participants' requests.

All celebrations where marimba music is played begin with a short set of four- and three-mallet sones de entrada (entrance sones) to welcome the ancestors, which usually takes place around 6 A.M. These entrance sones evoke happiness on the part of the living (because they are inviting and welcoming the souls of the ancestors) and nostalgia on the part of the arriving souls. Entrance sones are followed by the first cycle of four-, three-, and two-mallet sones. The three-mallet sones are considered the happy sones and are dedicated to the women preparing food for the festivities. Traditionally, these sones are played at dawn, when activity quickens; one of the first of these three-mallet sones is called *amanecer* (dawn) or *amanecido* (after dawn), a reference to the time of day it should be played (although it is usually mid-morning before they are performed). The last group of each cycle is the two-mallet sones. Then the cycle repeats.

The first cycle is called *primer sonido* (first sound), and the sones are called sones *con cera* (sones with wax) because wax is applied to all seventh-scale degree keys to lower them half a tone. The second cycle is called *segundo sonido* (second sound), and the sones are called sones *sin cera* (sones without wax), although only the four-mallet sones are played without wax. The sones are played in the same order as in the first cycle. Within each set of sones the repertoire varies, depending on the knowledge of each marimba ensemble, although the sequence, in terms of mallets, remains the same. Nevertheless, there is a basic number of very popular sones that all marimba ensembles must play. There are also certain pairs of sones that are always played one after the other, such as the three-mallet sones *palo seco* (dead tree) and amanecido.

At the end of the main ritual activity, a set of *surtido* sones (requests) is played for those who wish to dance and express their happiness or sadness. By this time participants are generally in various degrees of inebriation. The lack of structure in the order of the sones played in this set reflects the heightening of individual emotions at this time.

Finally, at around midnight, the sones *de terminación y despedida* (sones for the end and farewell) are played. These are in fact the same sones played earlier as entrance sones—mainly costa chiquita, *costa grande*, and Barreño. In the beginning and ending contexts these are <u>soon bis'ab'al'</u> (sones of sadness) because they evoke memories of the deceased. They welcome and bid farewell to the ancestral spirits. Musicians say that these sones are also a reminder to drunken participants to go home!

RADIOS AND CASSETTE PLAYERS

The buses traveling between the country's capital and its rural areas lack basic comforts and security but are well equipped with powerful stereos. These blast music throughout the landscape for the enjoyment of the fearless Ladino drivers and their assistants, who risk their passengers' lives at every curb and steep drop as the bus winds round the mountains. Traveling the roads between the urban world of Guatemala City and the rural world of Rabinal, more often than not squeezed between (largely Indian) passengers and their chickens and other goods, I was almost deafened by ear-splitting music—*canciones rancheras* (country songs), polkas, and *corridos norteños* (ballads originally from the Mexican-American border region), cumbias, *merengues tropicales*, and *boleros románticos*. These songs are also the staple of popular-music radio stations in Mexico and Central America and of some radio stations for the Hispanic community in the United States.

The music on the bus drove home the hegemony of the popular music produced in Mexico and Miami. This pop music is broadcast throughout Latin America and the Hispanic communities of Central and North America thanks to private radio stations and TV networks such as Univisión; local announcers provide minimal local color. Without exception, Rabinalense Achi listen to this music on the radio. Both men and women have a positive opinion of the radio; they say it breaks the "sadness" of silence and isolation, keeping them company at home. Local people do not consider this pop music an alien or imposed sound; on the contrary, it has been welcomed and appropriated (to form part of the pieza repertoire for the conjunto marimba), as have the connotations of power that Ladino and foreign culture represent. The musical journey on the buses to and from Guatemala City is a passage of transformation from straw hats to caps to straw hats, a prelude and coda of a powerful "trip" to and from the Mecca of Ladino culture.

Guatemala's first radio station was the state-owned TGW; transmission began in 1930 (Almorza 1994, 11); a private radio station commenced broadcasting a year later but soon closed down. At the time there were only about 250 radio receivers in the country, most of which were in Guatemala City and belonged to large stores or wealthy radio enthusiasts. Programming consisted mostly of music: Live popular and traditional marimba music alternated with operatic arias and other classical compositions. The dictator Ubico (1934–44) was very interested in developing radio and gave it his full support—so long as it remained under his control. The democratic regimes between 1944 and 1954 ended the state radio monopoly, and private radio stations multiplied rapidly. Radio has revolutionized the soundscape in Rabinal.[53]

The most important foreign radio station was the popular Mexican station XEW, which broadcast on the AM band. According to Rene Augusto Flores, a radio producer during the short democratic period, urban marimba ensembles could be heard in remote places by the end of the 1950s, although the number of radio receivers had only increased to 20,000. I believe this is an unrealistic estimate, because large areas of the country were without electricity at the time. Rabinal town's electricity plant was only installed (in the neighboring village of Chiac) in the late 1950s, and fifty years later many of the municipality's villages and hamlets are still without electricity. Even after electrification, there were few places to hear urban music in Rabinal—one or two cantinas or the homes of Ladinos or wealthy Indians. The records played over loudspeakers during the festivities for the town's patron saint and other fairs were another source of this music.[54]

The situation changed dramatically when ownership of transistor radios became common among the rural Indian population in the 1960s. Some sones popularized by the radio were added to the repertory of rural marimbistas throughout Guatemala; to a certain extent, radio created a common repertoire that influenced, albeit to a lesser degree, local playing styles. Even Esteban Uanché admits to reproducing sones originating in such places as Nahuala heard on the radio.

Radio's biggest influence has been in the dissemination of commercial urban popular music. This had an immediate impact on the growth of the marimba repertoire and transformed the practice of marimba music in Rabinal. Young marimbistas started adding bass and drums to their ensembles and adapting the melodies and rhythms of tropical (Afro-Caribbean) and *norteña* (Mexican–U.S. border country) music to create new versions of traditional dance dramas, and began delighting guests at Ladino and Indian weddings and baptisms (musical example on track 3 of the CD: cumbia pieza).

The broadcasting of popular music to rural areas has created a demand for urban music. The spread of radio-cassette recorders in the 1970s has led to the creation of local cottage industries to meet the demand for musical tapes.[55] There are two permanent stalls in the local market, supplying mostly bootleg cassettes of Rabinalense marimbistas and popular music, making music affordable (see Manuel 1991, 189–204).

There is a down side to this spread of pop music, however, as far as musicians are concerned: live son music at zarabandas and in cantinas has been largely replaced by juke boxes and cassette players, thus reducing the amount of work available. Nevertheless, musicians are among those who tape marimbistas in order to learn new sones, piezas, and playing styles (see Chapter 7). Esteban's solution to this intractable problem was to make recordings of his playing for sale. This way he got some financial compensation for the potential loss of income represented by other musicians learning either his repertoire or his playing style.

Also popular in the market stalls are tapes of evangelical religious songs—*alabanzas* (praises), hymns, and choral music. Following a 500-year-old precedent, evangelical groups aim to create a sense of communion with their target audience by adapting and playing ranchero and norteño music, to which participants sing and clap, in their religious services. These recordings are made by evangelical groups in Guatemala City and the towns of the western highlands, and are copied by local merchants and sold at low prices.

The Catholic Church has also benefited from this powerful medium. In recent years the Dominicans in Cobán City have set up their own radio station, Radio Tezulutlán, which transmits religious messages and cultural programs in vernacular languages about the ritual and musical traditions of the Q'eqchi' and Achi people. During my most recent visit to Rabinal, between 1999 and 2003, I discovered three radio stations in Rabinal. One of them operates locally without a license and takes a band from another radio station. The other two are legal. One is an evangelical station and the other is a highly popular commercial radio station called Superestéreo de Rabinal, which, according to my friends, most people prefer not only because it has good popular and traditional music but because they talk about the people and problems of the municipality. It was too early to assess the impact of this commercial local radio station, but it was fascinating to see people recognizing and identifying themselves with their favorite music and with news about people they knew and references to familiar places.

THE HISTORY OF THE SON and the marimba illustrate the fluidity and creativity of social and interethnic relations and cultural dynamics in Guatemala and other Latin American countries. The last two chapters have shown in various ways the importance of social and interethnic relations in the analysis of music. The previous chapter gave a structural perspective on how some dualities marking social and gender differences permeate and structure a discourse about musical concepts. In this chapter we again note how in Guatemala the history of the son (zarabanda) and the marimba is enmeshed with the conflictive dynamic of these social and interethnic relations. Here emphasis has been given to the (tri-ethnic) Mestizo origin of the marimba and its sones; we have observed the manner in which the urban Ladinos on the one side and the rural Indians on the other have mutually influenced each other in perfecting their instruments and repertoire of sones and piezas. The Ladino composers get their inspiration from the repertoire of Indian sones and create variations on these or invent new ones, sometimes even producing concert pieces. The Indians adapt the popular repertoire from the radio, including sones from other regions as well as new creations. The Indian musicians have also adopted the technical improvements of the simple marimba and new instrumental accompaniments to it, sometimes venturing into the use of the chromatic marimba. Nevertheless, this mutual influence is not symmetrical owing to social and economic inequalities; this is seen in the apparent traditional quality of the Indian marimba in contrast to a dynamic of modernization and renewal of the marimba in the Ladino segment of society. The dichotomy between tradition and modernity in the kinds of marimbas and repertoires is more the result of imposed social and economic differentiation by Ladinos than of resistance to change on the part of Indians. In effect, Indian marimba musicians use a discourse about the continuity of ancestral tradition—communication with past generations—in their understanding of the profound significance of music. In fact, despite Achi insistence on keeping to the ways of the ancestors, it is clear that the music they play for them has always been in a state of flux. Ultimately, this is not important, for the message stays the same, and it is the message that makes music work. And, while limited by economic scarcity, they are always in search of renewal and expansion of repertoire and capabilities, as we shall see in Chapter 8.

At the moment, the simple marimbas remain the favorite instrument and ensemble for son music during Indian celebrations, while the chromatic double marimba is preferred by Ladinos, who consider its music more sophisticated. In between is the marimba de conjunto ensemble, consisting of a single simple marimba de pieza plus double bass and drum kit, which is becoming increasingly popular among the Indian population for the latest dance-dramas, the groom's party at weddings, and other social events. But even here it seems that the new music is subordinate to its social context, which, as in all folk music traditions, has a central role in performance style and form. The sequence and timing of the son cycle correspond and are subordinated to the sequence and timing of the ritual occasion, as is the pieza music accompanying modern dance-dramas that are performed during cofradía fiestas. The structure and sequence of the day's events, which depend on the structure and process of ritual, remain stable, but the music changes.

This chapter has allowed us to understand some of the history of the evolution of the marimba, its repertoire and social contexts. Yet it is important to go deeper into the symbolic processes of this history so pertinent to Achi musical culture. In order to explain the symbolic capacity of music it is necessary to elucidate the symbols with which it is associated and to analyze the processes of how this identification is constructed.

In the next chapter we will look more deeply into the history, with the goal of discovering the roots of the symbolic association of the music with women and alcohol. This association is indeed common to many cultures. The following historical and ethnographic analysis seeks to unravel the intoxicating and transformational power of these three elements in the minds of the Achi people.

5 Good and Evil
Music, Alcohol, and Women

ALTHOUGH MUSIC, alcohol, and women have a positive symbolic role in terms of nurturing and sociality, in other contexts they are considered the embodiment of evil. As such, this trilogy makes people—especially men—vulnerable to a loss of control, which in turn can lead to transgressive and potentially dangerous behavior and may ultimately result in madness or death. Singly or together, music, alcohol, and women are both life-affirming and life-threatening.

This chapter explores the history of Guatemalan ideas about these things, beginning with civil and religious authorities' views on festivities in Indian towns during the colonial era. These authorities attempted to prohibit festivities where Indians (and others) played music, danced, and drank within a religious context rather than outside it, as was the European custom, and they understood their crusade as a struggle between good and evil. We shall then look at how this history has influenced modern-day views among the Maya Achi of the relationship between marimba music, alcohol, and women as they relate to sociality, social conflict, and male domination.

RELIGIOUS FESTIVITIES AND EVIL

Spanish missionaries saw the spiritual conquest of the Indians as a battle against the devil, whom they blamed for tricking Indians into their primitive beliefs and ways of life. The initial enthusiasm of the Franciscan and Dominican missionaries in Mexico and Guatemala evaporated as they began to suspect that Indians were continuing to worship their own deities in spite of their exposure to Christian beliefs. The missionaries' success—which they gauged by Indians' ability to learn, perform, and enjoy the stories of saints with song, music, and drama—was an illusion. Perhaps massive Indian "conversions" had led the missionaries to be overconfident about the imminent defeat of the devil and his minions;

Reprinted and translated from Sergio Navarrete Pellicer, "El bien y el mal: Música, alcohol y mujeres," *Latin American Music Review* 22, no. 1 (2001): 63–82. Copyright © 2001 by the University of Texas Press. All rights reserved.

or perhaps they just wanted to give a successful impression of their evangelization efforts to the Spanish Crown.

The numerous church decrees prohibiting Indian celebrations (Acuña 1975, 127–56) give the impression of a violent and irrevocable policy against such festivities, although Cervantes (1994, 34) has claimed that in practice provincial religious authorities tolerated them.[1] While the religious authorities were guided by Bartolomé de las Casas's famous dictum that "Indians are fundamentally good and their religiosity predisposes them to acquire the Catholic faith," they simultaneously doubted Indians' intelligence and capacity to be pious. Paternalistic attitudes led the Spanish to describe Indians as being "like children," a view that still prevails among Ladinos who refer to Indians in a diminishing way as "inditos" (little Indians). Indians were considered inherently weak and easy prey for the devil; Indian drunkenness at fiestas was commonly cited as evidence of this. At the same time, Spanish judicial authorities believed Indians were naturally prone to drinking, and the law considered drunkenness a mitigating factor in homicide cases (Taylor 1979, 104). This idea has served to obfuscate the real causes of violence in Indian communities, which were exacerbated by the introduction of sugar cane spirits and their illegal sale to Indians by other Spanish authorities.

The religious and royal authorities stressed the need to reduce the number of Indian festivities for economic, political, and religious reasons. The nascent economy of the Audiencia of Guatemala was hamstrung by what seemed to be an almost permanently drunken labor force. Both local Spanish civil authorities and the Dominicans who administered the wealth of Rabinal's *cofradías* tried to prevent these festivals in order to protect their own economic and political interests. They insisted that these celebrations were the root cause of neglect of work, excessive spending, and poverty among Indians. A royal provision to the mayor of Verapaz in 1799, which prohibited music, alcohol, and dancing during children's wakes (see Chapter 4) and vigils for the saints during cofradía fiestas, complained of the "daily feasts and continuous spree lasting nine days and the profane dances performed in front of the saints during the wakes at their homes and the many days of missed work by the whole town, with great harm to the public," which were seen as "consequences of these obligations whose purpose is the ruin of the participants" (AGCA, A1, file 4659, record 39868).

The document also reveals the conflict between the provincial civil authorities and the Dominicans who had economic and social control over the Verapaz region. The local authorities wanted to share the royal privileges of the missionaries over Verapaz and took every opportunity to discredit the Dominicans, blaming them for the great expenses of the Indians during religious festivities; they also criticized the music of the

Indians as inappropriate. Fiesta participants' priorities were wrong, their attitudes were wrong, and so too was their music: "it is not only the church expenses that ruin these wretches [Indians], but also the amounts of lights, fireworks, and music, commonly in terrible disarray and of a style foreign to the majestic depth of those august performances. Far from inspiring tenderness, devotion and a healthy dose of respectful fear, these excite instead delinquent memories and passions" (ibid.).

This complaint gets to the heart of the matter. Having incorporated Christ as a Maya ancestor, Jesus became an Achi; he was inside the spiritual system, not outside, beyond, or above it. He was therefore celebrated in the same way as other founding ancestors, with music, dancing, and alcohol. Admittedly, after the conquest, both the music played and the alcohol drunk changed, the latter with disastrous effects.

But while the royal authorities railed against Indian behavior, local Spanish authorities were more concerned with their own short-term interests. They turned a blind eye to the settlement of other ethnicities in Indian towns, opened clandestine alcohol shops and cantinas, and hosted *zarabandas* (social events at which drinking and dancing took place) where they sold cane spirits to Indians.[2] Indians' inability to resist the temptation to drink the new spirits may well have fed negative views of alcohol among both Indians and higher Spanish authorities. In the 1760s, Archbishop Cortés y Larras wrote that rural Spanish and Ladinos were responsible for introducing this evil to the Indians. The Indians were evil because they allowed themselves to be deceived by the devil; the rural Spanish and Ladinos were evil because they were dedicated to vice and bad habits (Alejos 1992).

Attacks on the moral depravity of the rural population, whether Spanish, Indian, or Ladino, continued throughout the colonial period. The 1799 provision mentioned above made a moral distinction between the folk music played by people in celebrations at home (which by this time included weddings, cofradía fiestas, and anniversaries of the dead), and the "cultured" music performed by orchestras and choirs in church. Attacks on Indian culture also reflect the loosening of the religious authorities' control over the local population and their festivities, as their own position was weakened by the spread of Enlightenment ideas from abroad.

What really upset the higher Spanish authorities was that Indians and Ladinos celebrated supposedly Christian festivals in a thoroughly inappropriate manner. One such inappropriate form of behavior was the dancing of women inside the sacred sphere; to make matters worse, these women appeared to be dancing, if not competing, for money from men. A 1669 document prohibiting this dance in the Indian towns of Zapotitlan province (where it was performed in Ladino cofradías) includes testimony from Spanish witnesses living in the towns of Cuyotenango, San Francisco Zapotitlan, Masatenango, and San Antonio Suchitepequez. One Spaniard's testimony reads:

> [He] knows and has witnessed that in all the celebrations in the towns of this province, the Ladino women captains[3] of the cofradías of Our Lady of the Rosary and St. Nicholas organize the dance they are accustomed to dancing and they call zarabanda, and they all dance, mostly women, for this is their purpose, and that in such dance there is a contest of men who, once a woman starts dancing, they approach her and set a *real* [Spanish silver coin] or more on her front, and then throw it in a dish that they have set for this purpose. (Ordoñez 1989, 99)

Other testimony in the same document states that this dance had been performed for a long time and that only the prettiest mulattas or Mestizas were chosen to perform it. After the men had made their donations, men and women were permitted to dance in couples. The reales went to the cofradía funds:

> [T]hat which is collected helps to pay the expenses of the celebration as well as the blood-procession which that cofradía organizes for the sake of the *penitentes* [penitents] in order not to dip into the cofradía's principal [capital], since upon leaving their charges they have to deliver every cent not spent with detailed accounts and explanation to the cofradía treasure, deposit it in the box, and sometimes they even add some jewelry as charity and they take care of the sick; after all that is their purpose. (Ordoñez 1989, 102)

This document portrayed women as agents of evil and gave weight to the edict, which concluded that these celebrations were offensive to God, using the façade of virtue to cover mortal sins, mainly of sensuality. The women's dance attracted the worst sort of people: Indians, Ladinos, mulattoes, Mestizos, muleteers, and foreigners "who had no home." These negative Spanish views of women influenced Indian perceptions of women as well.

A version of this dance survives in the modern provinces of Alta Verapaz and El Quiché.[4] The Q'eqchi, for example, perform a dance accompanied by the zarabanda *son* music of harp, violin, and guitar in their cofradía celebrations in front of its saint's image to collect funds for the cult; a cash offering to the saint entitles the donor to one glass of alcohol and the right to dance as a *devoción* to the saint. The substitution of alcohol for female sensuality as a reward for pious donations resonates with a contemporary myth about the origins of mankind and alcohol among the Maya Tzeltal of Chiapas, Mexico. The myth tells how the Virgin Mary transformed her blood into alcohol, seduced the Antichrist through dance, and got him drunk in order to trap him and prevent him from continuing his destruction of mankind (Navarrete Pellicer 1988,

151–52). In this instance, the female call to drink the Virgin Mary's own blood and to dance with her serves the purpose of eliminating the devil. Thus the dangers of alcohol and female seductiveness are inverted and become an instrument for the common good.

The demonization of Indian society was not only an ideological rationalization for Spanish control; it also reflected a Manichean notion of the world that was part of the rationality of sixteenth-century Spanish society (Cervantes 1994, 1–4). This notion was transplanted into a multiethnic colonial society, where it took hold and became part of the Achi cultural heritage. The clash between Ladino "outsiders" and Indian "insiders" for power and resources became for both sides a struggle between good and evil. That Indians internalized the negative view of themselves and their past certainly helped the Spanish and Ladinos to subjugate them. The conquest and subjugation of Indians has, in their eyes, transformed Ladinos into the devil's allies. Ladinos' greed for money and personal gratification, their accumulation of illegitimate wealth amassed from activities other than working the land, the exploitation and the ill treatment of Indians by Ladino bosses on the plantations were all seen as manifestations of evil (Cabarrus 1979; Warren 1992).[5]

Music and Drinking

All social musical occasions celebrating family and community life are called *alegrías* (happy occasions). At these events music, food, and alcohol are the most precious gifts exchanged among the living and between the living and the dead; they "open the path of communication" and express mutual recognition, sociability, and reciprocity within the family and community. Men make these offerings, though the gifts themselves are considered female.[6]

Marimba music is a female and "Marian" call to people and to the spirits of their ancestors to share the expression of *sentimientos* (sadness) and *emociones* (happiness). In a religious sense, this emotional channel is particularly intended to allow the release of feelings in an appropriate context, outside the realm of everyday life. The expression of feelings, desires, and intentions during alegrías also exposes participants to symbolic violence such as envy, jealousy, and vengeance through witchcraft, or to physical violence and accidents resulting from drunkenness. Even though music is immediately associated with gaiety, people also associate alegrías with drunkenness and fights, because "music invites drinking and drunkards provoke fights." Alcohol's unbinding and anxiety-relieving function (Horton 1943) contributes to the vulnerability generated in this social context. Participants' perception of music and alcohol (Taylor 1979) can transform the social event into a dangerous situation that can lead to conflicts and accidents.

Social drinking at alegrías not only encourages communication but is both a moral obligation and an expression of good will. To share alcohol is a gesture of trust between the person offering it and the one who accepts it and in time (on this or another occasion) returns the favor. To refuse a drink suggests a lack of confidence in the donor, who is likely to take this public rejection as an insult and may seek revenge. As specialists in ritual, musicians and *abogados* (prayer makers) are very clear about this principle, which is reflected in their acceptance of the drinks offered to them by the event's host and participants as a gesture of gratitude and in exchange for their prayers and musical offerings. The consumption of alcohol presents a challenge to musicians, who must balance their social obligation and their need to remain sober enough to perform. Musicians who take pleasure in the effect their music has on people also speak, often with annoyance, of the drunks who follow them everywhere they play. Many also express concern about their own and other marimbistas' alcohol consumption. They know that the constant pressure to socialize through drinking contributes to their own drinking problems.

But there is more to drinking in ritual contexts than relations among the living: drinking large quantities of alcohol, often to the point of unconsciousness, is a declaration of trust in the communion of souls. This "apocalyptic" pattern of drinking (Pages Larraya 1976) as part of the ritual celebration of the annual life cycle can be interpreted as a symbolic form of sacrifice. Individual will is delivered into the hands of the ancestors as an affirmation of the ties of reciprocity between the living and the dead. Collective drunkenness is, then, an affirmation of community spirit.[7]

This ancient form of drinking appears to be coming under increasing pressure, as people try to balance their views of marimba music and alcohol as a religious and social offering with the negative side effects of alcohol.

Perceptions of music and alcohol form part of a moral outlook in which sociality and conflict are interpreted as a battle between good and evil. Conflict is explained as the result of evil, often the evil of foreign or "outsider" influences. The evil intentions of other participants, stemming from conflicts between neighboring families over such things as land and water access, is a common perception. But even then, the story is told obliquely. For example, one man told me a long story about a fight he'd had over a girl, mentioning only at the end of the tale that he was already involved in a dispute with the other man over water access.

Others saw alcohol as the personification of the devil himself. Older people explained that alcohol consumption outside the places and times prescribed by ritual promoted evil. From the older generation's moral and religious point of view, one had to drink in "God's name," that is, within the social and religious aims of the community, while thinking of

God and seeking his protection. They criticized young men for using marimba music at cofradías as an excuse to gather outside in the street, the nighttime domain of the devil, where they drank and looked for trouble (cf. Warren 1992, 46–48). The elders accused the young of drinking *por puro gusto* (only for pleasure) like Ladinos, becoming evil in the same way. Cantinas are another of the devil's favorite haunts, where one can sense the evil spirit of the marimba, *la Siuanaba.*

Some people, especially evangelicals, blame the marimba for transforming alegrías into occasions for evil. Of musicians who have fallen under Protestant persuasion and abandoned their destiny, marimbista Francisco Ixpata said, "Here the evangelicals say that it is forbidden to play sones, forbidden to play *pieza*. Then they sell it [the marimba] because some say the marimba is a devil that imperils the person. So they say, that's why they sell it."

"THE MARIMBA IS A WOMAN"

While playing the marimba is an exclusively male activity, the instrument's spirit and sound are "female," according to the Achi. The view of music as feminine has many dimensions, but I shall cite only two of Achi women's social roles that are closely associated with the different uses and meanings of music. The first is the female role of food preparation, which is women's primary contribution to the family group and to the community during festivities: women's nurturing role is identified with the nourishing quality of food. Corn, the Indian staple, is viewed as a symbol of femininity. The Achi people of Cubulco say, "A fourteen-year-old girl and corn are alike because they don't tire of serving us day and night" (Neuenswander 1986, 7). The supernatural beings are also nurtured by women: In the rites of entrance during cofradía celebrations, the wives of the second- and third-highest *cargo* holders carry the offerings of wax and lard candles in their baskets. These are the food for God, the saints, the spirits, and the holy earth.

The musical instruments and their sound acquire female attributes because music is another of the offerings that nourish God, the saints, the ancestors, and the earth. Not only is music an offering in itself; its female voice also summons others to gather and make their own offerings. The female nature of music is also specifically assigned to the leading voices of the instrumental ensembles because, as first voices, they "pull" the others. It may be said that the perception of music as female permeates the concept of musical structure. The representation of the marimba as feminine also derives from its relationship with the earth, which provides food and other goods. As marimbista Esteban Uanché remarked, "The marimba is like a woman because it feeds us, provides sustenance like mother earth. We thank mother earth with <u>cuxa</u> [domestic alcohol beverage] covering the three spots [where musicians stand to play]. We also offer it to the marimba because both provide food for us. We walk on earth and she supplies us with provisions. The marimba also feeds us and provides <u>cuxa</u> and cigarettes."[8]

Five hundred years of Catholic instruction have been unable to rid Achi culture of the association between music, alcohol, and fertility.[9] The marimbista Lázaro expressed a similar idea, although for him the relationship between earth and marimba is not only imitative or iconical but causal or indexical: "We offer *guaro* to mother earth because she produced the tree which provided the wood to build the marimba. That's what I do."

Musicians illustrate the fundamental relationship between music and women in their discourse, in which music and instruments are referred to as though they are talking about women. This was brought home to me when Esteban and his nephews helped me buy a second-hand marimba in Kanchel village in Cubulco. As we returned to Rabinal town, Esteban began calculating the amount of work the marimba would need before I could play it. I explained that I had no money to pay for his work and that anyway it didn't need fixing as I wasn't going to perform in public but only wanted to learn to play on it. Esteban was so appalled that he offered to do the work for free. He said that marimbas are like women and that one must keep them properly dressed:

> Look, both have *chichis* [women's breasts; the resonators that hang underneath the marimba]. The cost of properly dressing a woman today is 1,500 quetzales for her *corte* [Indian skirt], her *faja* [cotton belt], her *huipil* [smock top], the ribbon for her head, her necklace with a cross and the *bambas* [silver coins] and *chibolita* [head-dress], her earrings and sandals.[10] And the marimba? The same. It is expensive to keep it tuned, well decorated, clean, and with new *entelada* [resonator membranes] every time it is played, so people can appreciate how beautiful she is.

After this convincing argument I realized that I was behaving indecorously toward my marimba and that I should treat it properly. I therefore left it to Esteban to bedeck it as well as he would a woman.[11] As the days passed, my impatience to start playing grew, but Esteban refused to hand over my marimba until it was totally renewed. I visited several times to see how the work was progressing and discovered how much attention is given to a marimba's appearance.

Women's valued role as conservers of tradition, as conveyors of customs, beliefs, and language to their children, has been transferred to the marimba. The equation of the marimba with women's role as living symbols of Achi culture provides another conceptual link between this somewhat recently introduced instrument and the ancestors.

One manifestation of women's identification with Maya tradition is the wearing of the traditional dress that Esteban described (men were prohibited from wearing their traditional garb in the 1920s, possibly in an attempt to give the country's labor force a more modern appearance). Most women, excluding younger women who live in town, take pride in the dress particular to their *municipio* (municipality), and in their own distinct embroidery and the brightly colored patterns of their huipiles, some of which they weave themselves.

The huipil (smock top) is one of the markers of tradition and social identity for all Indian Rabinalenses, if not all Indians. This is especially the case for women involved in market trading who travel with their menfolk to regional markets such as Cubulco, San Miguel Chicaj, and Salamá. When Celestino explained the differences in performance style between Rabinalense musicians and those of neighboring towns, he used women's dress as a metaphor for the different son styles, making a gendered construction of local tradition and its music: "Those from Cubulco play the *San Pablo* [son] and the *mixito* [little cat son] too, but in a different way, just like the women dress otherwise, different from Rabinal. Those from San Miguel wear yet a different uniform. Likewise with the son, they have changed the son."

The marimba also elicits certain ideas about male and female sexual roles. On the one hand, a woman is valued and appreciated because she provides for, and satisfies, the needs of the stomach; on the other, she is feared because she "calls" and "pulls" a man toward sin and the pleasures of the flesh, endangering his will. Consequently man tries to control her, frequently through violence, including sexual violence. Men and women's perceptions of their sexual relationships not only reflect but justify male dominance.

Sexuality is a sensitive subject among the Achi. Groups of men or women (rarely both) refer to sexuality through jest, making oppositions and reversals in their stories. Similarly, in neighboring El Quiché province, K'iche' women avoid speaking of sexual desire directly and generally face this theme with giggles and embarrassment. Yet they talk openly about sexual relations as part of their reproductive function (Zur, personal communication); they also speak freely of men's sexual desires but consider it sinful to talk of their own.[12] Catholic proselytizing over the centuries has taught men and women that lust and sexual pleasure are sins that may be punished with temporary madness and sometimes with death. They therefore abstain from expressing their own desires.

This modesty contrasts sharply with men's behavior toward women. From puberty onward Achi men besiege women. This sometimes begins at home, with advances from their own male relatives, even their own fathers. Fear of sexual assault corrals women into the company of female relatives; a girl or woman out on her own is considered sexually loose, an idea that had disastrous consequences for women who lost the protection of their menfolk, through death or flight, during the period of political violence.

The pursuit by male relatives continues after a girl marries, when children become their mother's protectors in their father's absence. This too works to keep women away from the world of men. This overt and aggressive sexual surveillance of women is coupled with extreme jealousy on the part of their husbands, which has been identified by health workers in Rabinal as a major cause of domestic violence. Men working away from home for extended periods are mistrustful and suspicious of their wives and blame them should any form of extramarital relationship develop while they are away. A man's tendency to hold his wife responsible means that he is prey to neighbors' gossip about his wife's supposed activities and male visitors during his absence. Together with a group of Rabinalense health workers, my wife Judith and I have produced sociodrama radio programs that address the most important social and health problems of the community. The workers chose to dedicate the first program to alcoholism and gossip. The storyline they created revolved around a man's reaction to a rumor that his wife had received another man in his house while he was away working on the coast. Malicious gossip, often fuelled by relatives who wish to weaken marriage alliances in favor of blood ties,[13] promotes conflict between husband and wife by raising doubts about fidelity. But it would be naive to think that men and women are merely passive victims of neighbors and relatives; gossip is used by both spouses to call attention to the faults of the other and to negotiate positions of advantage in their personal relationships and in relation to domestic tasks.

There is more truth to women's suspicions of their husbands' infidelity, which leaves them feeling threatened and afraid of abandonment. Men acknowledge that they may establish transient relationships with other women and even have other families in the places where they migrate for work, although this indulgence is usually only for those who can afford it.[14] A man's freedom of movement and his search for better living conditions outside his social sphere contribute to his access to other women. For their part, women assume that they are less likely to be abandoned if they continue to have sexual relations with their husbands, believing that their sexual disposition and ability to produce valuable offspring will persuade a husband to continue supporting the home. In other words, women justify and repeat the male-dominated dynamics reflected in their sexual relationships.

In contrast to the expansive gossip surrounding more conventional extramarital liaisons (those to which a woman is perceived to have given her consent), strict silence is the norm concerning rape. This is in order to avoid a multitude of negative consequences, such as threats from the rapist,[15] the victim's ostracism by her family, and her husband's rage and departure.[16] Female consent or provocation is generally suspected and the victim is therefore typically blamed for the attack and becomes an object of scorn and disapproval.[17] Nothing could better illustrate the prevalent ideology of machismo in Rabinal society, in which every woman is considered a potential prostitute.[18]

Men also believe that part of their sexual role is to satisfy women's unexpressed needs and desires, and they achieve this by asserting control over women, which includes violence, thus proving their virility. Thus men justify their domination and conceal their own (sinful) lust, which is projected onto women, whom men endow with an active sexuality that is not only demanding but sinful and corrupt.

These attitudes are made explicit through the perpetual comparisons men make between the marimba and women. For example, marimbistas refer to the activity of playing their instrument as *jodiendo* (fornication). Celestino told me that in order to control "her" it is necessary to play "her" frequently, because "the marimba is a woman and she gets jealous if one does not touch her. One must touch her at least once every five days." Through this metaphor, Celestino not only asserted the need to practice frequently in order to master the marimba but also alluded to the necessity of maintaining frequent sexual relations with his wife in order to exert control over her and keep her satisfied; he never mentioned his own desire. Sexual discourse has a *machista* (male dominance) content for both men and women; sexual relations are an instrument of persuasion for women and an expression of power and dominance for men.

In the male domination of women, sexual relations become an extension of the domestic violence women suffer from childhood at the hands of their fathers or other male relatives, including brothers and uncles, as a method of forcing respect. Women may respond to a drunken beating by their husband or other male relative by neglecting their duty as food providers or, in extreme cases, by abandoning their home and taking refuge with their parents or other relatives. Drunkenness relieves men of the responsibility of their actions and, while not condoned, is justified as a way for men to secure respect.[19] Influenced by the Christian belief that women, like Eve, not only tend to succumb more easily to temptation,[20] especially sexual temptation, but have the power to tempt men into following suit, men instill fear in their women in order to dissuade them from giving in to other men. Women generally prefer to tolerate a husband's drunken bouts and violence rather than be despised in their social environment.[21]

Machismo focuses on the negative aspects of femaleness. The attribution of an almost feral sexual power to women links them with the dangers of alcohol; their siren voices, like the marimba, call people to drink and dance outside the supposed safety of the ritual sphere, which is the domain of men. Thus women, alcohol, and music form an evil trilogy that makes men vulnerable, causing them to lose their senses and self-control and creating the circumstances that destroy the implicit safety of communal affirmation of communion with the spirits.

This is reflected in a favorite Achi myth about la Siuanaba, which is retold throughout Guatemala (Falla 1986, 67). La Siuanaba is a personification of death disguised as a beautiful woman who seduces men and then kills them. In every version of this story, the woman appears at night, during or after a man's drunken spree, taking the guise of a lover or a desired woman other than the man's wife. Other details vary, particularly regarding la Siuanaba's appearance, according to the narrator's taste in women. She roams dangerous, liminal places where she may bestow great amounts of easy (unearned) money on her victims; or she may try to kill them by guiding them into a ravine that she has disguised as a wide road. She may also scare them to death by transforming herself into a skeleton or the devil just when the man begins to embrace her. People describe la Siuanaba as well dressed and groomed, but if she shows her face, which is covered with her long hair, she appears to be a horse head or a skull. The easiest way to identify her is by looking at her legs and feet, which are turned backward.

One of la Siuanaba's favorite haunts is the cantina, which is considered an evil space because people drink with no sense of respect and devotion to God, prostitution is rife, and drinkers squander the money they should be spending on family necessities. Thus the marimba's summons to a zarabanda in a cantina is not a call to pay homage but an invitation to vice. In consequence it is believed that the marimba's spirit in these circumstances is none other than la Siuanaba.

Celestino related an incident that took place when he was playing at a zarabanda in El Motagua cantina, where a large number of people were drinking and dancing; suddenly a fight broke out, resulting in many injuries. He connected this incident with the apparition of la Siuanaba:[22]

> I did not notice it but I was told that a *patoja* [young woman] arrived dressed as a Cobanera[23] and began dancing and drinking with everyone all night. The man who reported this to me said that he had stepped outside to urinate when a woman came out of the cantina and called to him. He was a little tipsy and approached her. The woman made small talk and they started walking together toward the border of town around Pachalum. The woman was dressed like a bride and wore elaborate necklaces and a beautiful belt. When they walked by a huge tree on the side of the road, she invited him to go into the forest. Then this man said that he realized she was no woman but la Siuanaba because he noticed that her feet were

backward. So he circled around her seven times and he whipped her over and over again. The woman disappeared, leaving her clothes on the ground. The next day some people from Pachica went to the municipal authorities to report a bridal ensemble apparently stolen during the night from its bridal trunk. This man, upon hearing the news of the vanished clothes, went back to fetch them from the spot where the Siuanaba had disappeared. He returned the clothes and told the people what had happened to him and the people rewarded him with gratitude.

Celestino's story clearly illustrates the male perspective on sexual relations: In order to survive, a man has to exert control and dominance over woman's desire, which in fact is his own sinful desire and lust for a woman other than his own. By mentioning la Siuanaba, Celestino also implied that a woman caused the fight in the cantina. Invariably, in these stories, the intended male victim's faith triumphs over the evil seductiveness of woman, and man thus reigns supreme over womankind.

IN SUMMARY, THEN, OFFERINGS TO GOD, the saints, and the spirits of the dead are female symbols that share the attributes of being mediators and generators of social life with living women. These offerings are shared among the living and between the living and the dead, and there does seem to be an unspoken, even unthought, association between the sharing of music and alcohol and the presumed sexual looseness of women. The marimba, a "promiscuous" instrument, is played in religious and secular contexts, for Indians and Ladinos. Its music is both food for the spirits and a call to the devil.

Local Catholics believe that faith and devotion are the only means of maintaining control, keeping one's will, and avoiding becoming the devil's victim. Entwined with this belief is the pre-Hispanic practice of communal drunkenness at religious fiestas, which is seen as an expression of trust among the living and a form of communion with the dead. The balance between the two has been subverted by the introduction of late medieval Catholic attitudes toward women and sexuality. The negative connotations of music, alcohol, and women are clearly focused on the sinful sexuality of living women, overwhelming the value placed on them as actual and symbolic nurturers and positive emblems of fertility.

6   Musical Occasions

To the Rabinalense, all social musical occasions pertaining to family and community life are known as *alegrías* (happy occasions); the music is the "call" that invites people to come and celebrate the event with the *bulla* (bustle) of their presence and conversation. Alegría is synonymous with music and sociality; its equation with social gatherings contrasts starkly with *triste* (sad) moments of loneliness, silence, and isolation. Furthermore, sociality has a spiritual dimension because the spirits are included in all social events. Violinist Magdaleno Xitumul explains:

> We are happy because we are now a true gathering, and so are they [the dead]. Where there is alegría, there is revelry and they are there. Where there are people there are alegrías, because they are always with us [then]. When there is music, that is, marimba, when there is *adufe* [square drum], when there are drums, in a *cofradía*, a *cabo de año* [first anniversary of a death], a wedding, the souls are always there, watching.

Rabinalense Achi differentiate alegrías by context; they can be either secular or religious. The principal difference between them is that in the latter an *abogado*—the religious specialist who "speaks" through prayers to God and the souls of the dead (*ánimas*) on behalf of the living—formally invites the souls of the dead to participate in the event. But the ánimas are not invited to participate in secular alegrías such as *zarabandas* in cantinas during major festivities, the national celebrations for Independence Day (14–15 September) and the Day of the Revolution (20 October); nor are they invited to local events such as school celebrations or election campaigns,[1] because these recently introduced events are associated with the Ladino world and not with Catholicism. In this chapter I focus on anniversaries of the dead, addressing certain issues about the social context, ritual organization, and structure of the occasion. I re-create the activities, timing, use of space, and the kind of social interactions between musicians and the rest of the participants in order to immerse the reader in the social dynamics of a ritual context.

Alegrías are understood as specific pre-established contexts where music and socializing occur and in which musical performance evokes, shapes, and incorporates participants' memories and emotions into social life; indeed, musical occasions inform participants what and how to feel. The conventions, social significance, and symbolism of the organization, and the procedures and structures of alegrías aim to create sacred time and space in which to communicate with the dead and God.

OCCASION AND PERFORMANCE

Musical performance derives from the concept of "cultural performance" proposed by Singer (1958). Cultural performances are secular artistic cultural events and religious rituals are defined as the more concrete, observable units of culture that take place within a pre-established place and time. They are bound by a timetable, have a program of organized activities with a beginning and an end, and a group of participants (performers and audience). The main difference between musical occasions and cultural performances is that some musical occasions are not formally structured; there may be no program or sequence of organized activity, as is the case with zarabandas. Nevertheless, most musical occasions in Rabinal are cultural performances.

From a behaviorist perspective, it has been argued that "an organising principle in the ethnography of performance is the 'event' (or scene) within which performance occurs . . . . [It designates] a culturally defined bounded segment of the flow of behaviour and experience that constitutes a meaningful context for action" (Bauman 1984, 27). Performance is defined as behavior "situated within and rendered meaningful with reference to relevant contexts . . . in terms of settings for example, the culturally defined places where performance occurs" (ibid.). Place and time are defined in terms of significant behavior.

The concepts "occasion" and "event" are very similar; both are defined in terms of a context and a situated behavior (although "occasion" can imply one or more "events"). The term "event" has a more behavioral connotation, making reference to what happens, while occasion seems to be more related to the context in which performances occur. I have chosen "occasion" over "event" because it gives more immediacy or emphasis to the context. The demarcation between ordinary life and the celebration of life-crisis rituals or the specific dates of the festivity calendar is central to the study of alegrías: the time frame provides information about the type of occasion, what is meant to be happening during it, and how participants should behave and feel.

Cultural performances have also been described as modes of "performative reflexivity" (Turner 1984): "[C]ultural performances are not simple reflectors or expressions of culture or even of changing culture but may themselves be active agencies of change, representing the eye by which culture sees itself and the drawing board in which creative actors sketch out what they believe to be more apt or interesting 'designs for living'" (24). Following Van Gennep's (1960) three-stage concept of rites of passage (separation, transition, incorporation), Turner places special emphasis on the transitional or liminal stage:

> Liminality itself is a complex phase or condition. It is often the scene and time for the emergence of a society's deepest values in the form of sacred dramas and objects—sometimes the re-enactment periodically of cosmogonic narratives or deeds of saintly, godly, or heroic establishers of morality, basic institutions, or ways of approaching transcendent beings or powers. But it [can] also be the venue and occasion for the most radical scepticism—always relative, of course, to the given culture's repertoire of areas of scepticism—about cherished values and rules. Ambiguity reigns: people and public policies may be judged sceptically in relation to deep values; the vices, follies, stupidities, and abuses of contemporary holders of high political, economic, or religious status may be satirised, ridiculed, or condemned in terms of axiomatic values, or these personages may be rebuked for gross failures in common sense. (22)

Reflexivity and liminality are useful concepts in terms of understanding the alegría as "staged time" in which behavior and opinions about behavior are enhanced performances. Through aesthetic means such as the setting, music, prayers, offerings, and stylized behaviors ranging from tears to mockery, participants communicate meanings and feelings about belief, daily life situations, and behavior. Alegrías take place in a liminal time in which certain participants—the ritual specialists, among them musicians—must meet the ideal standards of behavior in order for the occasion to be successful; they have to maintain the measured politeness that is an esteemed trait of everyday Achi interaction, refraining from expressing a direct opinion, as this is considered ill-mannered and disrespectful. I was always struck by *marimbistas'* formal and serious manner of playing what they considered happy and playful music. They almost seem unaffected by their own music and oblivious to other participants' pain and pleasure, happiness and drunkenness. They appear as if they are not really attending, but in fact they are, for their music is very much in tune with what is occurring around them. The remaining participants are under license to mock the norms of sociality and express opinions and feelings more openly—although not with complete freedom—in the assumption that during the festivity, participants play a performative role. The collective "as if" attitude of participants during alegrías gives people the opportunity, to a certain ambiguous extent, to be direct without being considered offensive.

The ambience of an alegría stimulates communication and condones the expression of feelings that Indians usually try to control because displaying affection, affliction, or personal conflict is believed to make people weak and susceptible to gossip and illness. The feelings that the Achi prefer to leave unexpressed are classified into two categories: *sentimientos* (sentiments) and *emociones* (emotions), both of which come from the heart. Sentimientos are all forms of suffering, such as sadness, melancholy, worry, pain, love, hate, fear, jealousy, envy. Emociones include happiness, desire, satisfaction, and any activity related to these emotions, such as laughing, singing, whistling, running, shouting, and dancing.[2] Thus the license to express feelings granted by these occasions is not without danger, for everyone is exposed to everyone else's intentions and feelings, hence the ambiguity. This is particularly the case when the souls of the recent dead are invited to the celebrations commemorating their own deaths, as their presence fills the atmosphere with emotional memories that in the best of times generate public self-reflection and liminality and communitas between the living and the dead (Turner 1979). The years 1995 and 1996 were not the best of times; they saw the fourteenth anniversary of the massacres of 1981–82, in which many local men had participated.

Through musical performance, prayer, and dances, alegrías accommodate the disposition to serve and the opportunity to socialize and communicate feelings in comparative safety. Elaborate preparations for the event begin the separation from mundane daily life. The place where the event takes place is decorated, abundant food and drink and other offerings are prepared, and, finally, people turn their attention to their personal dress and appearance. The concentration of all social and material wealth on predetermined dates and sites displays the boundaries between everyday life, with its measured behavior, and the extraordinary world of abundance and full expression of the alegría, in which the participants' behavior is different but no less established.

Religious alegrías present an ordered sequence and highly patterned behavior. I heard music break the silence of the town at least twice a week, day or night, occasionally punctuated by fireworks to announce different phases of a cofradía fiesta or procession. Listening from afar, people can tell what the celebration is for and provide details of the rites being performed. Date, time, type of music, fireworks—all define an occasion and highlight each phase. Thus, merely by listening, people can "see" what is happening. Musicians' knowledge is more detailed; because the sequence and timing of *sones* depends on ritual sequence, they recognize the phase of the ritual according to the sones being played. Furthermore, the musical groups, repertoire, and performance style are determined by the type of musical occasion. When I questioned *pito* (cane flute) and drum player Eligio Gonzalez about the occasions when his instruments were played, he replied, "This drum, when it's time, because everything has its time, it's just like the fiesta, right? It has its day." He then named every occasion on which his instruments are played and gave the appropriate sones for each and described what happens as they are played.

The creation of a sequential order with its own rhythms, spaces, and behaviors, its own formal structures and conventions, is intended as a means of communicating with the supernatural realm; this is the main objective of religious rituals. Prayers and music are part of the ritual behavior that creates "sacred" time, establishing an orderly and safe "path of communication" that pleases the dead and assures a favorable response from them and God, the saint spirits, and the sacred earth. During this sacred time, the feelings, desires, needs, and intentions of participants are momentarily fulfilled and released from everyday silence, anxiety, frustration, and want. Music is the call to devotional participation, the path to sacred time and space, and the marker of the different stages and diverse activities of the celebration.[3] But, more important, music makes the sacred felt in the social body; some people say that music is the very body of the ancestors.

Religious rituals in Rabinal have a fixed sequence of actions that are followed (with varying degrees of strictness) in order to achieve the required communication between the living and God, ancestors, and the sacred earth. According to Bloch (1989), the efficacy of the ritual depends not so much on the semantic or propositional force of symbolic action but on the forms through which participants are restricted to certain orders and procedures and on the way in which the ritual is performed, though I believe it is an error to separate, oppose, and especially to exclude content from form. Nevertheless, it is true that in Rabinal, as in other highly formal societies, much of a ritual's efficacy lies in the repetitive performance of formulaic discourses, actions, and gestures. Tono López, a former sacristan and a linguist who helped me translate my recordings of Achi prayers, explained that not only are they highly repetitive in themselves but they are considered exact repetitions of the prayers the ancestors used. The repetitiveness, which follows the order established by the ancestors, is said to emphasize their appeals to God—"like a child crying and crying until he is fed," as a blind marimbista named Lázaro said. Whenever there is an interruption in ritual prayers, abogados resume them to assure God that they have not lost the path of communication and that they are continuing in the same vein as the ancestors. The orderly repetition of the prayers is a prerequisite to God's acceptance of them. The emphasis on ritual formulas and gestures rather than on content probably stems from early colonial evangelization practices—Indians were taught Catholic ritual formulas such as benedictions, psalms, and hymns, and liturgical gestures such as kneeling and the sign of the cross, before they knew the purpose of the ceremonial or the content of Catholic dogma (Breton 1979, 182).

Bauman (1984, 1992) acknowledges the referential aspect of performances as a baseline but emphasizes the form. He is not particularly concerned with the order and structure of performance; rather, he looks at

the relationship between performers and audience. To him, the performers' competence (skill and knowledge) and the response of the audience
to the expressive acts of the performer are key aspects of performance.
Bauman explains that the relationship between them implies the performers' responsibility or accountability to the audience for a display of
communicative competence above and beyond its referential content, on
the one hand, and the audience's evaluation of the performer's knowledge
and skill, on the other. Both Bauman and Schieffelin (1995) focus their
attention on the interactional credibility between performer and audience as a main condition of cultural performance. This is also valid for
the social performance in daily life (Goffman 1959, 1976).[4]

The interaction between audience and performers found in Rabinal is
not exactly what usually comes to mind when we think about audi-
ence/performer relationships. Behind this lie two other types of relationships: face-to-face patronage and religious advocacy, which go beyond
musical performance. Apart from their musical professionalism, one has
to bear in mind that musicians have an enormous moral responsibility
toward the community, particularly in helping people's appeals reach God.
The gift of musicianship places them in the position of moral guides, and
this determines much of the relationship with their audience. The audience expects them to be amenable to accepting contracts, to play for devotion and not only for money, to exhibit modesty, to behave respectfully
and with restraint during performances. Audience members also anticipate
that musicians will accept their many offerings of alcoholic drink, will play
with energy and endurance throughout the long celebrations, and will
maintain their alertness. The musicians' ability, both musical and social,
is at its peak when they simultaneously respond to people's feelings with
more elaborate performances, always contained by their professional conduct. All of these elements impinge on the credibility of musicians in the
eyes and ears of the other participants; this judgment depends not only on
the performance of the musician but also on the perception of the participants, both of which vary from performance to performance.

Provided that a favorable social image of the musician and friendly
relations between participants are maintained in daily life, the success and
efficacy of musical communication during musical performance rests on
fulfilling the social expectations of music and music making of the participants. This is brought about by musicians' skill, knowledge, restraint,
and endurance, which in turn establish the aesthetic, moral, and psychological conditions for the other participants to play their part. Within the
framework of religious alegrías, each group interprets and expresses the
moment in its own way and interacts with and responds to the other with
an intensity and complexity brought about through the general development of the occasion. The acknowledgment of the ancestors' presence and

the irrefutable proof of communication with them are revealed by the impact of abogados' and musicians' performances on participants' sentimientos and emociones. These sentimientos and emociones, experienced in the ancestors' presence, and their shared togetherness with the dead, are the emergent quality of successful ritual occasions.[5] Music is the audible evidence that the spirits have joined the celebration, instigating the flow of feelings between the living and the dead and the bond between them.

Recent work on the anthropology of emotions is helpful when thinking about emotions in the context of music, but it may be useful here to pause for a moment and look at the development of anthropological thinking about this theme. It took about fifty years from the time Bateson began his work on ethos for the idea that emotions may be socially or culturally constructed to enter into the anthropological literature. Up until then psychological and biological models had influenced the idea that emotions are purely subjective experiences of physiological events. There is now a large body of anthropological literature on emotions, ranging from relatively simple works on emotions in different cultures to more sophisticated works that discuss affect as a strategic social posture in relation to situations; the latter concern simultaneously self-creative impression management and individual identity feeling. An approach represented by cognitive and cultural anthropologists sustains a social view of emotion as a cognitive construction that is part of culture-specific meaning (Leavitt 1996). For example, Schieffelin argues that "Kaluli emotions, however privately experienced, are socially located and have a social aim. To this degree they are located not only in the person but also in the social situation and interaction that . . . they help to construct" (1985, 180). This view is useful in that it links feelings and occasions of feeling (including performance) with cultural views, strategies, and contexts, and therefore lends itself nicely to discussion of special performative occasions. On musical occasions that conjure up the dead, it is appropriate that people should feel most deeply moved and display themselves at their most emotional. Emotions are not only expressed on such occasions but are examined, shared, and given meaning. This kind of emotional display makes participants vulnerable, which suggests that the display of emotions here is equivalent to an emotional exchange, not only among the living but between the living and the dead.

Alegrías provide the cultural setting and the sound symbols representing emotions that are interpreted and embodied in the memories of participants; they are the contexts for public reflection and affection. While interpretations may be individual, they also hold collective meaning. In death anniversaries, for example, the memory of the deceased is embodied in the violin and, through the sones played on it, emotions are embodied in the audience. These are the embodied thoughts, which Rosaldo describes as thoughts permeated with the apprehension that "I am involved" (1984, 143). She states that "through 'interpretation' cultural meanings are transformed. And through 'embodiment' collective symbols acquire the power, tension, relevance, and sense emerging from our individuated histories" (141). Rabinalense violinist Magdaleno Xitumul echoes this view: "The violin means a lot, because if one dies the violin takes the signification that this instrument is going to play a son for the dead. The body will never come back again to us. Then one compares the dead person with this instrument."

Anniversaries of the Dead

Remembering and celebrating the dead by following custom is essential to ensuring the continuity of life. This is because, according to local Catholic belief, the dead remain in the world as the memory of the living (see Chapter 2). Abogado Pablo Camo expressed this in his prayer to the souls of the dead (ánimas):

> Revel in this alegría, in this blessing for all of you, since we are but your memories. We are your reminiscences, your children. We stayed here, we are a remembrance of you, to beg God the Father once more for your well-being, for the necessary rest of your souls, since in your time you were our grandparents in this world . . . we know that you also played music, you were great musicians and because of this we are here celebrating this memory of you.

The purpose of life for the followers of Catholic custom is, first, to please the ancestors by remembering them and acknowledging what they did to serve God and preserve life, and, second, to ensure the continuity of this teaching so that the dead in their turn will receive the blessings of the living. Victor Tum, abogado and musician, assured me that "the dead want to see a continuity and they rejoice when they see other people dedicated to the same."

Pablo Camo likewise begins his prayer: "We invoke our dead to ask for their blessing so we may have a new day here [on earth] with happiness, to thank our Father who is in heaven . . . . Thus we have reached the end of a year and are grateful to our God the Father." Gatherings to commemorate the anniversary of a relative's death are the most common musical occasions; they sustain musicians throughout the year.

Music and Mourning

The series of mandatory rituals commemorating a family member's death begin with the wake held on the night of the death and continue as long as there are relatives present to accompany the deceased's soul. There is no music during the wake. Wrapped in a straw mat (*petate*) and placed on the floor, the body receives the holy earth's blessing; it is then displayed in a coffin on a table, where people can view it for the last time. Together with the ánimas, mourners pray the three mysteries for the well-being of the deceased's soul. The ánimas are invited to accompany the deceased's corpse to its resting place in the cemetery and the funeral takes place the next day.

The family devotes time every day during the next seven or nine days to praying *novenas*[6] for the departed soul. They choose an abogado (known as a *padrino* in this context) to lead the prayers and a violin-and-adufe ensemble to accompany them; ideally, the same team of ritual specialists should be used throughout the fourteen years of commemorations. On the seventh or ninth day, and again on the fortieth day after death[7] the family gathers for prayers; the music of the violin-and-adufe ensemble "follows behind" the padrino's prayers, as it does on all subsequent death anniversary celebrations. The deceased's soul is invoked and welcomed, together with all other animas, and invited to pray the three mysteries and to enjoy the offerings prepared in their honor. This implies a degree of separation and distance and it is for this reason that it is necessary to invite the dead with music. The "little music" of the violin-and-adufe ensemble respects the deceased's transitional condition and suffering. It is still "fresh; it is soul not yet judged and is therefore in sin." The soul's suffering is shown in the overwhelming pain of the relatives. Marimbista Lázaro Cauec explains the grieving process:

> The first days after a person dies, it is very hard because he has just passed on and the family is sick in their mind and in their heart just feeling the pain and lamenting his departure, but after one year, the family is more or less calmed; time has gone by and it is acceptable to celebrate with violin and marimba. Because, as you may have noticed, the marimba speaks of many things traditional to the mind, that is, in spirit, because the sones bring alegría, emotions, and you are going to have some drinks.

Only after a year has passed will the soul be welcomed and remembered with marimba music at a happy social gathering—unless the mourners' grief is such that they defer the marimba music and social alegría until the seventh-year celebrations.[8] The celebrations of the first-, seventh-, and fourteenth-year anniversaries all follow the same procedure. The fourteenth-anniversary celebration ends the family's responsibilities to that particular dead relative.[9]

Musicians (violin-and-adufe ensemble and marimba de sones) are contracted because the event is a reunion between the souls of the dead and the souls on earth. Although people grieve when they remember the dead, they are also happy because this is a reunion and because they enjoy the things of this life. The ambivalence between feelings of sorrow and happiness is clearly expressed by the sones of entrance and farewell, which are the same. At the beginning they may evoke happiness and at the end sadness. But for some people, these four-mallet sones are always sones of sadness, whenever they are played. For them, it is the merrier three- and two-mallet sones that evoke happier feelings of sociality during the event. The feelings evoked by a son depend on the context in which it is played, the musicians' performance, and the individual's state of mind.

As marimbista Bonifacio Jerónimo explained, "We receive them with a son of sadness because they come and say, 'Ah! Look at this place I left.' That is why we receive them with their sones of sadness. Once inside [at the altar inside the house], then we begin with the joyful sones so they can listen and share with pleasure, right? Then, when they leave, we play again with sorrow, because maybe in one year, who knows who will or will not be still here?"

People rejoice to the sones of happiness, which indicate that the ánimas are sharing the alegría in the house where the celebration is being held; and they cry during sones of sadness, when they arrive from and leave to return to the cemetery; these sones are called <u>soon re okib'al keri qati' qamaam</u> (son for the entrance of our grandmothers and grandfathers) and <u>soon releb'al ke ri qati' qamaam</u> (son to bid farewell to our grandmothers and grandfathers). The sones for the souls of the dead, such as costa grande and costa chiquita, encourage people to express their sentimientos and recall past events and memories. Such sones are known as <u>soon bis'ab'al</u>, which literally means sones that evoke memories that generate sadness and nostalgia.

Celestino explained the relationship between his way of playing and the feelings of people listening to him: "I play the son more beautifully, with more *vueltas*, to make people cry and express their desires." Another musician, from the Lajuj family of La Ceiba village, commented on the musician's feelings: "Let's suppose a marimbista is performing a *son*. He will make more vueltas to ornament the son, he will then be putting something else into it, he puts feeling into it by making a vuelta."

THE FOURTEENTH ANNIVERSARY

The fourteenth-anniversary celebrations for massacre victims[10] fell between 1994 and 1996, keeping violin and adufe players very busy. Violinist Magdaleno Xitumul complained that he and Felicano, his adufe companion, had not been able to sleep because of the many obligations to the souls murdered in 1982. "The souls have many engagements now. All those who died in eighty-two are celebrating their fourteen years. You saw how it was in Nimacabaj [village] last night—there were many festivities because there were many who died in that dangerous time." I asked Magdaleno if I could attend one of his *compromisos* (commitments) and he agreed gladly. We arranged to meet at the Calvary Chapel the following Monday, when there would be a fourteenth-year celebration by the Pantulul bridge. Later I met marimbista Esteban Uanché, who told me he was also playing at the event and agreed to meet us at the same place.

As I walked to the Calvary Chapel the following Monday morning, I met padrino abogado Felipe Sis and Cristobal Gonzalez, the hostess's brother. Felipe had just finished lighting candles and incense for the saints in the main church. As we walked, Cristobal explained that this was the fourteenth anniversary of the death of his father, Juan Gonzales, who had died of a heart attack caused by fright upon witnessing the massacre in the town plaza on 15 September 1981. This was the last obligation Cristobal had to perform in order to commit his father's soul to God: "This is the end of our duty." Cristobal had celebrated two weeks earlier and now his sister Maria and her husband had organized this fiesta a few days after the end of the novena prayers.

Musicians were waiting for us to arrive outside the Calvary cemetery. We were the only people there; in the silence of the morning mist it looked beautiful, with bushes and wild flowers overrunning the plain Indian graves; only the big colorful mausoleums of the rich Ladino families towered over the greenery. Esteban searched among the graves for a flat surface on which to set up his marimba; Magdaleno and Feliciano sat on the gravestone next to Juan's grave. As they tuned their instruments, Felipe cleaned around the grave and decorated the stone with pine and cypress branches. He then knelt in front of the cross on the gravestone to initiate the "awakening" of the soul of Julián Gonzalez, his deceased kin, and the rest of the souls from Rabinal. As Felipe began the prayer to invoke the souls, both musical groups began playing, independently of each other, their own versions of the costa chiquita, which is one of the sones played to begin the celebration and summon the souls. The marimba broke the silence of the cemetery, overwhelming the murmur of prayer and the "little music" of the violin and adufe.

As an offering to the saints and souls, Felipe then placed several bouquets of basil between two rows of candles—seven yellow wax and seven white tallow—on the grave; a bottle of *guaro* (cane spirits) was sprinkled around the candles, which were then lit. Waving incense (another offering) over the four corners of the world, the corners of the space we all occupied, and in front of the musicians, Felipe began chanting a prayer of thanks to God and the saints for a new dawn over the world's four corners. Kneeling in front of the candles, he began a "roll call" of the spirits.[11] This general call is accompanied by the son <u>kotzij</u> (flower offering) and four more sones to summon the souls, played mournfully by the violin and adufe; the marimba simultaneously begins its repertory of sones *grandes* ("big" sones; entrance sones). The summoning of the souls lasted as long as it took the candles to melt, approximately one hour.

At the end of this general summons, Esteban packed up his marimba and the three musicians carried it to the house where the celebration was being held. The rest of us entered the Calvary Chapel, where a second invocation of the souls took place. Because it was a Monday, other abogados were also there praying on other people's behalf, and some were also accompanied by groups of violin and adufe musicians. Felipe approached them with the salutation, "Good morning, *compadre alcalde* [mayor], kajauxel, *principal*,"[12] and proceeded to search for a spot at the altar on which to deposit his offerings for Señor de la Misericordia (Lord of Mercy), who is the guard of the cemetery souls, and Señor del Cabildo (Lord of Town Hall). In the second instance, the abogado padrino lit four candles at the four corners of the chapel—representing the world—for those souls who died in pain at unknown locations, and placed some others at the center for the general congregation of souls. Finally he put two rows of seven candles each in front of the altar, where he knelt to pray until the candles were totally consumed. The musicians played sitting behind the padrino on one of the few benches available in the chapel. The violin and adufe sones accompanied the prayers. They echoed across the incensed darkness of the chapel and brought the sacred place to life (listen to the prayers and music on track 14 of the CD).

At the conclusion of this event, the padrino told me, "Now all the spirits are coming with us to the celebration." Thus "feeling" (I could only imagine) the great procession of spirits behind us, we walked to the house to celebrate the fourteenth anniversary of the deceased, Julián.

The house was a hive of activity. About thirty-five relatives, friends, and neighbors were busy preparing for the guests (which includes the dead). Men had been assigned to kill and joint the pig. Women were preparing the food (*chilate*, a drink often flavored with chocolate; *atol*, or maize gruel; tortillas; *frijol*, or beans; *chilmol* and *pinol de gallina*, stews; and *tamales de cerdo*, a maize dish filled with pork, and so on). Many of them had been there since very early in the morning to decorate the domestic altar in the main room of the house. The floor of this small room was covered with *juncia* (pine needles); fruit, a glass of water, candles, white Madonna lilies, and basil—the ánimas' favorite herb—had been added to the crucifixes and saints' images on the altar. Benches were set against the walls of the room and along the corridor of the porch.

In the midst of this bustle, the marimbistas remained almost aloof, behaving as if they knew no one there. Dressed, like everyone else, in their best clothes, they appeared very formal and elegant behind their colorful instrument. Carefully coifed, with cowboy hats tilted stylishly forward, and wearing clean shirts and trousers, machetes in hand-tooled leather sheaths hanging from their waists, their faces stern, they were an austere presence. They stood for hours, straight-backed, heads down, eyes on the keyboard, their bodies taut except for their arms, wrists, and hands, which moved constantly up and down in parallel and contrary motion, with two, three, or four mallets tangled in their fingers, their index fingers protected from blistering by pieces of plastic or leather. All marimbistas complain of great pains in their *pulmon* (lungs), by which they mean in their backs at the level of their lungs, and no wonder! Musicians' moderation, restraint, and general austerity indicate the respect, dedication, and care for the work they do and for the people and spirits of the dead for whom they are performing. Other than responding to a request for a particular son, they did not interact with the rest of the participants. They conversed with each other with reserve; from time to time they would disappear behind the house to relieve themselves. During more than eighteen hours of playing, the principal performers took only short breaks, when other players replaced them temporarily so that they could rest on a small bench behind the marimba (where they discreetly drank the guaro offered to them and ate the lunch brought to them).

The marimba began playing the son de entrada as soon as we arrived on the patio with the padrino. Felipe, accompanied by the violin and adufe musicians, then performed three blessings as a respectful greeting and petition to visit the altar inside the house: one at the patio, another at the *gotera* (entrance of the porch corridor), and the third at the entrance of the room housing the domestic altar.[13] This room holds only a few people at a time to join in the prayers, listen to the violin and adufe, rest and sleep, and eat and drink with the ritual specialists and the spirits, while the rest of the participants are outside the house, working or chatting, eating, drinking, and enjoying the big sound of the marimba, whose purpose is to promote feelings of happiness. Thus the division of space between the sacred (the altar indoors) and the secular (veranda, kitchen, and patio) is reinforced by sound differences. Both sets of musicians, one inside the house, the other outside, play independently, sometimes simultaneously and sometimes alternately.

Once inside, the violin and adufe players sat next to the altar and the padrino prayed for a moment. Later, the women brought lunch, which was served by Cristobal, the host's brother-in-law. After lunch, Magdaleno and Feliciano resumed playing while Felipe sat beside them to rest. Thus several hours passed. At one point, a young man tried to play the adufe under Feliciano's guidance, but he could not get the rhythm, and Magdaleno, the violinist, kept laughing discreetly.[14]

Meanwhile, outside, the marimba played for the men and women who were still preparing; guests begin arriving in the afternoon. Cristobal approached the marimbistas with an eighth of a litre bottle of guaro and offered them a drink, which they accepted, each one in turn drinking straight from the bottle. Esteban sprinkled what was left over the edges of the marimba keys to share it with "her" and to make "her" play better; he also offered some to the holy earth by tracing a cross on the three spots where his players and he were standing. By blessing the three spots where they stood, Esteban conferred sacredness on the space and obtained the holy earth's protection during the event.

Toward 11:30 A.M., Celestino pointed out that the marimbistas had begun to play three-mallet sones. This faster and merrier type of son is dedicated to the women working in the kitchen and is intended to encourage them to work happily and energetically. Considering how much they have to do before the guests arrive, it is probably just as well that three-mallet sones constitute the majority of the marimba son repertoire in Rabinal. Every so often, someone approached the marimba with a request, and the musicians interrupted the son cycle to play it. Esteban's son, Mincho, said, "The most requested sones are Amanecido, Zacualpa, San Pablo, Palo Seco, Mixito marcado." Later, when I asked Celestino whether it mattered that the order of the sones had been changed to accommodate requests, he replied, "It is definitely acceptable; that is why we are there, to serve the people."

Most of the guests arrived by mid-afternoon, bringing offerings of small amounts of sugar, beans, salt, or a couple of quetzales,[15] which they delivered to the padrino in front of the altar before going outside to listen to the marimba. Their children gathered around the marimba as usual. By this time the marimbistas were playing two-mallet sones to finish the first son cycle. They immediately proceeded with the second cycle (see Chapter 4). As the number of people grew, Esteban extended the length of each son. The more people gathered to share the meal, to drink and enjoy conversation, the greater his embellishment of the sones.

Julian Ordoñez, a marimba-playing friend of mine, arrived among the guests and we had a long conversation related to the *cabos de año* (first-year anniversary of death). Generally, during my conversations on the subject of the souls, people always began with the statement that many people do not believe in the souls nowadays, perhaps owing to the evangelists' influence. The evangelists say that death is the end of life and the end of the relationship with the deceased and therefore requires no more expenses or celebrations.[16] But they would proceed to relate an event that had allowed them to verify the existence of the spirits, as if to assure me of their faith in the souls. In the same manner Julian told me that during a recent lengthy cabo de año he had seen, through his dreams, the spirits drinking and dancing at the celebration.

> I was playing the marimba, exhausted, carrying a full day, one day and one night I had been playing, when a player friend of mine came and said, "I will help you." "Very well," I said. "Come inside, are you going for a drink?" "Fine." So I went inside by the altar and he and the others stayed playing outside. I felt sleepy and you should see, as you and I are here alive, the souls swallowed me, absolutely as one is here, I found myself there. Look, just as it is in this world so I am looking at them, some are dancing, others almost overturned the candles by the altar. Look, but it is full of people everywhere and they are dancing and others are drinking guaro, just as is done in this world. I saw it but in dreams. I alone was inside the house, everyone else was dancing in the porch corridor, I went to take a *cuajito* [nap] when I saw, they are coming, some overturning the flowers, but look, it is like this, [full] with people; they are souls, they are spirits. They are there, but invisible. We cannot see them directly anymore, but I have been in awe of this. That is what I saw. When I woke up I asked, "And the people that were here?" Mmmh! They were souls, they were the spirits that came because they were invited!

In Julian's story, as in others, one notes that the purpose is to hold on to personal experience or the experience of others who testify to the existence of the souls and their presence, especially on those occasions in which they are invited to share with the living. Julian's intention was not only to demonstrate that souls exist but also to create a psychological disposition to accept and feel their presence at that particular moment. His account was preparing me for what was going to happen during the late hours of the night.

The first recitation of the <u>ch'abal'</u> or *misterio* (rosary prayers) began about 8:00 P.M.[17] The room containing the altar filled with people, who spilled out into the corridor. The padrino and the violin and adufe musicians summoned the souls again so that they might receive the prayers. The marimba played the son costa chiquita once, to call the souls; then the violin-and-adufe sones were repeated in the same order as the morning performance at the cemetery and the Calvary Chapel—the son costa chiquita, the son <u>kotzij</u>, four more sones, and finally the son costa chiquita again, and with that the prayers ended. At the end of the misterio, the padrino, carrying a censer and followed by everyone who had been in the altar room, emerged onto the patio. By then the costa chiquita son had also been played on the marimba to indicate the exit from sacred time and space, and the marimbistas were continuing with their repertory of sones while guaro was distributed to everyone present.

The misterio, the music and associated ritual, was repeated at 10 P.M. and was followed by the distribution of tamales. Some people left after eating their tamales. Esteban disapproved, as the "prayer"—that is, all three recitations of the misterio—had not ended. He told me a story about a person who had been stoned by the spirits on his way home because he had not remained until the last prayer had been said.

The third and final misterio was performed at midnight, after which Felipe thanked the spirits for sharing the joy and wishes of Maria Gonzalez and bade them farewell. He asked the violin and adufe musicians to play the *rebix* son (singing son), that is, the costa coban son, commanding them to dance. I was reminded of something Magdaleno Xitumul had said some days before: "Sometimes when we sing, people start crying, they are overcome with emotion, with sadness. I really feel emotional, I am filled with sadness, because even if they stay, one knows that one way or the other one dies too."

Bread was distributed at the end of this prayer and the guaro continued to go around. Many guests were still enjoying the marimba music. The more inebriated participants began dancing, some by themselves, as if in meditation, others more merrily in couples, Ladino style.

Although people had requested a few favorite sones during the day, it is at this stage of the celebration, after 1:00 A.M., that most requests are made. The cycle of sones is completed and people's requests (*surtido* sones) can be played in any order. By now most participants were fairly inebriated and this influenced their requests. They asked for sones of sadness, the farewell sones: costa chiquita, *San Miguelito*, *Joyabateco*, *Barreño*. Some people cried as their request was played, others "danced," tumbling this way and that. The musicians responded to such expressions by prolonging and rearranging the sones. It was then that marimbista Julián Ordoñez told me:

> On the matter of sones they tell me, "Play my one son, the son chiquito, I will give you your one drink." And then—he died within the year! It's as though the body feels it, as if it is commanding you to go. And when they are leaving, they will cry in front of you, tears will come because you are requesting the souls to come and visit. That's what he told me: "Please do me a favor, play me the son chiquito to bid the souls farewell, to command them to return to their place, then play me that son because only God knows if we will be alive next year. Some of us do not know who is and who is not."

Esteban and his companions were also drunk and surely exhausted, but they kept playing with considerable energy, standing still, even though they had already played for more than eighteen hours. In the drunken scene they looked majestic! They seemed proud of themselves; they had fulfilled their commitment without failing. Cristobal, by then drunk and obstinate, begged them to stay and paid for a few more hours and, as there was enough drink to go around and they did not have a commitment for the next day, they continued playing. They were still partying when I left, intoxicated and exhausted, at about 3 A.M. Esteban told me the following day that there had been a fight after I left: A drunk had collapsed on top of the marimba, breaking some of the instrument's pegs. Visibly annoyed, he regretted having stayed longer for the sake of a few quetzales.

ALEGRÍAS PROVIDE THE SOCIAL and cultural contexts for musical activity in Rabinal. In behavioral and temporal terms, these occasions announce a "staged time." The literature on performance is helpful in looking at diverse performative aspects of musical occasions, especially with regard to musical performance as stylized behavior that communicates meanings and feelings between players and "audience" (both of whom are in fact participants occupying different positions). The sadness or happiness of the sones depends on the moment of the celebration and on the point of view of the living and of the dead.

As cultural performances, alegrías are organized to celebrate important dates and events of family and community life. I have emphasized anniversaries of the dead so as to focus attention on the ritual process through which Achi Catholics make a controlled exchange, offering devotion for protection, working through their grief, and disengaging from the involuntary painful and threatening memories of dead kin. The concept of reciprocity and exchange of blessings between the living and the dead is also a means of transferring the needs and feelings of the living onto the dead.

In the next chapter the issue of sentiments and emotions will be related to the style of playing of the marimba players.

7   Cognition, Values, and the Aesthetics of Music

MUSICAL RECOGNITION is based on the repetition of a musical order that gives meaning to music. Achi people say that *son* music does not change (which is clearly untrue) and that its performance is a continuation of the practice of the ancestors (which is true). Yet despite their claims that son music and its teaching methods have always been the same, the Achi do recognize change in both the music itself and the techniques for learning it.

The aim of this chapter is to illustrate how the traditional discourse concerning the transmission of musical tradition from generation to generation echoes cultural values. One of the purposes of teaching music is to reach consensus by repetition both within society as a whole and within the *marimba* tradition.

The discourses of music and culture are by their nature oral traditions and their consistency is therefore difficult to validate. Generally speaking, the historian has to be aware of the potential within oral tradition for variation, selectivity, and indirect evidence (Vansina 1973, 1985). But repetition and order are not simply components of learning, of ensuring the accuracy of transmission, or of absorbing the internal structure and sequence of tradition. They create or re-create the world. Among the Achi, the performer is more than a carrier of oral tradition; he has the freedom to be creative within the format. In fact, within the limits imposed by structure and sequence, creativity is admired and appreciated. Musicians recognize that the participants, in releasing their sentiments and emotions, maintain the link with the past.

I also demonstrate the ways in which both son music and learning methods are actually changing. Here my concerns are to address issues of creativity that assist in the adaptation and re-creation of roles affected by social and musical change.

This chapter is divided into nine sections that address four main issues. The first addresses strategies and method in the field. The second theme concerns how the Achi of Rabinal learn, understand, and contextualize music. The third describes and discusses material and social change and its effects on the son and the introduction of "Ladino" *piezas*. The fourth issue concerns perceptions of style in terms of the actual instrument, identity, and innovation.

Meeting the *Marimbistas*

When I first met the marimbistas (marimba players) of Rabinal, I told them that I was writing a history of the music of Rabinal and was interested in knowing, recording, and playing their music. My desire to learn to play proved to be the key to their interest.

Before I learned to play the marimba, my exploration of Achi ideas about music was hampered by my attempt to frame the questions in terms of the European theories of music in which I had been trained. The Achi often misunderstood my use of Western concepts, and in many cases I found them irrelevant. When I tried to concentrate on the specifics of organology, style, technique, and theory, I encountered conceptual difficulties of translation. Achi musicians had never been asked to reflect on their music and music practice in the way I was expecting them to do. Their answers to my conceptual questions were fragmented and of little use, for their knowledge is based purely on musical practice. Fortunately, we sang along to the marimba and I was able to use my own instrument (the orchestral flute) to illustrate my questions.

A further complication arose when I attempted to discuss the technical aspects of their music: Rabinalense musicians' vocabulary regarding musical concepts is sparse. A good example is the word *vuelta*, which has many meanings in conventional Spanish, among them turn, twirl, gyration, circuit, circumvolution, repetition, and rehearsal. Rabinalense musicians use the word to refer to different aspects of the son music that a good marimbista must be able to perform. First, vuelta simply means melodic ornamentation; in contrast to the simple, plain, ancient way of playing the melody of the sones, today's style is elaborate and sophisticated, with ornaments that require considerable agility. Second, vuelta means section, and refers to the son's musical form. There are sones of two, three, and four sections or vueltas. The two-vuelta son, for example the son San Pablo, is the simplest; three-vuelta sones such as the *amanecido* are more difficult; and four-section sones such as the *cubulero* and *coyotillo* are not only the most difficult but also the longest. Third, vuelta means a variation within a section, which is also known as a *coro* (chorus). These variations, which are generally rhythmic changes to the melody, are used frequently because the sections of a son are repeated over and over again; repetition is an important feature of son music, as it is of prayers. Son musicians assured me that repetition is the best way to gain the attention of God, the saints, and the souls of the dead: "All the repetition makes the son reach God's ears," explained marimbista Lázaro. Hence musicians who make a lot of vueltas are more convincing in their supplications and expressions of gratitude to God than those who don't. Furthermore, creative musicians who can vary the rhythms and play different ornaments give more color and movement to the son. Finally, vuelta can also refer to an improvisation of melodic phrases secondary to the main melody. The musical styles of the towns, villages, and individual musicians depend very much on the ways the vueltas are performed.

My problems diminished when I began to take marimba lessons myself, as I was constrained to limit my overly verbal curiosity to following their explanations—that is, to listening to their music, observing their movements and positions, and then copying them. I learned not only how to play but also how embedded the process was in Achi beliefs and attitudes to life.

Two families of marimbistas taught me to play the marimba de sones. One was headed by Esteban Uanché and the other by his nephew, Celestino Cajbón; with their distinct personalities and the almost forty-year gap between their ages, they well represented the different ends of the continuum of contemporary marimba music. Until his death, Esteban was the greatest exponent of son music in Rabinal; as an old man he remained faithful to the traditional repertoire, despite being the principal innovator within the genre. Celestino, who was in his mid-twenties when we met, was also taught to play marimba music the traditional way; most of his contracts to play sones are as a *mozo* (hired worker) for his uncle, for whom he plays center to Esteban's treble. Celestino also plays the marimba de pieza and the electric organ; he joined a short-lived tropical music group in Rabinal. While he shares his uncle's view on tradition, Celestino's experiments with nonreligious musical genres allowed him to simplify the learning process for me.

Celestino was also one of the few Rabinalense musicians to understand my theoretical interest. I had been curious to know how much the Achi knew about European music theory, considering that the marimba de sones is constructed in major diatonic scales. The short answer is that musicians do not know European musical theory, though some use a few of its concepts correctly. For example, they recognize that the marimba de sones has five octaves (*términos*), but they do not name the notes of the keyboard, nor do they divide the keyboard into octaves or refer to the tonic as the tonality center. The mallet positions of the harmony (center) and the bass players are learned not as chords but as a number of keys located one or more keys apart. The performers may learn to play different and alternative positions when they become experienced musicians, but all play open tonic, subdominant, dominant, and sometimes mediant chords.

Figure 7.1. Learning the marimba with Celestino and his brother. Photo by Judith Zur.

The Teaching/Learning Process

I was particularly interested to know whether a discourse existed about marimbistas' ideas about music and music practice, especially at the level of teaching and learning music. Conversations with different groups of marimbistas (which took place in the homes of the musicians who house and maintain the ensemble's marimba) revealed that not only does a discourse exist but that it is primarily a discourse about tradition and ethics, a statement about continuity and order.

Rabinalenses are familiar with traditional music virtually from birth. They hear it at the frequent festivities celebrating annual or seasonal rites, life-crisis events—principally memorials of the dead, weddings, inaugurations, and blessings of houses, chapels, and other buildings, and in the *cofradía*—and, until 1981, at *zarabandas* (social gatherings to drink and dance to the marimba de sones). When a Rabinalense male (whether child, adolescent, or adult) aspires to become a marimbista, he will go to such events specifically to listen to the rhythms and melodies of the sones and observe the movement of the mallets across the keys of the marimba.

To "have the sones in mind" is very useful. It enables him to concentrate on the positions and movements he is taught and allows him to arrive at an overall understanding of the son in its entirety fairly rapidly; soon he is able to think strategically in terms of the execution of the son rather than merely play his part mechanically. The advantages of lifelong familiarity with the music were brought home to me when I began to learn myself: I felt like a blind man feeling my way in the dark.

Any Achi male in Rabinal can learn to play the marimba at any age, with one proviso: Traditionally, becoming a marimba player is a matter of fulfilling one's destiny. It is believed that God mediates and determines everyone's individual fate. The will and application of the individual are indispensable attributes, but the crucial determinant is the will of God. Esteban Uanché told me that it had been his destiny (fate)[1] since birth to become a marimbista and that he achieved this through the grace of God. As a little boy, he had lined up corncobs as though they were the keys of the marimba and played sones as an adult musician does. On seeing this, his father had remarked to his wife that their son was a marimbista.

One learns to play the marimba much as one learns to do any other task. I had observed how people learn work skills in daily life—by watching for a while and then entering directly as a participant in the actual work itself. My first lesson proceeded in the traditional way: Celestino and his brothers played an abbreviated version of the simple, two-mallet son San Pablo so I could observe the movements and positions of the bass and listen to the rhythm and its changes. When the son ended, they pointed with their mallets to the different positions the bass had played to orient me to the keyboard. Then, without further ado, we began to play the son San Pablo!

Behind this method of instruction are assumptions about, among other things, the optimal time to learn any skill (childhood) and where to learn (in the family). Thus the basic conditions for becoming a marimbista are having marimba-playing relatives—father, grandfather, uncles—and ready access to a family-owned marimba. This approach is reinforced by the fact that it is generally extremely difficult to get an unrelated marimbista to teach one to play unless the teacher can see some way of incorporating the apprentice into his marimba ensemble. Adult apprentices face other difficulties; they have little time to practice and can play for only a couple of hours after the evening meal. Adults learn the repertoire one by one, learning maybe twenty to thirty sones, whereas a competent lad can learn twice that number in a year. Another problem for adults is that they are less flexible than children are and, perhaps, more conscious of the learning process; it can be years before they are ready to play in public. These factors make the adult beginner an unattractive apprentice. Many obstacles may lead to failure and the eventual abandonment of the marimba, especially when a man has no sons to take up the skill.

Another difficulty for adult apprentices is that the three-stage process of learning marimba sones incorporates the traditional principle of respect and subordination to the authority and seniority of one's elders. An adult faces the disorienting prospect of being taught by someone younger than he.

The traditional order in which the three increasingly complex positions are learned also corresponds to the hierarchical construction of Achi society. In the idealized schema, boys in marimbista families begin to learn by playing with the marimba as though it were a toy, at an age when they are too young to play in public.[2] By the time they are old enough to go to school or to work in the fields (around age six or seven), some boys spend all their free time playing the marimba, practicing at any time of the day or night. Tono Cajbón remembered the time when his sons were small:

> They played the marimba every day; you would find those "naughty" kids playing at any moment. They learned by themselves, only by observing what their elders did and by copying them. The sones remained in their heads. For instance, on a Saturday or a Sunday when I went out to gather wood, I would hear the marimba from a distance and they would be practicing and playing, and that's how the sones would remain in their heads.

Tono's wife interrupted: "The children heard the others playing and then they would play the same. There was no need to teach their hands because they learned by watching other people's hands playing. This is how the vuelta [sections] of the son remained."

These remarks are rather disingenuous. Marimbista families specifically send their young sons to fiestas to listen to the music of other players so that they can learn the positions, styles, and repertoire (older apprentices and established musicians also do this, taking their cassette players with them). This behavior, which is part of the development of the musicality of marimbista family, can cause resentment among established players.

Soon the marimba ceases to be a toy and playing it becomes a serious responsibility to the family, the community, the ancestors, and God. The education of Achi children is full of responsibilities linked to family survival, and they are expected to contribute to the household economy from the age of six or seven. Marimbista parents look to their boys to learn quickly so that they can be integrated into the family marimbista pool, making the family less dependent on mozos. Even relatively wealthy and ladinoized marimbista families, such as the Jerónimos (who used to own a marimba *doble*), subscribe to the concept of a family ensemble. Paulino Jerónimo told me, "When the older ones left home to study [in Guatemala City], the number of players decreased, but the younger sons began to join in—only those from the family, only the family."

Sometimes, when a boy is unwilling, a father forces him to learn. Tono's son, Celestino, may have learned by himself, as his parents claim, but his memories of his first proper lesson are very different:

> I was ten years old when my father began to teach me the marimba. He used to beat me when I began at the bass. He tried to teach me but I was unable to recognize the keys he pointed to, so he would grab my hands and hit them with the mallets. I would yell and run and hide in the kitchen, but he would come and take me back to the marimba. According to him, the task was to learn. In the end, after he repeatedly beat me with the mallets, I learned. At first I only learned the bass, but then I kept on playing and playing until I began to try the center position. From there I learned everything and then I moved finally to the treble. I only learned sones then. After that we started to play *costeno* and from there we learned piezas. That is how all of us in the family learned—it was a continual struggle until we learned everything.

Such treatment is quite normal in Rabinal. Education among the Achi is based on following preestablished procedures and actions and not in the development of abstract thinking, questioning, or looking for causality; the emphasis is on knowing the form rather than the deeper process of comprehending the content (Watanabe 1994, 87–89). Children under the age of twelve receive no explanations about anything because they are not thought to possess the ability to think; instead, they are given instructions and blows.[3] A young primary school teacher complained bitterly to me about his pupils' parents, who sought him out after school to encourage him to use corporal punishment and threats to discipline the children and make them learn; he preferred the technique of positive reinforcement.

In marimbista families it is customary to learn the bass position—the first and simplest stage of learning to play the marimba—before one is old enough to think for oneself. Boys often begin to learn when they are too small to reach the keyboard (they are given a little stool to stand on). They learn one of the two basic forms of playing bass, known as the *corrido* (both hands together) and the *marcado* (marking the notes). The corrido is the simpler and is accomplished by playing a triad chord, striking the keyboard to a determined rhythmic pattern with both hands simultaneously. In the marcado form, the bass plays a rhythmic pattern, striking the notes of a chord separately (an *arpegiatto*) with alternating hands, the left hand playing the stronger beat. Internalizing the rhythms at the bass position is one of the first skills an apprentice develops.

The ritual function of the music rather than ease of learning determines the teaching/learning process. This is "the way of the ancestors" and involves learning the marimba by practicing the sones in the same order as they are played at religious festivities and other events. It is important that the apprentice learn this and the purpose of the sones being played, and it is the way Esteban taught me. Thus, instead of progressing from simple to complex rhythms (Celestino's teaching method), the apprentice learns the four-mallet sones that open festivities and are the most complex before learning the three-mallet sones and finally the two-mallet sones. At the end of the learning/playing cycle, they return to the four-mallet sones, this time without using wax, which changes the tonality of the music. In fact, there are only a few basic types of rhythm on the bass, and sones of the same type (that is, four-, three-, or two-mallet sones) have similar endings. Because the rhythms are practiced while playing each complete son together with the other two players, an able young apprentice can learn the basic repertoire within a year. With experience, the bass player acquires the skill to follow the rhythm flexibly, according to the treble player's interpretation of the beat of the son. Some of the difficult challenges are the internalization of the syncopation and the changes from a simple ternary to a complex binary measure, which are required within some sones. Once an apprentice learns the vueltas of the sones, he is ready to play in public.

Bass players first perform in public when they stand in for their weary brothers, who take a couple of hours' rest. As engagements are rarely for fewer than twelve hours of nonstop marimba music, it is understandable that fathers insist that their sons join the family pool as soon as possible. Celestino's brother, Bernabé, was seven years old when he played his first six-day cofradía fiesta with his father. He was overwhelmed by the contrast with daily life, the abundance of food, tobacco, and alcohol, and the noise, bustle, and emotions of scores of people. He found it exhausting and terrifying. "I was playing standing on a chair, and the last day I was crying. I could not bear it anymore and I had to fulfill my obligation. I was worried and fearful of the elders because they drink [including musicians], and I was crying also because there was no one to take care of me, and the drunkards fight."

Few boys of Bernabé's age are expected to cope with such a heavy commitment. Most learn the difficult task of building up the stamina required for such long periods of playing by standing in for the principal marimbistas when they take a break. There is always someone willing to brave the marimba as a stand-in. Many young men play as temporary substitute bass players. Some play the rhythm of the one or two sones they have learned by observation alone, others taking the opportunity to demonstrate their skills, and all of them ask permission to play a piece as an offering to the saint whose day is being celebrated.

Thus music is not all the boy learns. Apart from gaining sufficient strength to fulfill their obligations, they also learn how to handle people, especially the inebriated, and to steer clear of fights.

From the outset, a boy is taught the correct attitude toward playing. A player must always be careful not to flaunt his skills for fear of awakening the malicious envy of other players, as this can lead to a witchcraft attack. He must always display a humble attitude as a sign of respect toward others; a lack of humility is potentially dangerous. Eustaquio, an able treble player, explained:

> And if a player tells us, "*Puchica mucha!* [Wow, guys!] You can really play better than me," then one replies, "Well, look, actually I have little skill." Even though I am able [a skilled musician], I would not reply, "Ah, because I can play, I am better than you." No! One shouldn't say that, as it would undermine the other person's feelings. As the army puts it, one would lower the other's morale. It is better to say, "I am able to do it a little bit," even though one can actually do it a lot more; that is the way to play it.

The idea that humility, as a sign of respect, is a virtue derives from the concept of humankind as just one kind of being among others within the cosmos, subject, like other beings, to God's will. The humble stance profoundly influences the way one learns any task as well as the way one appreciates it. A disposition to learn and an appreciation of the teacher's skill are greatly valued among the Achi; demonstrating such respectful behavior can be of great benefit to the apprentice, as I discovered myself. My teachers needed endless patience with me and had to repeat their instructions over and over again; fortunately they appreciated my interest, desire to learn, and the value I placed on their work, musical ability, and individual styles. Tono told me: "Thank God you have a great love of learning; there is nothing that one can learn overnight but if you have love you can learn. Everything is learned; there is nothing that comes without it. If you have learned [to play], there will always be someone who asks, 'Who is that playing?' And someone will be admiring the fact that one has learned. It is great to learn because there are always more occasions at which to play."

A related concept, also internalized during childhood, is the stoical Indian attitude to life, which is essentially a submission to destiny and the "law of God." Plans for the future are always provisional, *Dios mediante* (God willing). (I found this attitude exasperating). Living is a serious matter for the Rabinalense and requires deep respect and care for all the living objects: plants, animals, people, spirits, saints, gods they interact with, the work they do, and the instruments they use to do it. Musicians express their respect for and dedication to the commitments they undertake on behalf of the living and the dead by remaining almost stockstill when they play. Young musicians learn to contain bodily expression without thinking too much about it. This is not so much a matter of "impression management" (Featherstone, quoted in Csordas 1994, 2) as it is a stylized behavioral habit that is incorporated into learning practice.

In other words, musical culture is grounded in the body (ibid., 6). Bodily movement reveals as much about a performer's musicianship as do his knowledge of the repertoire and keyboard skills.

On one level, this lack of movement, the apparent separation from what is happening around them, is only a façade; marimbistas are quite aware of people's responses to their playing and may expand or ornament the sones to allow people to expand their feelings. In this respect, as I explain below, musicians—and the audience too—need to know what the music means and when to play each son. On another level, their physical disengagement serves as an energy-saving device. The stoical attitude of marimbistas (and indeed of Rabinalenses in general) enables them to sustain the enormous physical effort involved in playing for long hours without rest.

Boys learn all these things before making the transition to the second stage of the learning process: learning to play the center position, where the harmony of the son is played. By then they will have learned the ensemble's entire repertoire; they will also have learned the movement and position of the center player's left hand, as that hand has been their point of reference and guide at the bass.

The center position presents a major musical challenge because the player has different and more complex positions and movements in each hand. The center player's left hand guides the right hand of the bass and both move in parallel movement. His right hand frequently plays in parallel movement with the treble player's left hand, and both together carry a melody, at the interval of a third apart. At other times, the center player's right hand moves in parallel movement with the treble player's right hand at the interval of an octave. Sometimes the center player's right hand carries a short melody that repeats constantly in counterpoint with the melody of the treble. Above all, a center player must have the flexibility, ability, and dexterity to adapt and follow the personal style of the treble player.

If a center player is unfamiliar with the treble leader's personal style or is not of comparable dexterity, he may fall into the common error known as *encadenarse* (to play out of beat). The chords played to give harmonic and rhythmic support to the main melody are played a step behind and no longer correspond, which creates discord between the notes of the treble and the notes of the center and bass. Center player Marcelo Ixpatá remembered an occasion when he had been unable to follow the melodic evolutions of skilled treble player Esteban Uanché. Even though it is inadvisable to abandon a commitment, the humiliation made him feel so uncomfortable that he took the first opportunity to pass his responsibility to a marimbista friend, and left:

> The vueltas [ornamentations] were what made me go into *encadenamiento*. Yes, because when he makes his vueltas, I remained behind and the marimba didn't sound at the same time, but if I can go with the vueltas, then we are

together; the marimba does not sound in *cadena*. The sound is even. When the bass or the middle position is encadenados, the first goes alone, the others are left behind, and the voices change. One has to know with whom to play; it is not merely a matter of playing with anyone, like, for example, Don Esteban, as I did, because he already has his group and they know how he plays.

The third stage of the learning process corresponds to the treble position. The treble player is the most experienced and normally the eldest player; it is he who carries the melody and teaches and guides or "pulls" (*jala*) the second player, who not only plays harmony but simultaneously "pulls" the youngest player learning bass. The treble player carries the principal melody of the son and its variations. He directs the changes of section, its repetitions, and makes simple or complex improvisations with many vueltas, depending on his ability. He also indicates the tempo, intensity, and rhythmic changes, and plays the characteristic tremolos of marimba music. Celestino defined the position this way: "The treble commands the rest; when he starts, we, the center and the bass, begin as well. When he ends, we end as well. The first position is the most difficult because he is the one who has to make the most vueltas. He directs everyone, the center and the bass."

It takes more to master this position than long experience as a center player: The aspiring treble player must have a marimba in his house—he will not necessarily own it himself; it may be jointly owned or rented—and two reliable musicians. Apart from his musical prowess, the treble player's most important role is as an ensemble leader. Since the marimba is kept in his home, he has the last word on rehearsals. It is at this stage that his dexterity or ability is developed into a personal style and that he has to ensure the other players' subservience to that style. As leader, the treble player represents the group and has to obtain contracts for it; he also has to ensure that the other players will meet the commitments he arranges for them. The treble player's sociability is an important aspect of his success on both fronts (see Chapter 9).

CONCEPTS OF MEMORY

Learning to play like the ancestors involves traditional concepts about mind and memory, heart and soul. In the Achi language, the words for memory (k'u'xtal) and remember (k'u'xtaj) are derived from the word k'u'x, which means heart, will, or the center or essence of something (cf. Zur 1998). It is thought that the spirit or soul that controls a person's will is seated in the heart. A patient person who does not rush and carries out activities by "thinking well" is said to have a "big heart" (nimaal k'u'x). Marimbistas learn patiently and remember from the heart.

Feelings also reside in the heart. When a person is suffering, he or she may say, "My heart hurts [k'ax nuk'u'x]." The notion of the heart as the center of feelings, the will of the spirit, and of memory is vital for understanding the unitary relation between feeling and thinking. The word na'o (feeling, perception, understanding) is linked to the expression na'bal, which means "way of being" or "way of feeling"; the related term n'ooj can be employed more widely to mean wisdom, memory, comprehension, consciousness, idea, or significance. When a person has a good memory and a capacity to learn, it is said that he has a good memory (lik k'o una'ooj). Again, this expression reflects a unitary conceptualization of the way of being and thinking.

There are two ways to use memory when learning the marimba or any other instrument. One is to employ memory as a cognitive action and the other is to effect repetition or habit. Connerton (1992, 6–40), following Halbwachs (1980), defines it as a social memory incorporated in performance practice. Achi people never spoke to me about a memory of the body, but they did express the notion that the body has its own will. Apprentices' struggles with their untrained hands were expressed as though their hands had a will of their own. Despite their memory of a good part of the son repertoire, acquired though listening and watching, the challenge facing apprentices is to accustom their hands to moving and playing in accordance with the positions and rhythms of each son. I asked marimbista Francisco Lajuj whether he had the sones in his head before he actually began to play the keyboard. He answered, "Exactly, because they say that without the memory of the sones you will not be able to play. However, there is more to this: Even if you have memory, if you can't play with your hand, then you can't play. It is most difficult to make the hand learn. Memory is first because unless you know the sound of the son, you won't be able [to play]; how can you do it [without the memory]? You can't!"

Some musicians, when remembering how they learned to play, say that they only went "to listen to the vueltas and these remained in their mind"; other players, however, insist that the most important aspect of learning involved training their hands and their sight. Celestino's father, marimbista Tono Cajbón, told me that his sons' only inheritance was their hands and their sight.

When an apprentice learns a son, he remembers its familiar sound (the memory of the mind); sight is important because he has to observe the movements that have been shown to him so that he can remember and imitate them. As he is doing so, he feels the transformation of his own movements into sound. The marimba is a long instrument with big resonators, and the sensation of sound vibration is a powerful bodily experience shared by the three players standing side by side, striking the marimba. Practicing as a group, repeatedly going over the movements and positions of each son for hours on end several times every week until every son can be played without error, is the only way to accustom the hand and to internalize the rhythms in the body. To do this and enjoy it requires abundant patience and a "big heart."

Musicians liken learning the sones to any other task; once they have learned to play, they never forget. The hand's "memory" is not only as important as the mind's memory but seems to be a more persistent kind of memory. Again, musicians endow their hands with autonomy; each hand has its own will. But the older one is when one learns, the harder it is to "educate" the body. It was pointed out to me that the older a man is when he began to play, the more his body moves when he strikes the keys. The loss of physical flexibility that comes with age, together with a lack of internalization of the rhythm of the sones, makes it difficult for adult apprentices to strike the keys rapidly without moving their bodies. Celestino remarked:

> Because I was little [when I began playing], I learned to move my hand, but my father did not learn well until he was thirty years old, so he moves his whole arm. His body is obviously stiff. He plays with his whole body and he moves a lot. I have another uncle from Xesiuan village and he plays with his whole neck. Yes, there are some that play with their whole head. That's because their hand gets stiff.

The distinction Rabinalense musicians make between the mind's memory and the body's is not so different from my own experience. I learned to play the flute by reading musical scores; I noticed that my memory of the melodies became dependent on my capacity to sight-read, while my fingers seemed to remember where to move by themselves. When I let my fingers do the playing, the music flowed better than when I concentrated on it: My mind seemed to have a way of blocking my fingers. It was interesting to compare the teaching methods of Western music schools with the method used in Rabinal. Each has a different starting point: The Western method uses music notation as a constant reference for the memory, whereas the Rabinalense method depends entirely on observation and listening, imitation and repetition, to memorize the music.

Initially, I found it hard to play the marcado bass style. My inexperienced hands tended to move together rather than independently. I therefore concentrated on reproducing the rhythm and positions with one hand without moving the other and then I used the other hand to play its part before trying to use both hands at the same time. When I felt I had mastered the basic movements, I lifted my head and realized that a lot of children were watching; they were most amused by the way the gringo was playing. They laughed hardest whenever I made a mistake.

When we completed the first son, Celestino told me, "You are very able, but what you did with your hands is no good. The hands learn bad habits, so you must play with both hands from the start. If you are unable to make the different movements of each hand at the same time, then practice the movements slowly with your hands knocking on the table. This is what will help you."

Celestino was not only trying to prevent me from acquiring bad playing habits; implicit in his suggestion was the belief that to play one voice of the marimba one must play all voices. This is such a basic concept that on several occasions my teachers refused to begin a lesson when one of the members of the group failed to turn up. I had encountered this situation earlier, when I attempted to record the melodies (the treble part) of the oldest sones. The musician protested, "In my opinion, if you only play the treble, it will not come out prettily." The melody is not the son, and there is no value in a recording of only one of its parts.

Musicians see the sones as complete cycles that begin and end in the same way, forming part of major cycles that comprise the whole repertoire, which constantly repeats, much like the continuous cycle of seasons that rule daily life. To think of sones (let alone the parts played at the three positions) as separate entities is to remove them from their context, content, and function. Hence the practice of all three players rehearsing each son in its entirety. With or without repetitions, in their long or short versions, sones are always played all the way through from beginning to end. When I went to Celestino's house for my first lesson, I was rather daunted by the fact that I would be taught while playing the repertoire as a member of the marimba group. Unlike the Western method of dividing a musical piece into melodic phrases, sections, or difficult passages, Rabinalense musicians make no allowance for apprentices and continue playing, regardless of errors or temporary pauses such as those created by my inability to keep up. This strategy of nonstop playing is used in the West only when the apprentice musicians playing in a group are already familiar with a piece or are practicing sight-reading. I soon discovered that this method of learning is one of the most useful characteristics of the traditional teaching process. Practicing in a group allows the apprentice to learn bass and rhythm in an integrated way, with harmony and melody.

Continuity and Change

Social and material change over the past forty years has influenced the music played in Rabinal. One of the most important influences has been Ladino-controlled Spanish-language radio stations that broadcast mostly urban popular music (piezas).

Until the late 1960s, when radio ownership became common among the indigenous population, the division between Indians and Ladinos was clearly expressed in terms of their respective musical repertoires, types of instruments, and the contexts in which they were played. In Rabinal town and villages, traditional sones played on the diatonic marimba were expanding from cantinas to Achi ritual celebrations; piezas, interpreted on the marimba doble (by only two ladinoized Achi families and by foreign musicians) were played exclusively for the town's Ladino population.

This separation has become blurred by modernization and its effects on folk-urban interaction.[4] Many marimba musicians play both sones and piezas for Achi and Ladinos as well. The pieza genre and styles of playing it have greatly influenced the son and its playing style. Nevertheless, the meaning of both sones and piezas continues to represent Achi/Ladino interaction in Rabinal's ethnically divided society. This social opposition can be analyzed in terms of the interrelationship among three overlapping categories of opposition: the ancient son vs. the modern pieza; villages vs. towns; and Indians vs. Ladinos.

These categories are related to each other but the third encompasses the first two. People make a distinction between traditional music (the son), which has been transmitted for generations among the indigenous population, and the newly adopted pieza music, with its diverse musical forms.

People also distinguish between villagers and town dwellers. This is not strictly a matter of population distribution but a cultural category, since indigenous people predominate in the villages and Ladinos in town.

Achi people also see a difference between towns and villages in terms of musical genres and personal styles. The small populations of most Rabinal villages support only one cofradía, dedicated to Santa Cruz; apart from Xococ, Pichec, and Nimacabaj, there are virtually no Ladinos to create demand for piezas. Village marimbistas therefore have few opportunities to play in public and develop their skills, and little incentive to expand their repertoire. Village musicians do play in town every so often and it is not the case that they have nothing to offer their more sophisticated fellow marimbistas; their contributions do enrich the styles of town musicians, and vice versa.

Marimbistas from Rabinal town have always been in more demand because there are many more festivities there, including the vast annual festivity cycle organized by the sixteen cofradías (see Chapter 2). The competition for work promotes stylistic innovation and musical skill. Celestino told me that, unlike the villages, where only *naturales* (indigenous people) live and play sones, there is great demand from town Ladinos who like marimba de pieza music for their weddings, baptisms, and other events but don't like playing the instrument themselves. His comments reflect his personal experience; Celestino was born in the village of Plan de Sanchez, fleeing with his family to Rabinal town at the age of ten following a massacre perpetrated by the army and local vigilantes in 1982. There were two marimbas in Plan de Sanchez, but only his family's was used; with few opportunities to play, their repertoire was small, their style simple. All this changed when they moved to town and began to hear other marimbistas, particularly Celestino's maternal uncle Esteban. Soon the Cajbóns were asked to play for the cofradía de San José, where Celestino's brother got his first opportunity to play a six-day fiesta; later he learned the music of the traditional dance-dramas, piezas, and other musical styles.

The development of musical styles and genres in Rabinal can be explained as a process of folk-urban interaction based on interrelated notions of time, space, and ethnicity. The process of cross-pollination was slow until radio ownership became common among Indians in the 1960s (see Chapter 4). As indigenous marimbistas began copying and adapting the melodies of famous composers from the capital and other cities such as Quetzaltenango, Totonicapán, and Huehuetenango from the radio, the musical exclusivity of Ladino dance halls disappeared. Audiences began to demand piezas, as they too heard them on the radio.

It tended to be boys and youths who, in the mid-1970s, began incorporating this new repertoire into *conjunto* marimba groups. Youngsters' openness to new rhythms and their ability to copy melodies attracts them to the treble position. This openness, together with their greater free time, allows boys to experiment with pieza tunes at the treble. The decision to incorporate piezas into the repertoire modified the traditional relationship between the adult treble player and the younger partners at center and bass; the teaching/learning process became more reciprocal. Ten years later, after *la violencia*, youngsters were involved in the resurgence of marimba music; in both instances, the knowledge and leadership they learned from playing the treble position gave them increased respect and power and hence privilege in the family, overriding the traditional value of seniority. Younger players became their own masters and exercised the power of their position as treble players over the center and bass players, who were sometimes their elder brothers, fathers, or uncles. One can see such youngsters calling the tune within the family in ways that go beyond music.

I knew two family ensembles with an established tradition of incorporating piezas into their repertoire that dissolved when the younger generation decided to buy pieza marimbas. A power conflict arose between the generations. The elderly fathers made their opinions known by continuing to play sones, and only sones, on their family's son marimba, and they employed mozos in order to do so. Beyond the generational power struggle, older people found it difficult to learn to play in a completely different way, on a different type of marimba, and were reluctant to risk making mistakes in public.

BOOTLEGS

The spread of tape and radio-cassette recorders in the 1970s[5] accelerated the process of incorporating urban music into local repertoires. Musicians, who have always listened and learned from each other, now began to use tape recorders, hastening and reinforcing the exchange of melodies and styles. As a marimbista of the Lajuj family put it, "We do not play the same as others, they are teaching us and they always record what we are playing; they are always taking from us as well." Esteban feigned to despise this new method of learning the son repertoire. He complained that there was always someone taping him wherever he played; listening and watching is one thing, he said; that is a form of respect, but flagrantly using a tape recorder is quite another. At the same time, though, the bigger and more obvious the cassette recorders or ghetto-blasters people use, the more Esteban actually liked it, because he saw this as a form of homage and a sign of his musical prowess.

Of course Esteban himself surreptitiously taped other marimbistas, but he proudly claimed that he had never been caught. This is not as big a contradiction as it seems, because he never taped other Rabinalense players and always recorded from his customary long-distance listening position. He dared not do otherwise, lest he sink to the same level as everyone else and thus lose his status as a master teacher. To protect his reputation, he preferred to travel to Cubulco town to listen to the sones played there. "I copy from the Cubuleros," he told me. "Before, I didn't have such good sones. They were okay. But then I heard the sones of Cubulco, which consisted of four [mallets] and they stayed [were memorized]. But I am not a copier. I listen while I am there without them knowing it."

Copying Cubulco musicians was acceptable in Esteban's eyes because he did not live with them and so was not subject to their criticism. This did not stop him from being criticized by Rabinalenses, however. The distinct playing styles of these adjacent municipalities are but one manifestation of the age-old rivalry between them. Celestino, who learned much from Esteban's personal style and admired his flexibility when playing, believes his uncle's ability had nothing to do with the origin of the sones he played. According to him, Esteban's creativity lay in his improvisations of sones from both Cubulco and Rabinal:

> The people from Cubulco play their own sones, they are different, and Esteban goes there to record them. Esteban plays the sones from Cubulco but he plays them better than the Cubuleros. His hand plays beautifully,

unlike the hands of the Cubuleros. Yes, they play the Cubulero son, but they do not play it beautifully. He puts something else in it; he invents, and that is why it is beautiful. I do not invent like he does. I can play as he does but I do not invent, I don't know how to. But he does, he can invent. It is his destiny to play beautifully.

SOCIAL CHANGE

When I asked individual musicians how they themselves had learned to play the marimba, I discovered a large gap between the purported norm and their own experience of learning to play. Although I did come across marimbistas who had begun to learn in childhood, I knew others who did not take up the instrument until they were in their twenties or even their early thirties. To some extent, this pattern of learning reflects external influences such as that of Catholic missionaries in the 1950s and, a decade or so later, of Protestant evangelicals. Both tried to dissuade Indians from playing their traditional music for various reasons (see Chapter 5). Another important factor was the repression of Indians and indigenous ways following the political violence of the mid-1960s and early 1980s. The resurgence of interest in marimba music following the end of la violencia can be seen as a statement of identity. It is also, considering that many of the younger generation see pieza music as indigenous, a statement of change. The adoption of piezas as the musical accompaniment of new dance-dramas (or new versions of old ones) manages to be both things at once: new music, old meanings.

Most men who learned to play as adults did not come from marimbista families. Some had had access to a neighbor's marimba as children and learned a little that way. This childhood knowledge encouraged them to acquire a marimba or become apprentices as adults. It is, for instance, fairly common nowadays to find soldiers in their early twenties who are marimba enthusiasts saving to purchase a marimba. They get together with relatives and marimbista friends to make a cuchubal (a business or work-related partnership) and buy a marimba collectively.

Other men began to learn after the deaths of marimbista kin during the two periods of political violence. Like Tono and his late father, they had not learned to play as children. Tono was nearly fifteen when his grandfather and great-uncles, renowned marimbistas, were killed by the army in 1965; it was only then that his middle-aged father bought a marimba so that they could continue the family tradition as a means of remembering their murdered kin. All of Tono's sons have been incorporated into the family marimba pool; they learned to play on the same marimba in the traditional way. It has taken three generations to recover the technical level and restore some of the family's prestige as marimba players.

This is a common story. Many marimbistas were among the hundreds slaughtered in local massacres. Musicians' testimony reveals that nearly a whole generation of older musicians disappeared virtually overnight; with them went a good part of the musical repertory. As families disintegrated, so did marimba groups. Some marimbas were abandoned as people fled to safety; others were partially or totally destroyed during the army's scorched-earth campaign. Some families sold their marimbas quickly and cheaply because they needed the money. I met a young man whose dreams of becoming a marimbista were thwarted when his mother was forced to sell the family marimba following the murder of his father and uncle during la violencia. He is only now beginning to achieve his goal.

The periods of intense violence in Rabinal resulted in generational ruptures in the musical traditions of several marimbista families. In some, the tradition has been lost forever; in others, there has been a regeneration of marimba groups, led by surviving players who lost their partners to la violencia, young adults, and even enthusiastic children whose non-playing fathers have bought or rented a marimba for them to play.

Another reason for renewed interest in the marimba is that an instrument represents social capital; it serves as a nexus for maintaining and extending social networks, an important factor in a society fragmented by violence. Traditional musicians say that playing marimba music perpetuates custom, as the sones they play are the music the ancestors left to the living and like to hear at community festivities. And of course the marimba can also generate work and income.

"The Good Marimba Calls to the Four Quarters"

When people refer to a "good marimba," they are judging two things: the sonority of the instrument and the competence of its performers, particularly the treble player. People prefer not to be asked their opinion of specific marimba groups or marimbas and only did so when I insisted, an act of great rudeness on my part by local standards. Even then they took great pains to avoid comparing or undermining marimbistas or marimbas.[6] Perhaps it is not so surprising that I found very similar opinions about music among children and adults, men and women, musicians and audience; the only difference was the more elaborate discourse of marimba players.

I learned what constitutes a good marimba during the long search for a marimba of my own. Esteban, Celestino, and his brother, Bernabé, tested several marimbas in different towns and villages on my behalf. Each test consisted of playing several sones; they then gave me a detailed analysis of the marimba's qualities. Their evaluations encompassed aesthetic aspects such as its decoration, color, and name;[7] they looked at the woods used and the construction; they assessed its weight and ease of handling and decided whether or not it would fit in the various places they wanted to use it or would be stable on uneven ground; and, of course, whether the marimba gave a good sound and was balanced between the ranges. Provided the price was reasonable, the marimba's sonority or loudness was the most important criterion.

There were two key issues. First, that the marimba feel soft to play, while still having a big, full, and solid sound. Second, that the three positions sounded balanced and of equal loudness; it is often the case that the center position has a fuller sound than the bass or treble. The sound of a good marimba can travel long distances and so the best test is to listen to it from afar, as Esteban always preferred to do.

Little is ever said about the skillfulness of the players who make the marimba's voices sound the way they do. This does not mean that people never evaluate a player's capabilities but that their skills are often judged by the quality of the marimba they play and not the other way around. For example, Bacho, who comes from the Ladino-dominated village of Nimacabaj, considers himself one of the municipality's best marimbistas because his marimba is the "sister" of one owned by the best player in town, Esteban Uanché (it is one of two that Esteban bought in Totonicapán).

The sonority of the marimba is of great value because the instrument is used to call people to participate in the *alegría* (joyous occasion) that is being celebrated. Esteban told me that Ladinos pay for *notas de duelo*, that is, broadcasts of funerary music by classical composers over private loudspeakers announcing the death of a relative and inviting people to participate in the vigil for the dead. The Achi prefer to let the marimba reach people's ears: "The marimba is the announcement itself. When the people hear it, eeee! People come from the four quarters and from the villages. They come to celebrate, to drink rum, eat tamales, see the body of the deceased, and listen to the sones."

For players, the "softness" of the marimba is as important as its loudness. Softness refers to the lightness of the keyboard; players should not have to strike the keys too hard in order to obtain a loud sound, nor should the audience hear the keys being struck. The relationship between the greatest volume and the least effort is very important, especially when considering the length of performances, including the exhausting cofradía fiestas, which test the endurance of any marimbista. Lasting six days, they comprise four twelve-hour performances and two twenty-four-hour performances.

People say a good player is one who has the endurance to play with the same sonority during an entire musical event; they drink alcohol in an attempt to keep up their energy levels, although this tactic often has the opposite effect. It is common for the volume to fade as the event progresses. At the beginning of a festivity in a town house, the music can be heard at least two blocks away (about 100 yards), but little by little the volume diminishes, so that by nightfall the music can barely be heard from two or three houses away. People say this is evidence of a bad marimba and they make oblique remarks about the marimbistas' drinking habits.

STYLE AND IDENTITY

Marimbistas often compare their styles with those of players from other municipalities, especially Cubulco. The municipalities of Cubulco and Rabinal, which are both in the *departamento* (province) of Baja Verapaz, are the main centers of Achi culture. The towns of these municipalities are only eleven miles apart; an active market and cultural exchange exists between them and their surrounding villages. Although each municipality has its own repertoire of sones, many are common to both areas. I saw Rabinalense marimbistas playing in festivities in Cubulco villages, indicating that there is a fair amount of exchange of musical styles. The sones may be the same, but differences in playing style are important, as Celestino explained. "Although the same sones are played, they have changed; the sones vary in the same way that a woman's clothes vary from town to town." Son playing, like women's traditional clothing, incorporates style elements peculiar to their municipality.[8] The stylistic differences between the son music of Rabinal and Cubulco are connected to their inhabitants' sense of identity or, to put it the other way around, the differentiation between municipalities is part of the process of style and identity formation. Local styles evoke a sense of belonging to one's municipality and its distinctive cultural style, which is comforting to Indian musicians and audience alike.

But there is also an ambivalent attraction to the inherent power of the other, a simultaneous attraction to and rejection of the dominant Ladino culture and the power it represents. Some people with less traditional tastes admit that they are attracted to the Cubulero style because of its similarities to modern popular music. This is hardly coincidental: Cubulco's Ladinos are more powerful than Rabinal's and exercise greater control and dominance over the Achi population. One result of this is that pieza music has had more influence there, and this is reflected in the faster tempo at which Cubuleros play sones, imitating the fast rhythms of the piezas favored by Ladinos and young people of both ethnicities.

Rabinalenses criticize Cubuleros because their playing style is too fast and "choppy"; they say that listeners cannot distinguish the vueltas. But a certain amount of envy is detectable in this criticism; it takes skill to play so rapidly, and few Rabinalense players can duplicate their speed and dexterity. Rabinalenses explain their slower and simpler style in terms of pleasing their ancestors; they always make comparative references to the way their ancestors played because they believe that the son repertoire was the ancestors' creation. They want to play the way their ancestors did because the ancestors long to hear the music; they believe that if one changes the way the sones are played, the dead will not be able to recognize them.

The contrast between Rabinal's simple, slow, peaceful musical style and Cubulco's fast and violent one is reflected in their iconographic interpretations of their respective patron saints. Rabinalenses say that their patron, San Pablo, has a peaceful stance, as he holds his sword pointing at the floor, whereas Cubulco's patron saint, Santiago, is mounted on a horse like the cattle-raising Cubulero Ladinos, with his sword held ready for battle.[9] This metaphor speaks perspicaciously of the violence meted out to Indians by Ladinos. Implicit in Rabinalense criticism of Cubulero son players' style are their historical disputes concerning other aspects of life and livelihood such as race and land.

It is not that all Rabinalense marimbistas play one way and all Cubuleros play another. Villages adjacent to Cubulco (especially Pichec) boast that their fast-playing neighbors influence their playing, and some have converted their marimba de sones into a marimba de piezas. Juan Ordoñez, who actually plays the marimba de pieza, recalled playing with a marimbista from the Juarez family of Pichec: "Oh, that guy played with us but he left us behind once and for all. One doesn't understand his playing. Everyone has his own level. I was intimidated because he is a musician. You should have seen him; he grabbed the mallets and kept on striking, kept striking, kept striking! Yes, everyone has their own way, but those who work fast always make mistakes. Those who work with calm play with more security."

Rabinalense marimbistas also make comparisons between their playing style and that of neighboring municipalities such as San Miguel Chicaj (in Baja Verapaz) and Joyabaj (in El Quiché). They identify with the towns of these municipalities because their players' slow-paced style is, they say, similar to their own. I never had the opportunity to hear San Miguel marimbistas and so I cannot say if there is any truth to this claim. Given that Rabinalenses came from the Joyabaj region in the fifteenth century and that San Miguel Chicaj developed from lands belonging to Rabinal's cofradías, this statement could be an allegory for their common ancestry.

PERSONAL STYLE

When people want to compliment a marimbista, they say he is *mero travieso*, a very playful or "naughty" performer. This positive character attribute can also be applied to a whole population. For example, when

I asked about the musical life of the coastal *fincas* where Rabinalenses work for a few months every year, Tono explained that people who live there do not have marimbas because they are not playful people.

The joyous spirit of the marimba is, to the Rabinalense, an expression of their cheerful and happy character; the epitome of this is the "naughty" (playful) treble player, who can perform all the vueltas of each section of a son. Judgments about his personal style are based on these abilities. This is not to say that the Achi do not recognize the important roles of the center and bass players; it is just that they give more attention to the director of the ensemble, the treble player.

The marimbista whose character, ideology, and personal playing style raised the most controversy was Esteban Uanché. Both Ladinos and Indians acknowledged that he was the best sones player in Rabinal; yet he also generated more change within this genre than anyone else. This combination of tradition and innovation provoked both admiration and contempt. Esteban boasted:

> The people know me; it is true that I am unique. Our God, our Lord and celestial Father, gave it to me and that is why the people tell me that I am a good teacher, the best among us, the *naturales*. "If you die," someone told me, "will there ever again be someone like you in this town of Rabinal? There is no other treble. We have gone to listen to everyone and they are not the same."

Esteban's life history may partly account for his prickly nature. He was born and raised in the Ladino-dominated village of Pichec, which is closer to Cubulco town than to Rabinal. Pichec Ladinos have the same attitudes toward Indians as their urban neighbors, viewing them as inferior and treating them with contempt; they are in perpetual conflict with the village's Indian population.

Esteban epitomized the contradiction between identification with tradition and attraction to power. He was antipathetic toward Ladinos and had a clear understanding of the repressive role of the army. Yet Esteban referred with pride to his four years as a soldier, when he served in the special presidential battalion in the democratic Arbenz era; his stories were full of references to the army's power and clearly reflect the militarized mentality that pervades Indian life. He constantly referred to his friendships with the powerful. Despite his claims that he would never play for any political party for fear of being identified with it, he could always be found playing for the richest and most reactionary parties. His ideological ambivalence, saying one thing and doing another, caused him many problems. While they admired his playing skills, many musicians kept their distance because they saw him as a difficult, selfish, mean, grumpy character (summed up in the term *delicado*). Many marimbistas were surprised that he had been generous enough to give me classes and that I had been tolerant enough to accept them!

Most Rabinalense marimbistas do not make changes to the tempo of the son other than to slow down just before beginning the final cadence or coda; they maintain a constant tempo within the son. The style is continuous *fortissimo*, although they might add or subtract double notes of the chord to give a richer or simpler sound. Only a few "playful" marimbistas (such as Esteban) use dynamics and constantly change the tempo, bringing contrast and expressiveness to the son. Lázaro, an experienced marimba player, explained:

> The son has a limit. At the beginning one has to play loud and slow, then the rest goes slower, and at the end one plays low in volume. There are sones with two strophes, others have three and four strophes, and then in those sections, wherever less is required, one has to do it less, and when loudness is required, one can do it louder. The end has to be played low and slow because it is the end.

It is always interesting to compare what people say with what they do. Lázaro's concept of son tempo is one of progressively slower movement, yet he is one of the fastest marimbistas in town. His ideas concur with the general concept of the ancient, slow style, whereas his playing is influenced by the fast beat of other musical genres played on the radio.

Esteban was innovative because he improvised. He insisted that many people play the sones in the old style, but he liked change and introduced new vueltas all the time. This is why he had difficulty finding center players who wanted, or were able, to play with him, excepting his nephews, Celestino and Bernabé. He complained about his previous center player, who abandoned him:

> Not anyone can [play with me]. Francisco Alvarado behaved badly, that fucking man was [playing] with me. He wasn't such a good player but because I am the real naughty man, I told him, "This is the way we are going to do it and this is the way you are going to play." And while I was teaching him this, he started to get upset with me. He didn't like to be taught the vueltas I was teaching him. I said, "I don't like the vueltas that you are playing because they are the old ones, so stop doing them. Let's make new ones. Let's make a business, because this is a business." I only make new sones.

Esteban took an innovative approach within the traditional genre and his success lay in combining the musical form of the traditional sones, which people recognize and like, with the introduction of many variations, including the improvisation of vueltas. While it is true that his transformations were novel, people questioned whether he was creating new material or merely re-combining old. Lázaro, who told me that he likes to invent new melodies adapted to preestablished harmonic and rhythmic patterns, was scathing about Esteban's style:

> There are invented sones; the mind invents some of them. First one has to qualify if what one is playing is all right; then, if it is good, one keeps adding and adding until the son has three strophes. Then one leaves it there. Then one looks at the repertoire to look for names that do not already exist and finds a new name for the son. But there is this man whose name is Esteban Uanché. He puts six sones on top of every son he makes. No, he doesn't play well, because if one plays one over the other, it is not doing any good. One has to make them so they are independent, without material from others.

Another marimbista from the Ordoñez family criticized Esteban's playing for similar reasons, claiming that he only made arrangements (*composturas*) and that he introduced sones from other places: "People like to listen to the old style, not those sones that who knows where they come from."

Purist suspected that Esteban's innovations were derived from popular music, and there does seem to be some truth in this. Within the pieza repertoire there are certain pieces that have an improvisational section (*montón*) just before the pieza ends. In this section, the fourth marimba player, the piccolo who accompanies the higher range of the marimba de pieza, stops playing to let the treble player improvise on the theme and show his ability and dexterity. The montón is a kind of cadenza in the style of cadenzas played in classical concertos of the late eighteenth century, in which the musician showed his improvisational abilities just before ending the movement. Esteban's playing style did resemble the improvisational form of the monton.

Esteban's innovative style separated him from what he most wanted to protect, that is, the traditional concepts that underpin son music. Some people said that the dead would not recognize or understand his music any more than they do piezas.[10] This was a terrible insult to a man who rejected the idea of dedicating piezas to the dead, saying that piezas are for Ladinos:

> Pieza is not allowed at the cemetery. I can't imagine my son playing pieza with counter-bass for me when I die. Has anybody seen me dancing pieza? That music is for the people with money! If I die I want the players to play a pair of sones on the top of my grave so I can listen to them. Some people say that the dead do not listen, but I am sure they do!

There was also the danger that the living would not recognize Esteban's music, either, or would at least be distracted (as some people claim to be) from its purpose as a form of communion with the dead. It is not just musicians who need to learn the sones but the audience too. Bacho explained:

> People who know the sones can hear their sadness, and those who do not know do not hear them as sad. For example, you will not hear a particular son as sad if you do not know the sound of that melody, but for those who know the sones, it makes them cry. Haven't I told you about the time when my brothers and I went to pick up the marimba Esteban sold us? He told me, "Go and get the marimba, guys, but before you leave play for me a son of sadness." "O God! Of what?" Back then I didn't know anything. "Sorry, Don Esteban," I said, "but which are the sones of sadness?" "Don't you know?" he said, very surprised. "Well, there are several of them, like costa grande, costa chiquita, joyabateco, san miguelito, eeee! There are many." "Which of those do you want to hear?" I asked. "Any of them," he replied.
>
> Then we put down the marimba under the big *morro* [gourd] tree he has at the entrance to his house and we played one. Suddenly he started to cry and at the end we took the marimba and left.

It is only through knowing the context, name, and purpose of each son that the listener can understand its meaning and participate in an exchange of emotions. This tends to limit the degree of change found acceptable within the genre,[11] and changes, especially to the son genre, are roundly criticized (even though they are also admired, often by the same people). Esteban kept his public in a state of uncertainty, their normal expectations of the sones and their vueltas thrown into confusion. In his attempts to distinguish himself from other musicians, Esteban stretched the boundaries of acceptability and expectation, distancing himself from his friends and jeopardizing his popularity. Concerns over the validity of Esteban's playing style gave some musicians an acceptable reason for not playing with him; to be forced to admit that one does not have the ability to play would be unforgivable and socially dangerous. Criticism based on envy of his ability to obtain the most and the best contracts are, of course, completely unacceptable.

Ordinarily, the will of the audience directs the musician and the music, but Esteban tended to impose his will on both music and audience. Nevertheless, he subscribed to and indeed was a strong advocate of traditional principles concerning musical performance: Son marimbistas consider themselves servants of the people and feel it is their duty to please them with their favorite sones. Marimbistas become surrogate agents, liberating people's emotions (while holding on to their own as a sign of respect to the audience, both living and dead); together with the violin and *adufe* players, they are intermediaries, communicating the feelings that flow between the living and the dead.

THUS TIMES CHANGE, music changes, but the discourse about music and music practice remains the same, at least for the time being. The Rabinalense musicians I met were at their most confident when discussing the ritual aspects and procedures of traditional son music; the long-established discourse on the subject gives their work a sacred aura, a sense of usefulness and satisfied purpose. It seems that all marimba music (so long as the audience likes it) comes under the rubric of serving the community. This probably helps to account for the survival of the traditional discourse about music in the face of a dwindling support base of local Catholics and new methods of learning that turn the traditional authority structure upside down. Thus traditional concepts of religious and social duty survive innovation within the traditional genre, the introduction of pieza music, and the increasingly business-minded attitude of musicians themselves.

It is noticeable that most critics of innovation are of Esteban's generation, that is, grandfathers in their sixties. As elders (<u>mam</u>), their traditional social role includes reinforcing the boundaries of the acceptable. They tend to forget that when they were young they too were at the forefront of innovation, bringing the marimba into ritual practice. Esteban was a part of this but, unlike his contemporaries, he never stopped learning and experimenting with the genre.[12] His music, then, was the antithesis of the much-valued concept of "repetition" through which consensus is reached and the ancestors/God appeased, and as such was considered disturbing—perhaps more disturbing than the introduction of something completely new. The assimilation and transformation of the new is one thing; genuine creativity is clearly another.

8   The Economy of the Son
       and the Pieza

ONE OF THE FACTORS driving musical change over the past few decades has been a shift in musicians' survival strategies, which have responded to social and economic conditions in general and to the death and destruction of *la violencia* in particular. As ritual specialists with an essential role in community celebrations, musicians are highly visible; many were killed during the violence of the early 1980s. Those who survived faced a demoralized and impoverished population whose ability to invest socially and economically in fiestas had been dramatically reduced. They were therefore forced not just to seek new ways of supplementing their income but to address what this meant to them in terms of their identity, the value of their work, and their reputation and prestige within the community.

THE MORAL ECONOMY

The ways in which Achi musicians take part in the commodity economy while retaining their social and religious roles as moral obligations to the community recalls discussions of "moral economy" in both the anthropological and historical literature (Thompson 1991; Scott 1976; Bloch and Parry 1989; Harris 1995). For some writers the moral economy means nothing more than the political economy in capitalist and noncapitalist societies (Sahlins 1977; Brocheux 1983; Parker 1988).

Discussion of moral economy has often focused on a false dichotomy between capitalist market economy rationality and the precapitalist economy centered on peasant subsistence, with its principles of safety and reciprocity. For example, Taussig's (1980) work has been criticized on the grounds that market "rationality" is always influenced by ideological conditions, political interests, and moral, social, and religious values, thus giving a much more complex rationality to economic practices of production and exchange (Trouillot 1986; Turner 1986; Englund 1996).

The impact of commoditization in Rabinal is not a new phenomenon. The inhabitants of Rabinal, like those of all Indian societies, have been integrated into the market economy through wage relations with the capitalist sector for at least fifty years, that is, since the "revolutionary" (democratic) period when compulsory work was abolished and minimum wages were established. Older musicians remember plenty of paid work in local road construction during the mid-1940s, which pushed the municipality's economy toward the monetary. Referring to the Arbenz era, Estaban Uanché said, "When that president came to power, then there was money for the poor." People had the money to go to the cantina and to *zarabandas*, where they listened to the increasingly popular music of the marimba de sones. Others bought marimbas, which were rapidly being integrated into Achi religious life, adopting other musicians' traditional attitudes of service to the community while increasing their income. The marimba soon became so embedded in Achi life that it is difficult to remember that musicians' need to juggle moral obligations with financial needs is nothing new.

The strength of these moral obligations should not be underestimated. It is the price musicians pay for their gift from God, and they take their responsibilities seriously. Violinist Magdaleno told me,

> Sometimes my wife gets upset because I work too much, but what can I do? If I refuse to play, the dead will punish me, too. The dead will come to knock at my door for not obeying, for not going. It is an obligation to the *ánimas* and, like he [Feliciano] says, if somebody comes to ask me to play, what am I going to say? I can not say I am ill if I have nothing [wrong with me]. They may even think I am going to die.

Felicano, his adufe-playing partner, agreed: "You have to go because otherwise the dead will think you just do not want to work. That is why I do it too, for my work."

I frequently heard explanations like these, particularly from musicians and *abogados*. These men's deference to the demands of their work reflects the social responsibility of having to mediate between people, God, and the spirits, keeping all parties happy. From a religious perspective, maintaining good relations between the living and the dead (and God) prevents failure and illness and promotes community well-being; people have high expectations of their musicians and abogados. Ritual specialists' God-given talents determine their destiny, and while this is a privilege, it does have its price.

Because musical talent is seen as God-given and as determining a man's destiny, musicians understand their profession as an obligation to the community, which is ruled by sanctions and punishments should this responsibility be neglected. They view their work as a duty to the living and the dead, who may take revenge if they refuse a contract or a request for a son or fail to fulfill a contract to play. *Marimbista* Filemon Lajuj told me:

> If you make a mistake, then you will have bad dreams. The spirit owner of the marimba [la Siuanaba] appears in your dreams. She will ask you, "Did

you do such and such? You did not carry out your obligation." It is the marimba spirit owner who talks to you, because this instrument is not like one of us. If you make an error, you may go mad or something will happen to you for not fulfilling your obligation. A player in La Ceiba hamlet did not meet his obligation. At the last minute he decided to go to the plantation to work and his arm shrank. It happened because of his error. You look and think this [the marimba] is just wood, but we are not the same to her. She has an owner who will punish you for not doing it.

When *segundero marimba mozo* Marcelo Ixpata walked away from a commitment to play a *cofradía* fiesta, he lost Esteban's sympathy for good. Although Marcelo did find someone to finish the gig for him and although Esteban himself could be said to share some responsibility for the affair (in that he hired someone he should have known couldn't keep up with him), these are minor considerations. What is at issue here is a breach of faith, not only with Esteban, the cofradía for which the ensemble was playing, and the participants, but with the ancestors, God, and, for some musicians, with the spirit owner of the marimba, the female Siuanaba. Although no great calamity has yet befallen Marcelo, he has lost his most precious asset—his reputation, and this has dented his earning capacity.

The connection between duty, status, and wealth is an old one. The Rabinalense have an economic view of religiosity and devotion that is most evident in the traditional hierarchical prestige structure of the cofradía *cargo* system (see Chapter 2). Individuals express their religious devotion by taking cargos (positions or burdens) of progressively greater religious and economic responsibility. The greater the economic expense, the greater the devotion to God and the saints and, therefore, the greater the *carguero*'s prestige and status in the community. From this economic view of religiosity, musicians who play as a *devoción* at a cofradía fiesta gain considerable prestige (and more work). The blind marimbista Lázaro takes pride (ki'koteem; jorob'eem)[1] in playing for "the sake of God" and charging modest fees. "I do people favors because I like it more that way. I do not charge big amounts of money. What for? I know whoever hires me will serve me, will give me food, because it is God we are serving. I put a little bit of devotion, a little collaboration." Lázaro is regarded as a good person because his modest charges make his work affordable for everyone.

Musicians oscillate between a devotional attitude toward their work, which brings spiritual benefit and social prestige, and a pragmatic stance of valuing their music as a commodity. As a commodity, music is tied to a different—Ladino—prestige system centered on economic and political power (this does not, of course, prevent musicians from negotiating their wages for playing at religious events as forcefully as they can within the bounds of politeness). But musicians who clearly and systematically opt to play within the Ladino sphere are considered ambitious, which is not a virtue in Achi society. They may be labeled <u>itzel winak</u> (evil people), no different from Ladinos, whose social interests center on making money and personal gain (<u>ku' an nim che riib'</u>).[2] It is to avoid this that pieza musicians occasionally play for the modern dance-dramas as a devoción.

Despite the weight and importance of traditional values and beliefs, financial considerations are becoming increasingly important. Most peasants' incomes are as modest today as they were during the revolutionary period.[3] But musicians, like other Indian peasants, were less dependent on wage work fifty years ago because the subsistence sector was stronger then and their expenses lower (see Chapter 1). Musicians claim that they could afford to play as a devoción to God, the saints, the holy earth, and the souls of the dead, that is, free of charge. Today's economic circumstances make it impossible for them to dedicate an entire performance as an offering. Devoción has been reduced to extending the contract by one hour to show good will to the people who hired them and to God and the spirits, from whom they hope to obtain protection in return. Only a very few marimbistas (such as Lázaro) will agree to play an entire event as a devoción, and then only when a collective prayer is needed to ask (for example) for rain or a similar communal need. It is not that Rabinalenses are less religious than they used to be, just that their devociones have been simplified to reduce cost. The same applies to their fiestas and dance-dramas, which have been scaled down and are performed less frequently for lack of funds.[4] Rabinalenses themselves say that the number of fireworks thrown by children and young people on Christmas Eve is a good indicator of the health of the community economy. Few fireworks and silent streets after midnight indicate a poor crop, a lack of wage work, or both, rather than any loss of religious faith.

In other instances, the simplification of ceremonial life has been interpreted as a result of the secularization encouraged by the commoditization of society. Sociologists interested in this phenomenon, which is generally understood as a decline of religion (Hamilton 1995), have found that it tends to be closely related to modernization and industrialization (Wallis and Bruce 1992)—in other words, to capitalism, which again places modernity in opposition to tradition. But Guatemala's peasants have been incorporated into the capitalist system for several generations, though modernization seems to have passed them by. It is also reasonable to suppose that the politicization of Indian societies before, during, and after the political violence of the 1980s accelerated the secularization process, but this has not been the case. The Catholic Church, which took a leading role in political consciousness-raising prior to the violence, adopted a similar role in the human rights movement of the past fifteen years.

Yet despite the social change and political upheaval of the past forty years, the practice of music still constitutes social and political capital that can be transformed into income to supplement subsistence agriculture. Musicians therefore consider the social and political benefits as well as economic advantages before accepting an obligation to play. For instance, a musician who plays for a religious ritual as a *devoción* receives food but no cash, yet his gift of his music makes him look generous and pious in the eyes of the living and the dead; he gains prestige. When the musician plays for a political event, such as FRG's election campaign,[5] he knows he will be paid handsomely, but he worries that he might be identified with the party's political agenda or its representatives, who are the living symbols of the dreaded army.[6] The benefits and dangers associated with any commitment to play are not necessarily mutually exclusive, although I have set them in opposition to illustrate extreme considerations. Many musicians today strive for a larger market balance, playing primarily for money with only the occasional performance for *devoción*, which protects them from malicious gossip.[7] Musicians' decisions to expand and transform their repertoire or change their instruments carry similar advantages and risks. This strategy opens up their market and generates greater income in less time, but it requires a bigger investment, both in cash and commitment. Men who make this gamble gain additional prestige and status as musicians "who can [play] sones and piezas."

Again, it would be reasonable to assume that these new economic strategies, which increase income at the expense of the devotional aspect of performance, are the result of an expanding market culture and the consequent secularization of social interactions. I observed neither loss of piousness nor any displacement of religious devotion by money. Flautist and drummer Eligio Gonzalez explained the nature of money from a religious point of view:

> People ask for *pisto* [money] with their candle. Or ask for their life, to be able to earn pisto on a job already started. Or if their pisto has no remedy, it means, pisto earned and gone, which bought nothing, nothing done with that pisto; then it's necessary to make a devoción to God. That's why I set a devoción to be encouraged, to be working, to have *corazón* pisto [never-ending money]. Always the name of God is behind the work and the pisto. The heart of pisto is never to lose sight of God. Never leave God for anything. Because he is the owner of everything. The owner of the pisto and of our lives.

"Corazón pisto" is money invested in God's name. It guarantees a return, which may be health or more money. From this perspective, there is nothing wrong with a person's accumulating money so long as it is done in God's name.[8] And even if the money is spent on alcohol, so long as it is drunk in the "name of God," God will ensure that one drinks *con medida* (with moderation). In other words, God can mediate the potential opposition between individual and collective interests in the use of money. Catholic morality concerning money, which Taussig (1980) incorrectly interpreted as a critique of capitalism, is understood by Rabinalense Achi as a need for reciprocity; there is no trace of the idea that seeking money, let alone money itself, is evil. A lack of reciprocity is behind the frequently heard complaint that the goods and labor that used to be offered for free now have a price tag: "Ahora todo es pisto" (today everything is money).

THE WORK ETHIC

The notion of *compromiso* (a verbal commitment to play music for an event) and the fulfillment of that compromiso are moral values with religious origins.

As we have seen, marimbistas are at the service of and accountable to the people, the spirits, and God. They are morally compelled to play for others. To refuse to play, or to leave a performance unfinished because of some disagreement or drunkenness, is a sin that exposes the musician to punishment by God and the spirits, the wrath of the people, and possibly failure in life.[9] The musician thus assumes his compromisos from beginning to end, honoring a contract out of respect but also out of fear of the consequences should he fail to honor an agreement. As we have also seen, marimbistas can nevertheless and sometimes do look for indirect ways to refuse a contract if they do not want to play.

The economic aspect of a contract is thus immersed in moral concepts of respect and sociability. Although contracts to play pieza music are better paid, musicians keep their word if they have already committed themselves to play son music, because credibility, friendship, and new contracts depend on the fulfillment of their obligations. As Bacho, a marimbista who adopted new musical and economic strategies to generate more income, put it, "We can do both things, we can play piezas and sones. Now, when they come to ask for so many hours of pieza music and we already have an obligation for sones, I reply, 'I'm sorry, go search for another because we already have a compromiso for sones.'"

Some Indian musicians told me that they do not play pieza music, nor will they change their son marimba ensemble to a *conjunto* ensemble, because that is not the music the dead want to hear. They say that musicians who change their music become evil, like Ladinos, because that is the music they like (Ladinos, by contrast, think pieza ensembles play the only "decent" music). The purpose of these musicians' statements is to identify themselves with their ancestors and to demonstrate their devotion to the souls of the dead—in other words, to differentiate themselves ethnically from the Ladino world. But these statements also mask the technical, social, and economic difficulties they encounter when attempting to incorporate the new music genre and its musical instruments.

CONTRACTING A MARIMBA

Son marimba groups usually contract by shifts of one day (twelve hours), or one day and one night (twenty-four hours); they also play by the hour or by the son. A wedding celebration at the bride's house is a twenty-four-hour contract; a cofradía fiesta contract is for six twelve-hour days and two nights. Ladinos tend to contract son marimbas by the hour for their family gatherings and for institutional events. Marimbas are only contracted by the son at the cemetery during All Saints' Day and All Souls' Day celebrations on 1 and 2 November.

The price of hiring a son marimba and musicians depends on the men's place of origin. Village marimbistas charge 30–35 quetzales (about $5) for one day, but marimbistas from the municipal town or its largest villages charge 70–120 quetzales (up to $20). Village marimbistas, *los de la montaña* (those from the mountains), are considered less competent players than those of the town because they have fewer opportunities to play and thus less experience. I have met groups in the villages close to Rabinal town who often play there and are as good as, if not better than, the groups in town, yet because of their place of origin their price is lower. A marimba's history and quality also translate into different prices and thus into different clienteles. Socioeconomic differences between poor and not so poor Indians or Ladinos are also expressed in terms of quality of performance in the music market.

It is more expensive to hire marimbistas by the hour, as they charge double for an event of only a few hours in order to guarantee a minimum income. Village and town son marimbistas charge 10 and 20 quetzales, respectively. Conjunto marimba ensembles (six musicians) charge 30 quetzales an hour, and double marimba ensembles (nine musicians) charge 100 quetzales; individual musicians earn 5 and 10 quetzales an hour, respectively (see below). The price also increases if the client is a Ladino.

Rabinal's leading marimbista during my time there, Esteban Uanché, set the maximum prices annually when all son marimbistas gather at the cemetery to play for the dead on All Souls' Day. His nephew Celestino explained:

> Don Esteban is the director of all marimbas, he sets a price and everyone will ask him how much should they charge. This year a short melody costs one quetzal. He is the head chief because everyone recognizes that he plays the son beautifully. They do not play beautifully in the villages. If compared with Esteban's son, they do not measure up. There is a difference. Don

Esteban embellishes the melodies, playing the cycles where others can't. There are some who may try and play the amanecido without caring if they make the turns or not; they do it clumsily. Esteban instead does it complete.

The primary selection criterion when contracting a marimba de sones is price. When explaining the different prices and options, Bacho, a marimbista, said, "If people are poor they don't call on Don Esteban, because Don Esteban does not compromise, he demands his price without question. He is the most expensive." Customers are willing to sacrifice a little in terms of the quality and trustworthiness of marimbistas in order to better distribute their limited resources on food and other essentials for their celebrations.[10]

Different criteria apply if people want to increase their prestige by staging a memorable event. Encompassed under the concept of the marimba's "sound," these include the instrument's resonance, the personal style of the *tiplista* (soprano player), the players' stamina, and the extent of their repertoire. Last but not least, the duty performance of the marimbistas is also considered, in other words their ability to play as long as possible before abandoning their instrument in order to drink.

A Marimba's Economic Value

Apart from earning musicians a modest income to supplement subsistence agriculture, the marimba also serves as a domestic savings and emergency fund. Like livestock (usually a pig or cow), the marimba can be sold when the family or a fellow member of the <u>cuchubal</u> (partnership) needs to raise cash to pay for a funeral or other unavoidable expense such as an illness in the family. These are frequent occurrences because of poor health conditions, especially in the villages. Esteban Uanché told me that when his father was dangerously ill, some Ladinos wanted to buy his marimba and coaxed him, "Sell your marimba, Don José, you will get cured with that marimba." Many marimbistas stressed that if it were not for illnesses in the family, they could have built better homes or bought land. The possible disintegration of a group is a very real threat, which deters many men from investing in a marimba.

A good second-hand marimba *sencilla* (son or pieza marimba), unrestored but in fair shape with a good sound, can be obtained in Rabinal for between 800 and 1,200 quetzales ($133–200), which is equivalent to a season's work on the plantations (*fincas*). Tono Cajbón's relief, when he managed to recover his marimba following his escape from Plan de Sanchez after the massacre there on 18 July 1982, is understandable: He had his most precious asset and a means of earning a living for his family in their new landless home in the municipal colony. "The marimba was left in Plan de Sanchez and my brother-in-law returned to get it, he returned at night to rescue the marimba and came back with it by eight the next morning, but that was all. Everything else was lost, kettles, bed, tape player, hoe, cane-knife, grinding stone, dishes. . . . We came with our hands crossed, not even clothes, we had nothing.

THE CIRCULATION OF MARIMBAS AND PLAYERS

By my count, there are forty son marimbas and eight conjunto marimbas for pieza music in the villages of Rabinal municipality, and five son marimbas and two conjunto marimbas in town. The bigger villages—Xococ, Pichec, and Nimacabaj—have more than three son marimbas each. Conjunto marimbas are found in Ladino-dominated areas; there are five in Pichec alone. The musicians I interviewed not only knew the number of marimbas in their own and neighboring villages but their final destination when they were sold. They also knew the reason for the sale—for example, the separation of the group, or the owner's need for cash. Players' cohesion or mobility affects the circulation of marimbas that, with the exception of some better-quality instruments, make the rounds of marimbistas and apprentices. The history of ownership becomes the instrument's provenance, its pedigree, and affects the price musicians can charge to play at an event.

The most stable and also the oldest marimba groups are those formed by relatives; the ideal is a father and his sons. Family solidarity helps maintain cohesion in a group, but when sons marry and acquire new economic responsibilities, they often leave the group temporarily and sometimes permanently. In such cases the father usually employs marimbista friends to work as mozos (daily paid workers) until his son returns, which he usually does, at least occasionally; sometimes, however, the son works as a mozo for someone else or creates his own group.

The least stable groups consist of unrelated and often landless young men who form a marimba group for secular motives—the former conscripts, for example, who buy a marimba between them and learn to play simply for something to do. For them, playing for the ancestors or earning money is not always the prime consideration. Such young men will withdraw their investment in the marimba should a better employment opportunity arise. They can earn more on the fincas where the work is regular and the day shorter; they can also meet girls from other communities away from the censorious eyes and gossiping tongues of village elders. As they move around, as young men do, they hear marimbistas from different communities and learn new music and styles as they listen, sometimes playing as mozos in marimba groups wherever they happen to be.

"Equality" of Income

A son marimbista group's income is divided equally between the three players and the marimba; each gets a quarter of the contract fee, as Celestino explained: "Esteban says how much we will earn. If it is a day, he charges 120 quetzales and tells us immediately, 'the price is 120 quetzales divided by four [which] is 30 quetzales each' because the marimba earns a salary too, no more, no less."

Just as a marimba is treated as a living creature whose spirit or *dueño*[11] is la Siuanaba (see Chapter 5) and with whom drinks are shared to entice it to play better, so it receives a salary for its participation in the performance. The transferred value for wear of the instrument results in an extra salary for the owner, but instead of understanding this as a productive investment by the owner in the common work tool, the apparent inequality between owner and mozo is concealed. The extra payment is not the natural right of the marimba owner but of the female marimba. Once each musician has received a quarter of the income, what remains of the added value produced by the marimba mozos is appropriated by the marimba owner as rent and in recognition of his rights over their labor during the term of the contract. Exploitation takes the cultural form of an extra wage because the marimba (a living agent) is also a creator of value. Whenever musicians are given a round of drinks, alcohol is poured over part of the marimba to make her happy and sound better, so why not give her a wage, too? This idea is reinforced by the notion that marimbistas' competence is a quality of the marimba herself. However, these practices can also be seen as a way of making the private ownership of the marimba culturally and socially acceptable to ensemble members.

For all of that, owners make no profit from the marimba's share. Marimbas require little maintenance except for the replacement of the membranes (*tela*) at the bottom of the resonators, preferably each time the marimba is played at an event. Few marimba owners can afford to do this, as a set of membranes (*muda*) costs ten quetzales; as a result, the marimba sounds muted and thus reduces its players' modest income. Parts like ropes, pegs, and mallets are changed infrequently; only the tiplista's mallets are expensive, involving a trip to Guatemala City.

Despite these expenses and low earnings, economic motivation is significant for son marimba owners and musicians. Esteban was the only marimbista to refuse to play piezas to make a living from his music; the rest rely on subsistence agriculture and a couple of months' work on the fincas every year. Pieza musicians tend to be more business-minded, augmenting their repertoire and their income by playing the latest piezas on the conjunto marimba. They play more often and are considerably more expensive, some earning enough to avoid going to the fincas. The Jerónimos even managed to send the youngest generation to secondary school in Guatemala City on the proceeds.

THE ANNUAL CONTRACT CYCLE

The annual cycle of marimba contracts relates to the annual cycle of religious celebrations, the agricultural cycle, and plantation work. The busiest season is the dry season, called "summer," between November and May. People begin leaving for the fincas after the Day of the Dead on 2 November. This is marimbistas' biggest work opportunity of the year; there is work for everyone. And because they charge by the son, musicians earn as much over the two days as they do over a six-day fiesta. Others leave after the *maíz criollo* harvest in December, returning for the celebration of the town patron saint's fiesta in January. Most labor migrants are home by Easter, and all are back for the festival that marks the end of summer: the three-day fiesta of Santa Cruz on 1–3 May. This is the only cofradía fiesta celebrated in every village, and as such it is marimbistas' second-biggest annual work opportunity. Young people save their finca earnings and marry between January and May, before the rainy "winter" season starts and corn planting begins, providing marimbistas with fairly reliable income.

Marimbistas estimate that musicians who play only the son repertoire work about twice a month; at maximum rates, a musician averages sixty quetzales ($10) a month for twenty-four hours' worth of music, plus travel and expenses. Members of a conjunto ensemble (four marimbistas, bass player, and drummer) who can play up-to-the-minute piezas may have contracts to play each week, as they can meet Ladino and Indian demands for popular music, thus generating a maximum monthly income per musician of eighty quetzales for sixteen hours of work. The increase in monthly income for fewer hours of work does not compensate in the short term for the high price of the instruments and the cost of their transportation. Only a few families can afford to swap their son marimba ensembles for conjunto marimba ensembles or, alternatively, they consider the change too much of a financial risk.

MUSICAL STRATEGIES FOR SURVIVAL

In Rabinal the marimba has acquired greater importance than other instruments because the popular urban music Rabinalenses listen to on the radio and cassette can be incorporated in its repertoire. The commercial music industry has opened up a labor market for marimbistas to which other traditional instrumentalists have no access. The market for son music in Rabinal is constant and diverse, but the combination of many marimbistas and limited opportunities to play can and does lead to envy and conflict. The market for pieza music is growing, but as yet only a few marimbistas have changed to conjunto ensembles and incorporated the pieza repertoire. Some reasons for this are the cost of establishing a conjunto ensemble, the difficulty of keeping such a large group of musicians together, the continual threat that some domestic crisis will force a musician to withdraw his investment, and the difficulty of learning a new repertoire and music techniques.

To increase their income, many marimbistas have either become more mobile or changed to the marimba de pieza. Experienced players often prefer to be as mobile as possible, hiring themselves out to marimba owners as marimba mozos. In this way they avoid the cost and responsibilities of buying and maintaining a marimba themselves while at the same time getting work with various marimba groups and thus increasing their repertoire of music and styles. A successful marimba mozo must be skilled and adaptable enough to work easily with any tiplista; he also must have the type of personality that can build and maintain good relations with other marimbistas.

The second strategy is more suitable for groups composed of family members, as it requires a great deal of group cohesion and solidarity. The family buys a marimba de pieza or, if it already has one, upgrades to a conjunto marimba by adding a drum kit and double bass, and learns the pieza repertoire. This strategy involves considerable risk because of the large investment in terms of money and time. It also offers the best financial rewards: conjunto ensembles can charge more, and with only ten of these ensembles in the municipality there is little competition for work. There are also opportunities to play for Ladinos and Indians every week. The gigs are shorter, too, though more intense; people expect conjunto marimbistas to play continuously in ninety-minute sets so that they can dance for a long time in a Western style in couples. Musicians consider pieza music much more difficult and challenging than son music, where the sets are shorter and danced by older people who can manage only one or two sones. The exception to this general rule is weddings (the party at the groom's house), where they are only required to play for four to six hours, but then they charge even more for their work.

It is a paradox that son marimbistas who wish to maximize their earning potential do so with minimal investment, whereas conjunto marimbistas, who no longer play the "music of the ancestors," maximize their earning potential by exploiting their domestic resources—in this case, sons—in the traditional manner. The family relationship facilitates the organization of collective work, including the coordination of frequent rehearsals. The authoritarian structure of the family also maintains the necessary group cohesion, as the father or elder brothers control the younger boys (even in those cases where a younger child takes the lead in the pieza-learning process; see Chapter 7). This ensemble may remain stable for years, until the sons begin to marry.

Switching to a conjunto marimba is not an attractive proposition for the son marimba owner who hires marimba mozos. The larger number of musicians he would need to hire would threaten his control and authority over the group, jeopardizing his prestige in the eyes of his clients and hence his investment. A related reason for not playing piezas is the loss of face involved in being forced into a subordinate position to other, younger musicians, who find it easier to learn the new music. Although some men do find playing piezas difficult, social difficulties far outweigh technical ones. For these reasons men will think twice about changing to a conjunto marimba, for all that it seems a good idea in financial terms.

MUSICAL CHANGE IS A CULTURALLY ACCEPTABLE means of confronting challenges resulting from the effects of market economy expansion on a debilitated subsistence economy. The consideration of socioeconomic musical conditions and the calculations musicians make in terms of market and prestige economies indicate that rational economic thinking—as defined by Western capitalist thought—is only one part of the issue. The urgent need to increase income presents musicians with an apparent choice between profit and devoción, that is, between self-interest and a generally strongly felt obligation to serve community needs. Most musicians solve this problem more or less successfully. Another factor is whether one can afford the purchase of a conjunto marimba or, if choosing the alternative, whether one has the requisite social and technical skills to succeed as a mozo. Both options can be financially and socially risky, and the Achi are not known for taking risks.

9　Music within Social Interaction

MUSIC IS A FUNDAMENTALLY SOCIAL PHENOMENON because it is a form of communication whose messages are constructed and interpreted socially.[1] During social interactions musical communication takes place in the experience of playing and listening to music, and also, not least, in conversations about music and musicians after the performance is over.

Goffman's comprehensive definition of performance includes every situation in which an individual engages in social interaction. "I have been using the term 'performance,'" he writes, "to refer to all the activity of an individual which occurs during a period marked by his continuous presence before a particular set of observers and which has some influence on the observers" (1959, 32). Because everyday social interactions are included in this definition, there is an interpretative continuity between interactions that occur during musical performance and those that occur among musicians and between musicians and the public in daily life. While it is necessary to determine the specific frames in which both types of performances occur (Bateson 1972; Goffman 1974), there is a close and abiding relationship between them.

The evaluation and interpretation of a musical performance directly affects both the prestige and status of musicians and clients and their social roles and relationships in everyday social life. At the same time, these social relationships have a direct impact on musicians' access to contracts. It also affects the open disposition of musicians to play and the coordination among them while they are playing, as well as the receptivity of the audience to the musicians and their music. This is because it is in the course of daily interaction that agreements and disagreements are constantly negotiated and influence the ways of appreciating musicians' work.

The interpretation of musical performance transcends the ritual times and spaces of cultural performances; interpretation is in a state of permanent flux, always open to negotiation and adjustment, depending very much on musicians' sociality and their capacity to project desired images and intentions. There is a correspondence between their technical skills and the social skills needed, both within and outside musical performance. The highest value is assigned to those musicians who are committed, respectful, and sympathetic to the public's and musicians' needs, capacities, and preferences. This chapter looks at the "extra-musicality" of social interaction, which I argue is part of the process of musical communication.[2]

Marimbistas seek friendships and patronage not simply to obtain more contracts but to acquire status and prestige through playing for Ladino audiences as well as serving the Achi community in the ways I have described in earlier chapters. By fulfilling their social and religious obligations, they protect themselves from exposure to envy and witchcraft, which can result from social conflict and act to ensure social accountability. Friendships are a means of preventing potential conflict and gaining greater access to and control over the conditions of music production and consumption (while simultaneously blocking others from such advantages). Friendship is usually expressed in terms of idealized family relationships; the subtext is the connection with the ancestors.

THE FAMILY

The family is the social base of Achi society and provides an idealized model for social relations, including friendships and patronage. The family is viewed as providing the ideal conditions of cohesion and loyalty as well as the hierarchical authority structure necessary for the success of any enterprise, from subsistence agriculture to forming a *marimba* ensemble. In the latter case, the ideological emphasis on the family (as opposed to the individual) encourages a family's male members to stay together, develop competency, and acquire prestige as a group.

In real life, things are not always so simple. Esteban Uanché, until his death Rabinal's premier *son* marimbista, bitterly regretted that he had only one son, Mincho, and so was unable to achieve his ambition of organizing two marimba ensembles within his immediate family. For most of his career he had to hire at least one marimba *mozo* for every performance, and once Mincho got married and set up his own marimba ensemble, Esteban was back where he had started. Esteban moaned constantly about the mozos he taught, who, once they were competent to accompany him, began giving excuses for not playing with him and eventually abandoned him. Certainly his improvisational style created difficult challenges for his apprentices, as they had to be constantly attentive to his movements and ornamentations; competent but uninspired mozos need not apply.

After losing several mozos, Esteban found apprentices among his extended family and began training his nephews, Celestino and Bernabé Cajbón, who had begun their musical training with their father, Tono. By the time I arrived in Rabinal, Celestino and Bernabé had been playing for Esteban for two years, and he had finally achieved a degree of stability in his ensemble. The young men had great respect for their uncle, and he in turn admitted that they are talented young musicians. But even they were getting fed up with his demands.

Tono has the much desired and envied marimba *de hijos* (literally, a marimba full of sons) but has lost his older sons' respect because of his drinking problem. When drunk, he becomes verbally and physically abusive, fighting everyone in sight and hitting his sons whenever they play together at fiestas. Although Tono claims his sons do not play with him because they are busy with other commitments, the truth is that he himself destroyed the trust and solidarity between them.

The *conjunto* marimba ensemble (marimba, counter bass, and drum set) depends even more on family relationships because it requires the unity and loyalty of a larger number of musicians. Economic cooperation is also more likely when all the instruments are owned by the family; then there is no threat that the ensemble will collapse because one member withdraws his investment or claims personal ownership of an instrument.[3] Common storage of family-owned instruments tends to ensure that they will not be stolen, handled roughly, or destroyed. Finally, rehearsals are easier to organize within a family.

At the same time that hierarchy within the family is emphasized, the Achi have a strong notion of equality between families. This may derive from a sense of community and a cultural inclination to conform. The idea of equality is reinforced by the sharing of limited resources in general conditions of poverty, where everyone faces the uncertain outcome of seasonal subsistence agriculture and annual epidemics. These are palpable facts of life for most Indians (and poor Ladinos) and provide the basis for the belief that one person's gain is another's loss and that someone's success actually causes others' misfortunes (Foster 1965). Musicians' God-given talents and their role as ritual specialists set them apart, as does their ability to buy and hold on to what is, in local terms, an expensive piece of equipment. It seemed to me that musicians' discourse on the family was partly influenced by this negative view of their social position and was, to some extent, a means of downplaying their importance by placing them on a level with everyone else.

THE MARIMBA MOZO

A mozo de marimba is a musical contractor, an individual with experience and knowledge of the musical repertoire who offers his services to marimba owners who need an extra player for an event. Mozos generally work for friends or with groups with whom they feel comfortable. Marcelo Ixpata boasted of his skills as a mozo *segundero/centrista* (second/center player, who carries the harmony) in a way most uncommon among the Rabinalense Achi: "Because I am a professional player I can play with anybody. As long as there is someone who can *jalar* [lead; literally, to pull] in the first position I go behind, following as second, tailing, tailing."

Celestino, who is a much better musician than Marcelo, explained why he liked being a marimba mozo:

> I play with the Mendoza family and with Mincho Torres, and I always play with Matilde Castro from Chiac. I have played in many marimba groups like Ecos del Valle [Echoes of the Valley] from Pachica. They are a family group of children. Another group I play with is the Juarez family from La Ceiba and with Esteban here [in Rabinal town]. I keep myself busy with all of them. There are times when *compromisos* don't come from this side but that side, and that one will come to me in advance and give me a date [to play] and they say, "a gig is coming up on the thirtieth," and I record it, and if Don Esteban seeks me out for that day I refuse him because I already have an obligation, so then he has to hire another mozo. I am not tied to anyone.

When I asked if that was best way, or if it was working for him, he answered, "Oh yes, because there are always opportunities any day. There are not always opportunities for everyone, only once every few weeks. But I work with whoever because each of them has an opportunity coming up."

Experienced treble players who own their own marimbas are usually responsible for hiring the mozo to play with the ensemble. It is uncommon for a marimba owner who plays second or third position to hire a mozo to play the treble, or first, position. It is socially confusing, not to say risky, for a marimba owner not to occupy the musical position with the greatest decision-making power. Nevertheless, a successful segundero mozo must have sufficient experience to follow the treble leader, and many are more skilled than the *tiplistas* who employ them. Mozos who take the third position, playing rhythmic bass at the left side of the instrument, do not need this level of experience.

It is essential that a mozo have extensive knowledge of the son repertoire and, in the last decade or so, of at least some of the public's favorite *piezas*. Although marimba groups share a common repertoire, they all have some sones and piezas that they say only they can play and that they sometimes claim as their own creation. These claims help to explain why, when marimbistas told me that the repertoire contains some 150 sones, they either could not or would not name them all.[4] They certainly avoided naming sones they played themselves, and this secrecy is a means of self-empowerment through keeping uncommon sones their sole preserve. As mozos work with the different marimba groups, however, they learn these allegedly exclusive sones and piezas, as well as the personal style of the treble leader of the ensemble that claims ownership of them. As mozos pass on different ensembles' knowledge, skills, and styles, they become the medium through which Rabinal's repertoire is both expanded and homogenized; they become the generating source of Rabinalense style. Mozos' mobility, which has become an important aspect of social interaction, particularly in terms of musical practice, may explain the present dynamism of Rabinal's marimba tradition.

A mozo must have good technical skills and a developed aesthetic sense. Of greater value than individual dexterity is his skill in coordinating with and adapting to other musicians on a personal level, for this encourages leading marimbistas to prefer one mozo to another.[5] While all musicians must form friendships in order to integrate themselves into the group and develop a clientele, this ability is even more essential to the marimba mozo, for he has the additional challenge of forming friendships with a variety of different marimba owners. Because the mozo is a bystander in several ensembles, his interests and intentions can be different from and conflict with those of marimba owners, which makes the forging of friendships a challenge requiring constant attention. No matter how good a musician a mozo may be, he will not be asked to join an ensemble unless its treble finds him congenial. At the same time, however, the more accomplished the mozo is, the greater his power will be in negotiations with marimba owners. They will try to keep a good marimba mozo as a permanent part of the ensemble. A favorable relationship between treble leader and second player (who carries the harmony and part of the rhythm section) is essential and must be demonstrated outside the musical performance as well as within it. When the second player is a mozo, this relationship becomes a very delicate matter.

Becoming a mozo gives a musician the opportunity to learn new music and playing styles that, once mastered, increase his reputation and his earnings; it also allows him to extend his personal social network (and to avoid identification with any one group or faction). All he needs are his mallets; he avoids the financial burden of marimba ownership and maintenance. Celestino is a case in point. Clearly a musical man, he developed a reputation for himself by playing for Esteban and created a network with other musicians who regularly asked him to play.

CONFLICT, ENVY, AND WITCHCRAFT

Face-to-face relationships are still the primary mode of communication and social interaction in Rabinalense society. But conversations can be oblique to the point of incomprehensibility, because musicians will go to great lengths to avoid arousing the envy of others or falling victim to gossip.

Avoiding direct confrontation in social interaction is an important ethical principle of Achi society and explains why conversations tend to be indirect. When conflict or disagreement occurs, people attempt to reach consensus in a circumlocutory way, which can be a protracted process. If this fails, people try to avoid further contact. They physically withdraw to allow things to calm down, or, if this is not possible, they keep their silence, accepting the terms and conditions of the other party to the interaction, however unjust these might seem to be.

When people told me myths, legends, and stories, they nearly always began with "they say"—or, if there is a particular interest in identifying an individual, with "they say he says" or "he says they say"—in order to avoid responsibility for a direct accusation. The information is presented as common knowledge, which also gives it credence. This form of communication is particularly useful when the aim is to criticize or to gossip maliciously about someone about whom one feels resentful or envious. Gossip is an indirect form of communication about diffuse ideas and beliefs and the need to conform, and it is by definition unattributable.[6] People who malign others are said to be evil, with "bad hearts" (itzel winak); the phrase derives from the Achi word for witchcraft (itzib'al). Fear of witchcraft, like gossip and rumor, operates as a mechanism of self-control and as a means of enforcing the rules of social behavior, ensuring that no one stands out, either above or below anyone else.[7] The politeness that characterizes all Achi social interactions is a form of self-protection.

Mistrust and envy lurk beneath the surface of most conversations and are never expressed directly, least of all to the person(s) toward whom one has these feelings. Schulze Jena's (1954) description of personal relationships among the neighboring K'iche' in the late 1920s could easily have been written about the Achi in the 1990s:

> [A] secret envy awakes in the less fortunate and drives him to premeditated action. It only takes someone to be successful in an enterprise, to wear better clothes, to buy a piece of land, or to restore family happiness in a broken marriage. The Indian takes the happiness and good fortune of others as personal and direct damage because his lack of fortune is interpreted as having been set against the ancestors. To defend himself from this, he consults a diviner, begging him to put him in contact with the ancestors and to request punishment for the fortunate person in the same way he has caused the damage to him. In these situations mistrust develops, and envy may turn into a satanic hatred when the less fortunate feels degraded by another person. The person who suffers misfortune desires the greatest suffering, which is death, for the fortunate enemy and misery to his wife and children. He firmly believes that the witch's curse can bring his enemies illness, sadness, poverty, and death. In this way vengeance is diverted from direct violence. (43–44, my translation)

Awareness of these dangers drives people to do their utmost to convey a friendly and favorable impression when addressing someone directly. The friendly treatment I received throughout my stay in Rabinal was a subtle and effective way of neutralizing the potential danger of interacting with a stranger and reducing the differences between us arising from my status as a foreigner. They use the same mechanism to avoid conflict with their more powerful Ladino neighbors and thus protect themselves from harm.

Collective representations of envy and vengeance as a cause of failure and death are lived and interpreted daily through reference to the lives and fates of saints. The martyrdom of the saints functions as an archetypal model that is reenacted in the fate of the Achi people (cf. Eliade 1987). Midwife and ajq" mes (healer) Vicenta explained, "The saints did not die by natural illness but by envy. Yes, they died because of people's envy, they killed them. Isn't it written in the sacred book? All the saints died in that way. Just like us, we have resemblances with the saints and with Jesus here in life."

Musicians are the object of envy simply because they are endowed by God with knowledge and musical ability; they are also exposed to the dangerous consequences of competition for contracts. Each marimba ensemble and its musicians present a potential enemy from whom revenge can be expected; they come from another village or town. As marimbista Filemón Lajuj explained, "That is what happens with this instrument, it has envy, it creates envy. To play is dangerous, and sometimes it is a shame to play because there are evil people who are envious. There are other people who can play but perhaps they are not invited to come out to work. Perhaps they do not call them to play and one is selected to play, that is why they are envious."

Julián Ordoñez told me about the great envy of another family of conjunto marimba players, who were considered ladinoized because some of them had become professionals (lawyer, photographer, and accountant):

It was my son Juan who began to learn the pieza music. That is why the Jerónimo family don't like us—because we learned that music and bought fine instruments from Guatemala [City]. We bought a good drum set and some other things. . . . We went and played in other places and they started bothering us because they stopped playing, while we started playing more. When the drum set arrived by bus, they heard and came to see.

"Hello guys, did you come from Guatemala [City]?"

"Yes," I said.

"What did you bring?" they asked.

"Bread," we replied.

"Bones!" they said. "You are liars."

Later they came home to see and said, "Now you really kicked us well, guys!" and I responded, "You have your work, you are professionals, and us, what do we have? We only have hoes. We are just doing a little bit." That is why they don't like us.

This is typically disingenuous. The Ordoñez family is actually a wealthy Indian family; apart from having land to cultivate they are craftsmen potters as well as marimbistas. The Jerónimos, by contrast, have been marimbistas for a century. The Ordoñez family's acquisition of a conjunto marimba made them competitors in an arena that the Jerónimos felt was theirs. In an attempt to avoid conflict, Julián Ordoñez responded humbly to the Jerónimos when they first met, and again when they visited his home. But this time he could not resist adding a little criticism; by calling the Jerónimos "professionals" Julián implied that they had adopted a Ladino lifestyle. His reference to hoes suggested that the changes within his own family were "only those of peasants making a little improvement." Both parties were well aware of the other's circumstances, but this formal self-abasement is an essential means of avoiding conflict.

The Ordoñez family fell victim to the envy and vengeance of the members of another conjunto ensemble. Juan said, "We went to play at a party, and look what they did to us." "Who?" I asked.

> The Double M group. They had played for that family before, but this time they wanted the payment in advance, so the organizer of the party did not give the contract to them. Instead, he came to see us. And you know what they did because of that? The house was full of people, it was very happy, but they threw fireworks behind the marimba. Do you think people could stand that? Eeeeh! It was like chili! But we did not stop, playing although it was unbearable; I did not take a breath. All the people went outside the house. They did it because the party was going so well, that is what they did to us.

Esteban Uanché's antisocial and distant nature was also attributed to envy. According to Tono Cajbón, Esteban never came to pay his respects or chat with him when he was playing—which is not surprising, considering that Tono is usually drunk and abusive. But Tono was convinced that Esteban envied his playing: "Esteban is not a friend, because he is only watching us from afar in front of the church, he does not come to visit. The truth is that he feels uncomfortable if my marimba mozos play well and if my marimba has a good sound. He does not like it."

Because of the belief that one man's gain is another's loss (cf. Foster 1965), envy can lead to retaliation through witchcraft. I asked violinist Magdaleno Xitumul if he had feared witchcraft during the early years when he was learning to play. "No," he answered, "because how could I know if someone felt envious of me? In my thoughts, this instrument was only a toy." The responsibilities of musicianship do not apply to apprentices, so Magdaleno felt immune to envy. But once musicians acquire knowledge, older people are always challenging them by requesting difficult sones: "It seems they only do it to screw us and to see if we can play them."

Envy can also lead to allegations of witchcraft, as Victor Tum's experiences illustrate. Both an *abogado* and a musician, Victor was held responsible for a severe drought that caused crop failure in the valley lowlands. This was clearly witchcraft because Victor, who planted on higher land at the foot of the mountain, had a bumper crop that year. Naturally Victor was envied. But what generated the accusations of witchcraft was not simply that as an abogado Victor knew how to contact the spirits and direct rainfall his way; it was also what Victor and his crop partner did with their surplus, which was to stage the <u>Xajoj Tum</u> (Rabinal Achi) dance-drama. They were seen as paying their respects and expressing gratitude to the ancestors for their generosity, which was to celebrate publicly the misfortune of others. Local Catholics had a related but slightly different interpretation; they thought the drought was a punishment from God and that it was inappropriate to stage a dance-drama while the community was in disgrace. People were unimpressed by Victor's assurances that he had merely attempted to show the younger generation that the dance-drama had survived, despite its not being staged for a long time.

Witchcraft and Vengeance

The Achi people position themselves in the world through elaborating myths that give meaning to their lives. An example of this is the creation myth in which Jesus avoids becoming a victim of the Maya Wise Men's witchcraft by ignoring them (see Chapter 2). During and after *la violencia*, such stories enabled many religious-minded people to explain the persecutions and killings of community leaders and whole communities.

Local words for witchcraft include <u>itzib' al</u> (to make evil), *brujear*, *hacer brujo*, *maléfico*, *hechizo* (to practice witchcraft), and *mal hecho* (evil thoughts thrown into the air).[8] Witchcraft is a means of taking secret revenge on people toward whom one feels envy, jealousy, hate, or other "bad feelings"; it is a deliberate act that is believed to cause its victims genuine harm. It is performed in secret because people fear awakening others' "bad feelings" and provoking retaliation.

People who perform witchcraft are known as <u>ajq' itz</u> (evil ones). Their identity is kept secret, but people know where to find them if they want to. The Achi say there are witches among the *principales pasados* (past principals) of the *cofradías* who work as abogados; such men know how to call and address the spirits. Two abogados were identified to me as witches because they had abused other *mayordomos'* women during cofradía festivities and were considered evil. The evil <u>ajq" itz</u> is opposed to the good abogado, the <u>ajq" mes</u> (healer) and <u>ajq" iij</u> (diviner).[9]

Vicious forms of witchcraft against musicians include secretly ruining their musical instruments. Esteban Uanché told me that there are still many witches in the neighboring town of Cubulco; one of them is a fellow marimba repairer named Raymundo, who ruined a marimba that Esteban had taken to him to tune because he had been unable to repair it himself.[10]

> He has done [witchcraft] to me. Some time ago I had a marimba and we were rehearsing the Costeño dance in Palimonix hamlet. I realized that one of the keys was not tuned properly, so when we played the music we skipped that key. The next day I took the marimba to Raymundo in Cubulco to repair the key. When I arrived I asked him to fix the key, and you know what this man did? He planed the whole keyboard, and when I returned to test it, neither the sones nor the Costeño dance could be played, only the piezas and one or two sones like the Zacualpa and the Mixito Marcado. I was furious, so I only gave him four quetzales (then equivalent to $4) because I had not asked him to tune the whole keyboard. But what could I do? I returned with the marimba on horseback and arrived home by four o'clock. That night I tried to play again and nothing, it was worse! It sounded like knocking on a piece of wood board. That man Raymundo had done brujo because I had not paid for his work because I did not ask him to plane the whole keyboard. I was very sad, crying. The marimba had cost me eighty quetzales and now I had nothing. I wanted to burn it, to get rid of it once and for all, but my wife did not allow me to do so. As you know we have our patron [an ajq" itz] in Cimayac Mazatenango. They are *chingones* [excellent] at carrying out witchcraft there. Then we wrote a letter to him and sent it. I was desperate, but in two weeks we got a letter back saying that I should not worry, he was going to get the voice of Huehuetenango [a town famous for making good marimbas] for my marimba. I only needed to send forty quetzales to do a mass, to make a devotion [to pray with candles], a responsory, and a *novena*. He said that I should not worry because what they had done to the marimba was to tune up in B-flat. The following day I played the marimba and it sounded beautifully. But I did not like it anymore. The marimba is like a woman and it seemed as if it had been raped, so I did not want it, knowing that someone else had already abused her. I decided to sell it to Gaspar, the marimba merchant from Huehuetenango. In the end Gaspar sold it to Raymundo from Cubulco.

As Evans-Pritchard (1976, 25) explains, "the attribution of misfortune to witchcraft does not exclude what we call its real causes but is superimposed on them and gives to social events their moral value." Esteban knew that some of the son repertoire sounded wrong because Raymundo had planed the keyboard, but he did not know the technical details of changing the tuning by that procedure. Instead he thought the change in sound was the result of Raymundo's having taken revenge for not receiving proper payment. It was not until Esteban received a written response from the ajq" itz from

Mazatenango and read his words of power and authority that he started to hear that the marimba sounded better—although in a different key.

A similar connection is made when a musician falls ill; people believe that someone has poisoned him. The *atol* or *chilate* (corn-based gruel) or *trago* (sugar cane spirits) given to musicians during festivities may be laced with something deadly. A case of witchcraft by poisoning was related to me by Maria, the violinist Magdaleno Xitumul's wife. She claimed that her father was poisoned and killed because people were maliciously envious of him for being a musician.

This case reveals not only the conflict arising out of envy for musicians but the conflictive relationship between evangelicals and Catholics within families. Maria told me:

> My father died because he played [music]; they poisoned him [because of this]. He played the violin and they killed him because of that. Back then my father was living with my evangelical brother in town and people were constantly begging him to play for them. On one occasion he went out to play, and he says that their first stop was the cemetery where they went to bring the souls of the dead; it was only a forty-day celebration. When they returned to the house, he said, they were waiting for him with a tasty-looking gourd, filled with atol and *cacao* [corn beverage containing cocoa]. Because he was thirsty he took it and drank it, but he soon discovered that it did not go down [well]. He felt like his heart, his stomach was full. So he went out of the house to vomit it all up, but not everything came out. The atol came out but the poison remained inside.
>
> My father did not tell us anything, he only said he was dying. Then he told me that somebody had given him something to drink; he did not tell us [before] because of my brother. My brother gets angry and scolds us. He used to say to my father: "Why are you going out to play? Leave all that nonsense [referring to the musical performances of Catholic custom]. You go to play but when you get sick the money you earn will not be enough to cure you."

Perhaps the potential exposure to harm during every social occasion where musicians perform contributes to their obsession about fulfilling their obligations to both the living and the dead. Behaving in the proper way according to their special role gives them a sense of protection.

FRIENDSHIP

The daily cultivation of friendship—musicians' political strategies to prevent social conflict, expand their social networks, and gain greater access to and control over musical production while blocking others' access to these advantages—is a crucial survival technique. Musicians have to create and maintain friendships not only among themselves but also with the people they serve.

Acting respectfully, courteously, and reliably is essential to establishing friendship. Again, the family is considered the best model, for family relationships—at least among male family members[11]—are based on trust and respect, which is why the marimba should be taught within the family. The important principle of hierarchy and a concomitant respect for seniority within the family is duplicated in both learning process and performance. Yet despite the cultural emphasis on the respect due to elders and their knowledge, an overly hierarchical relationship (where seniority means authoritarianism) can lead to the failure of an ensemble. The treble has to approach his center and bass players, including mozos, with modesty and humility, as though he is asking a favor and looking for their companionship. This is a general social rule among adults and contrasts strongly with the treatment given to boys.[12] Tono Cajbón was not the only impatient father who mistreated his sons to such an extent that they lost interest in playing with him. Yet Tono told me that "friendship is everything." I was looking for a marimba to buy at the time. "There is a marimba in Chiticoy hamlet," he told me. "Julio Oxlaj just bought it in March this year, but he is selling it because he could not find *compañía* [other musicians to play with]. He could not find compañía because friendship is everything. If he does not have friendship, he will not have compañía. If you have friends you can go wherever."

A lack of respect for the principle of seniority can have the same result. In two cases fathers left the family group because they could not bear the loss of authority they felt when their sons had to teach them the latest piezas.

The creation of trust and respect is of the utmost importance at rehearsals, when musicians from outside the household, especially mozos, share the intimate life of the marimba owner; his family might gossip about them, which would have a negative impact on the owner's opinions of them. Celestino and Bernabé temporarily stopped playing with Mincho Torres because he accused Bernabé (who, like Celestino, is married with children) of courting one of his daughters; he even went so far as to tell Bernabé that a member of his family had seen the couple together in the fields. Bernabé flatly denied the accusation and he and Celestino promptly left the group.

Friendships among young men, whether related or not, facilitate the conditions of trust and sociability essential to sharing the cost of buying a marimba and investing the time in learning to play. Marcelo Ixpata told me, "I learned when I was twenty-two. I became interested in playing because my friends pushed me to learn. They said, 'Play, man, play; it is easy to learn.' That was in the hamlet of Nimacabaj; I learned to play there. I have friends there and in Xococ."

But for Bonifacio Jerónimo's father, joining a marimba ensemble was an excuse to socialize and get drunk among friends. "My father tried to play," said Bonifacio, "he bought a marimba with two other friends. They were kin, but not brothers, and so they gathered to play and play but they developed the vice of drinking while playing, so they were learning more to drink! My grandfather did not like it and admonished my father, who then decided it was better to stop playing."

Friendship gives musicians access to contracts and thus increases their opportunities to play. Musicians are keen to point out that they have friends (social contacts) all over the place. Success is measured by enumerating the different places where they have played; the inclusion of remote hamlets and villages indicates that their reputation extends far and wide. Musicians often say, "We have been all over Rabinal municipality," by which they mean those settlements that correspond to their sense of community. Only a few son Marimbistas and members of conjunto ensembles whose reputation extends beyond Rabinal mentioned performing in nearby municipalities, such as Ladino-dominated Cubulco or predominantly Ladino El Chol and Granados.

ACHI–LADINO RELATIONS

The common Achi assertion that the marimba is the creation of the ancestors should be understood as a metaphorical statement describing the instrument's acceptance in Rabinal's ritual life. As I have shown in Chapter 4, the marimba was first introduced into the municipality 100 years ago and was played primarily by Indians for Ladino social occasions before moving slowly into the Achi social sphere.

In fact, the marimba only became widely accepted for Achi religious celebrations in the 1950s. The changes instituted by Arbenz's reformist government—abolition of the old labor laws, institution of a minimum wage—meant that many Achi people had small amounts of money to spend. Some invested in marimbas; others went to the cantina, where Ladino cantineros hosted *zarabandas* to attract business. Several new cantinas were opened in the early 1950s.

The second impetus for change came from an unexpected quarter: the Ladino mayor. In 1951 municipal mayor and teacher Mario Valdizon, together with a group of teachers from Rabinal, tried to boost civic education and culture within a nationalist framework. Aware of the enthusiasm with which Indians celebrated anniversaries of the dead and of the impact of the recently introduced marimba on these events, Mario and his friends decided to inculcate civic virtues by organizing the same kind of celebration for the anniversaries of the Revolution (20 October) and Independence (14–15 September).[13] To ensure marimbistas' cooperation, the municipal authorities decreed that marimba ensembles could play in the cemetery for the celebrations of the dead (1–2 November) only after obtaining a license from the municipality. This license was granted exclusively to those groups that agreed to play in the plaza on the national holidays, performing for twelve hours on each occasion, free of charge. This much-resented decision actually gave Rabinal's nascent marimba tradition a large boost.

The alliance between Rabinal's teachers and the municipal authorities has continued to the present day. They are still trying to determine the practice of the marimba tradition and attempting to manipulate, adjust, and adapt the Indian community's conventional symbols and meanings to serve as a symbol of national unity. They are party to the state's systematic exploitation of the sociopolitical power of the musical tradition, which is achieved mainly through its ideological institutions for education and culture and serves the hegemonic interests of the powerful elite. Self-serving Ladino and Indian teachers promote Indian folklore as part of the national identity and the cultural heritage of Guatemala. They have, for example, occasionally hired both son and pieza marimbistas to perform at folklore festivals in Salamá, Cobán, and Guatemala City.

Participation in these folklore festivals is ambiguous and problematic for musicians. One the one hand, the patronage of these teachers gives musicians prestige; on the other, they pay the price of being manipulated by the Ladinos who organize these events for their own political and economic ends.

Well-known musicians are also hired by ladinoized Indians and Ladinos to give credibility to the events they sponsor. During the 1995 election campaign, for instance, local Ladino political campaign managers hired Rabinal's most respected son marimbistas to play for them. Almost every political party used son marimba music to identify their political agenda with Indian tradition and to suggest that both shared the same ideological interests. Apart from periods of political unrest, election campaigns are the only occasions on which Ladinos show any interest in marimbistas' many friends and extended social network. They rely on these friends and fans to come and listen to the marimba, which is set up near the entrance to the political party's offices.

The party whose policies come closest to Indians' interests is probably the Comité Cívico de Mejoramiento Municipal (Civic Committee for Municipal Improvement); it expresses an unusual amount of social sympathy but lacks political and economic power. It too hires marimbistas, but of the kind that like to play for *devoción*, which can also be read as playing for poor people. During my stay, the Comité Cívico chose these marimbistas not simply because they couldn't afford more expensive musicians but to convey a democratic message.

During these elections, I traveled to Cubulco with Esteban Uanché. Walking down the main street, we heard marimba music emanating from the PAN (National Advancement Party) stand. "Hey, listen, that's my marimba," exclaimed Esteban, who dashed in to make enquiries. He greeted everyone present and then asked if they knew who was playing.

"I don't know, but I think the tape comes from Rabinal."

"Well, yes, it's me playing."

Esteban then asked who had supplied the tape and appeared satisfied with the answer. As we continued on our way, he remarked proudly, "Everyone here knows me." Although he remained suspicious about the tape's origins, he was extremely pleased to know that a powerful party in Cubulco—a musically respected town—was using his music to attract people. He was equally happy that he had proved to me just how famous he was. I could not tell him that these Ladino politicians were unlikely to know that son styles vary from municipio to municipio, let alone understand what these differences represent. In fact, it was highly incorrect politically to play the marimba style of Rabinal in the land of prestigious Cubulco musicians.

Ladino Patronage

Economic, social, and political power in Rabinal is generally in the hands of ladinoized Indian merchants, teachers, and town Ladinos generally. The Achi population regards them as the "other" part of Rabinalense society because their cultural and social interests are different from their own, an attitude that reinforces the gap between them. Because of the power Ladinos hold, Indians try to bridge the social distance between them by forming "friendships," thus empowering themselves through this identification (Tumin 1952).

Musicians who enjoy the prestige of having Ladino clients would never substitute them for their Indian clientele, who provide them with most of their contracts. But playing for Ladinos gives them higher status and recognition as good players; this in turn provides them and their playing styles with authority over other musicians, and they thus become the de facto representatives of—and often the innovators within—Rabinal's marimba music tradition. From the Ladino perspective, playing for Ladino celebrations grants Indian musicians a special place as representatives of the Indian tradition, which absorbs and encompasses a popular repertory and is their festivities' source of joy. There are very few instances in which Indian knowledge and tradition exert such definite power in a Ladino context and where Ladinos, sometimes grudgingly, have no alternative but to accept their central role in the celebration.

With the requisite air of modesty but nevertheless making sure I understood that his group played for Ladinos, Julián Ordoñez told me how Indians wearing <u>caites</u> (Indian sandals) overcame the Ladinos' disparaging attitude toward Indians through sheer endurance, playing throughout the celebration while the audience got blind drunk.

> Somewhere in Chol, we went to play and one of them [a fat man] told me, "This is the Indian who is going to play here." He said, since he was already drunk, "These are *caitudos* [people wearing <u>caites</u>—a derogatory reference to Indians]; I know them, those who come to play." Ha! Son of a bitch, I thought. Then the companion of the man who was talking came and embraced him [in order to overwhelm him] and said, "Look here, Alpidio, stop talking, he's caitudo but you never know. You are full of yourself, but this caitudo is going to trash you later, remember," he said. "Balls," said the fat man. By nine o'clock people started to dance. Ah! the fat man was thrown on the floor and there he lay once and for all. Where was all that he was talking about? He couldn't even hear what we did [played] anymore. Well.

Julián adopted a subordinate, humble, and controlled posture when recounting the derogatory remarks made by the Ladinos about Indians, thus indicating that he responded to their provocation without aggression. He also demonstrated that he was stronger than the Ladino. His quiet and stoical endurance gave him power.

Ladinos' general ignorance of son marimba music increases the prestige of piezas as far as Indians are concerned. Some musicians cultivate relationships with Ladinos not just to expand their work opportunities but as a means of identifying with them; learning piezas to accommodate Ladino musical preferences makes musicians more versatile and is a form of social capital that gives them power and authority.

THE MILITARY

Some musicians' friendly relations with army officers, paramilitary police, military commissioners, and PAC chiefs, initiated at the height of the political violence (1981–83), still give rise to suspicion, even though friendly relations were essential to both economic and literal survival at the time. The possession of a safe-conduct pass from the army not only spared musicians' lives but also allowed them freedom of movement, which they needed if they were to win contracts. This gave "approved" musicians an advantage over others who, for one reason or another, could not or would not play, especially over musicians from the remote mountain hamlets. Included under the rubric <u>aj paq'ees'</u> (mountain people), hamlet dwellers fell victim to the phrase's symbolic meaning, that is, someone who lives outside God's realm—hence a devil, savage, pagan, or rebel. This association hampered mountain marimbistas' attempts to secure contracts, as the public strictly avoided anyone or anything the military considered subversive.

Because the army banned social gatherings with marimba music during the violence, contracts had to be approved by the military authorities, which frequently meant playing for the army. For example, a few weeks after the massacre of everyone (including marimbistas) in Rabinal's plaza on Independence Day (15 September) 1982, the army co-opted marimba ensembles to play for twelve hours on market days (Thursdays and Sundays) to provide a false sense of security and encourage people to come out of their homes and shop. In return for playing, these marimbistas were exempted from patrol duty. Tono Cajbón was one of these privileged musicians:

> When we settled in Rabinal after escaping from the massacre up there in Plan de Sanchez, the first gig we got was in the cofradía of San Jose. During the first day the *judiciales* [paramilitary police] came looking for us. They were following us again. But because I knew Don Lucas, the chief [military] commissioner, I rang him from the military headquarters and asked him to tell the soldiers and judiciales not to kill me because I was already fulfilling my obligation to perform in the town square, that is, my Sunday shift playing the marimba at the square every week. Yes, every Sunday I was forced to play there, and that is why I am still alive. Otherwise, ugh! I would be dead. I am friends with all the military commissioners and the chief, so they know me and that is why they gave me safe conduct, which they presented at the military headquarters; and then they released me.

These safe-conduct passes bestowed some of the army's prestige and power on the holder long after they ceased to be necessary. Only when the army itself lost some of its power and prestige did these pieces of paper lose their symbolic potency.

The general public responded ambivalently to the position in which musicians found themselves. They envied musicians' privileges, which derived from their musical knowledge. They also saw them as the army's allies and, as such, treated them with the same respect and distrust as they did the military. This ambivalence produced in the musicians a sense of power, in the same way that people feel the protection and power of the military in wearing camouflage suits, army boots, or belt buckles made from bullets.

THE LOCAL CONCEPT of "friendship," which extends to and overlaps with patronage and protection, permeates the Achi musician's world. However the concept is defined—and the Achi define it in terms of family attitudes and feelings of respect and trust—friendship has gained increasing importance in the aftermath of la violencia, as people reconstruct their families and social relationships in the face of (often huge) personal losses.

Friendship is particularly important for musicians whose position in the social structure has always been ambiguous. While they are agriculturalists and migrant workers like most everyone else, their musicianship sets them apart. Musicians have always been envied simply because of their good fortune in receiving the special gift of musicianship from God. Musicians need good social skills to manage their personal relationships and to prevent the harmful effects of envy and revenge. Their respect for and acknowledgment of other people's needs is seen as effective protection from witchcraft.

People also envy musicians' role in communicating with the supernatural world and their ability to call forth in people the expression of emotions usually suppressed in everyday life. Marimbistas are particularly vulnerable to envy because, unlike other musicians, their music has a wider audience, outside the ritual context. This means that their personal behavior and social relationships come under closer scrutiny than those of other Achi musicians. It also means that marimbistas' ability to form the relationships so essential to getting contracts with people outside the immediate community can and does come under suspicion. Some people still harbor resentment against marimbistas for what they deem a misuse of the very social and musical skills that enabled them to survive la violencia. This resentment is complex and extends not only to musicians' survival but to their exemption from the civil patrols, which means that they were not forced to kill anyone.

Sociality and musical competence are, then, interrelated if not indivisible. Prestige is not simply vested in a musician's musical technique or in the breadth of his repertoire but depends on visible evidence of his social skills, namely, his ability to obtain contracts and his capacity to satisfy people's demands, both musically and socially speaking. The satisfaction of participants' intentions and desires extends from the performance of daily social interaction to the musical performance, and from the social interaction in musical performance to performance in daily life.

Friendship, understood as musical patronage, emerges in full force in the conflictive context of Indian-Ladino relationships. I have shown how Achi marimbistas look for friendship within the Ladino population as a way of gaining power and legitimacy, especially within their own social or ethnic group. Without a doubt, they also value the respect and recognition gained from Ladinos in the process, for with this comes not only a greater sense of self-affirmation and safety, but also the promise of additional contracts.

10 Conclusion

"Who Am I to Know Better Than the Ancestors?"

FOR THE RABINALENSE ACHI, son marimba music is the tradition of the ancestors, which goes back to the dawning of the sun and the creation of the World of Light (the introduction of Christianity). In fact, however, Rabinal's marimba tradition began in the twentieth century.

Drawing on historical sources, life histories, myths, and rites, this book has endeavored to shed light on the emergence, diffusion, adoption, and transmission of a musical tradition that is understood locally as a way of making sense of the world. "We cannot do anything more or create anything different from that which already exists," said Juan Manuel Jerónimo. "Who am I to know better than the ancestors?" Musician Eligio Gonzalez was even more explicit: "Everything we are doing now was already done before by the Lord, it was done by the Maya. We are not doing anything other than that which God left for us. . . . We cannot make anything just like that. Not us, not even the United States [can]."

"Making sense of the world" becomes even more important during periods of rapid and sometimes extremely violent change. Belief in the dead, which is the heart of local Catholicism, provides a sense of historical continuity and cultural integrity. Past generations of Achi have passed down *el costumbre* (the custom or tradition) that "allows the world to continue," so long as subsequent generations continue to perpetuate its practice. For the Rabinalense Achi, son music and prayers open the path of communication with God and the omnipresent ancestors (who include Jesus, the saints, the spirit owners of the world, and the dead). Men whose God-given fate is to be musicians or *abogados* have the lifelong burden of guiding ritual activity with their offerings of prayers and music. Enacting and reenacting the deeds of the ancestors "helps make tradition," which pleases the ancestors, who, as a gesture of the goodwill thus generated between the living and the dead, assist the living with their appeals to God.

Colonial and national authorities have tried for centuries to suppress or at least reduce the number of Indian celebrations on the grounds that they cause social disorder (and especially sexual license) and contribute both to Indian poverty and to Indians' reluctance to work. One of the difficulties facing the authorities has been that these celebrations took place largely within the framework of the *cofradía* system, which they had themselves introduced as a means of encouraging Indians to celebrate the festivities of the Catholic ritual calendar. Another difficulty has been the conflict between central and local authorities for the control of the Indian labor force. The outcome has been ambiguous policies, such as the central authorities' ban on the sale of alcohol to Indians at the very time that local authorities were establishing cantinas to sell it to them. Thus, on the one hand, celebrations were being prohibited while, on the other, local business interests were encouraging them for commercial reasons. These opposing positions are reflected in the Achi moral ideology, which differentiates between the positive connotations of male music making and female nurturance and the negative connotations of male drinking and female sexuality. This ideology identifies women with the Marian or demonic voices of the marimba; women are both the living carriers of Maya tradition and the cause of men's selfishness, loss of will, failure, and death. This belief legitimizes an ideology of male domination within both ritual and everyday life. Female sexuality is still seen as potentially disruptive to social life. Yet there are limits to this; self-interested behavior is more commonly associated with Ladinos, who are seen as lacking community values and therefore as evil.

Music is a metaphor for women, just as women can be a metaphor for music. The son and the marimba have a common origin in the cofradía celebrations and *zarabandas* of the colonial era. The central authorities' numerous attempts to control the former and ban the latter have been internalized in terms of the positive and negative associations of womankind.

In the past forty years the cofradías and the *cargo* system have gradually lost their role as the primary institution through which Achi people gain status, prestige, and political and religious influence, and justify individual economic differentiation. Victor Tum, an elderly abogado, once told me that Protestantism[1] and schools were the two main forces that were "finishing off the Achi race." Victor believed that religious conversions and a Spanish-language, Ladino-oriented education were the most tangible ideological reasons for people's reluctance to speak Achi or to "make the service of God" (hold a cofradía cargo). As far as he was concerned, neither the capitalist market economy nor the political violence is directly responsible for the decline of the cofradía, because these things are beyond people's control. Nevertheless, capitalism and political violence have led people to pare down traditional celebrations, though religious belief itself seems unchanged. Anniversaries of the dead are not in decline at all—or at least they weren't during the time when the clandestine graves of people murdered during la violencia were being exhumed.

Abogados and musicians were in constant demand, celebrating the four-teenth and final celebrations for relatives who had been assassinated or "disappeared" during the violence. During this period, son music, played on marimba and by violin-and-*adufe* ensembles, played their customary religious role, adapting to special circumstances of mourning during the celebration of collective anniversaries of the dead.

Most of the Achi people's politically conscious leaders supported the organization of these collective celebrations for the exhumed remains of victims of the massacres. Belief in the dead, central to Achi identity, was brought to the forefront of political action. Even if the cofradías are in decline, it is likely that demand for the services of son musicians and abo-gados will endure.

The simplification of ritual practice has also affected the variety of instrumental ensembles and repertoires, resulting in an increasing empha-sis on the marimba. For instance, the reluctance of the younger genera-tion to learn the "little music" of the violin and adufe suggests that this ensemble could disappear. The marimba is already playing alongside vio-lin and adufe in invocations of the dead (though not yet in front of the altar), and allegedly playing the same *sones* for the souls. It has also become the music of choice for zarabandas, weddings, modern dance-dramas, and, most important, celebrations in the cemetery on the Day of the Dead.

Performance of Rabinal's rich dance-drama repertoire has also been simplified and reduced. Nowadays, only a handful of dance-dramas are performed, although the most popular one (*el costeño*) is staged by sev-eral groups simultaneously at virtually every cofradía fiesta. The marimba is now the most popular instrument for this genre and it is also proving to be the means through which the popular urban *piezas* associated with Ladinos are infiltrating the musical tradition.

This situation echoes the introduction of the marimba around fifty years ago. The new music and dance styles are popular with the dancers, who, with a few exceptions, are boys and young unmarried men to whom piezas represent sophistication and knowledge of the outside world—just as the marimba did a generation ago. Nevertheless, the roles they perform, the choreography they follow, and the iconography of their costumes are all part of the oral tradition of el costumbre. This merging of new trends with traditional dance-drama forms and ritual practice allows the rising male generation to learn and participate in el costumbre without losing face through association with the old fogies of local Catholic circles. It allows them to be protagonists in social and religious events without the need for much knowledge or skill (at least in the minor roles) and with-out having to participate in the economically onerous cargo system. Participation is attractive to boys and youths, as it provides opportunities for social interaction and a means of gaining admiration and prestige. Dance-dramas' religious function is a secondary consideration for these young people, although the dance-drama still functions as a playful, dynamic, and creative link with the ways of the ancestors, drawing boys and young men into the cofradía. As dance director Domingo Alvarado told me, "without dances there is no cofradía."

The introduction of pieza music into ritual practice is, on an ideological level, quite revolutionary. Pieza music is associated with Ladinos and interpreted within the framework of the conflictive dynamic of Ladino power and Indian subordination.[2] Thus, on the one hand, the music is associated with Ladinos' lack of (Achi) social values, while on the other it is seen as a source of empowerment that stems from an identification of piezas with urban Ladino power. This does not necessarily mean that the Achi people aspire to a Ladino identity; these days, being Indian has acquired greater positive value—even a Ladino taxi driver in the capital refers to Guatemala as "GuateMaya"! Rather, this empowerment can be considered a form of appropriation—since piezas are produced by Achi musicians for both fellow Achi and Ladinos—invested with connotations of power challenging. At the same time, musicians hope to meet the expectations of the majority, especially the older Achi generations and the dead—beginning with the recent dead, who heard the music during their time on earth.

That so many people (including the dead) are familiar with piezas is largely due to technological modernization. For example, feeding the "green revolution" with fertilizers and pesticides assured modern dependence on wage work and commodities and hence increased population movement; migration to the cities for work exposed many people to pieza music. For others, the introduction of transistor radios and cassette recorders brought pieza music to their rural communities.

These and other forces of social and cultural change have caused significant changes in the Achi musical tradition. Within a decade of the introduction of radios and cassette players, the political violence of the early 1980s wiped out almost an entire generation of *marimbistas* in Rabinal; with them went some of the older sones. Perhaps this gave an added impetus to the current, almost compulsive practice of taping music, whether live or from the radio. The death and destruction of the early 1980s certainly led to changes in teaching and learning methods, and many young men now learn from the radio and tapes. These and other changes in teaching and learning methods, the innovations within the tradition, and the incorporation and adaptation of new instruments (such as the marimba de pieza or the marimba de conjunto), styles, and repertoires into Rabinal's ritual life indicates that musical change is not only welcomed but rapidly assimilated into the sacred realm of exchange between the living and the dead. In other words, it is interpreted within the framework of what is still the most important source of Achi identity, the belief in the dead. By bringing the innovation into this framework, continuity is assured.

Modernization and the incorporation of the marimba and its son and pieza repertoire into the ritual life of the Achi people has resulted not in westernization but in the syncretic adaptation and appropriation of new instruments, repertoires, and styles, and has transformed them into what the Achi believe is an ancestral tradition. Once accepted, these new cultural elements are deemed to have existed since the beginning of the World of Light.

For decades, anthropological studies in Guatemala have been concerned with ethnicity and cultural change. For example, anthropologists (e.g., Adams 1959) once believed that, as a consequence of the rapid and violent modernization of Guatemala during the mid-twentieth century, the nineteenth-century dream of ladinoizing (assimilating) and integrating Indian societies into Western ways was finally being realized. Social scientists have seen discrete changes in clothing and language as major cultural indicators and interpreted them as loss of Maya identity. While the massive population movement to the major cities, particularly the capital, during the 1980s might seem to support this view, my analysis of the indigenous marimba music tradition suggests that change does not necessarily mean loss of identity.

Indeed, the contemporary emergence of a pan-Maya cultural movement and the increasing presence of Maya leaders in the national political arena contradict the conventional prognosis. Adams (1994) has retracted his linear view of social evolution and, acknowledging that, despite "civilization," the ladinoization of Indian identity is not taking place, now proposes the co-evolution of Ladino and Indian cultures. Other anthropologists (e.g., Warren 1992, 1993; Watanabe 1994; Wilson 1995) have also attempted to explain the revitalization of ethnic movements and the continuity of Maya identity within the context of deep and rapid social change. Warren (1992) has studied the endurance of Maya ethnic ideology in the contemporary Kaq'chikel concepts concerning Ladino domination. Wilson (1995) has documented the new attitudes of Q'eqchi' urban catechists who have revitalized ancient myths and turned them into political and cultural symbols of Q'eqchi' ethnic identity. The symbols they used in their struggles against the traditional power structures of Catholicism in the 1970s have now been reoriented to support the search for a unified Q'eqchi' identity in opposition to Ladino society.

AMONG THE ACHI, as among most Maya groups, identity is based on descent; hence social and material change in the conditions of musical production must continue to please the musical taste of the ancestors, which is portrayed as static and unchanging. It may be argued that the musical changes analyzed here do not amount to a change of musical system but are adaptations to new material and social circumstances. This is because the musical strategies continue to be framed within the paradigms of ancestry and of a divided bi-ethnic society.

One of the central aims of this book has been to analyze cultural change and cultural construction and to demonstrate how older forms and relationships are adapted to new situations. The inventiveness of tradition (Sahlins 1993, 1999) goes beyond the resiliency of Maya cultures. Certainly it is not a view about the essentialism of deeper structures or, on the contrary, a frivolous approach to political manipulations of culture by local agents. It underlines the ways musicians and audiences appropriate cultural changes and construct a view about their cultural practices that corresponds with previous worldviews. Modernity does not oppose tradition; it is appropriated and interpreted as part of Achi tradition.

The argument that musical communication is not limited to performance but extends to the social relations between the participants springs from the Achi people's pervasive preoccupation with friendship. Friendship (and/or patronage) is essential to maintaining a good image and gaining contracts; it is also vital in order to avoid gossip, envy, and witchcraft. Musicians' views about their own music take into account the views

FIGURE 10.1. Flying "souls" over cemetery. Photo by Judith Zur.

of the community. My analysis therefore goes beyond musical performance per se and addresses social issues as well. Feld's idea of musical communication, which is limited to the context in which music is heard (1984), is therefore of limited value for my purposes.

I hope with this book to have made a small contribution to the anthropological study of music as part of a larger social process. From this point of view, music making or, more precisely, social interaction in musical performance, is only a stage of the social relationships of musical production.

Contents of Compact Disc

Maya Achi Marimba Music Recorded by Sergio Navarrete Pellicer. Time: 37:52

Track 1. Cofradía soundscape with music and prayers. Recorded in Rabinal, Baja Verapaz, 1994. Time: 1:28.

Track 2. Amanecido son. Marimba La Reina Rabinalense. Esteban Uanché (treble), Celestino Cajbón (center), Mincho Uanché (bass). Recorded in Rabinal, Baja Verapaz, 1995. Time: 2:57.

Track 3. Cumbia pieza. Marimba Marim-Balam. Celestino Cajbón (treble), Bernabé Cajbón (center), Trinidad Cajbón (bass). Recorded in Rabinal, Baja Verapaz, 1995. Time: 1:47.

Track 4. Son for the Negritos dance-drama. Pipe-and-tabor ensemble. Brígido Coloch (pipe and tabor), Melesio Coloch (pipe and tabor). Recorded in Rabinal, Baja Verapaz, 1994. Time: 2:18.

Track 5. Cofradía son "Guerra." Flute-and-big-drum ensemble. Juan Juarez (flute), Francisco Cortéz Piox (big drum). Time: 2:17.

Track 6. Son music to raise the souls of the dead. Violin-and-adufe ensemble. Magdaleno Xitumul (violin), Feliciano Chen (adufe). Time: 2:29.

Track 7. Son of the Rabinal Achi dance-drama. Tum-and-trumpets ensemble. Jose León Coloch (tum or slit drum), Victor Sarpec Tum (trumpet one), Pedro Morales Kojom (trumpet two). Recorded in Rabinal, Baja Verapaz, 1994. Time: 2:09.

Track 8. Contradanza. Marimba pieza. Marimba Marim-Balam. Celestino Cajbón (treble), Bernabé Cajbón (center), Trinidad Cajbón (bass). Recorded in Rabinal, Baja Verapaz, 1995. Time: 1:45.

Track 9. Marimba pieza: Danza de la muerte. Marimba Marim-Balam. Celestino Cajbón (treble), Bernabé Cajbón (center), Trinidad Cajbón (bass). Recorded in Rabinal, Baja Verapaz, 1995. Time: 2:48.

Track 10. Waltz. Naranjales de Rabinal (by Antonio Luna). Marimba Reina del Ejercito. Time: 2:25.

Track 11. Marimba son: Entrada. Marimba La Reina Rabinalense. Esteban Uanché (treble), Celestino Cajbón (center), Mincho Uanché (bass). Recorded in Rabinal, Baja Verapaz, 1995. Time: 1:52.

Track 12. Marimba son: Costa chiquita. Marimba La Reina Rabinalense. Esteban Uanché (treble), Celestino Cajbón (center), Mincho Uanché (bass). Recorded in Rabinal, Baja Verapaz, 1995. Time: 3:14.

Track 13. Marimba son: San Pablo. Marimba La Reina Rabinalense. Esteban Uanché (treble), Celestino Cajbón (center), Mincho Uanché (bass). Recorded in Rabinal, Baja Verapaz, 1995. Time: 5:23.

Track 14. Prayers and violin-and-adufe son for the dead. Violin-and-adufe ensemble. Magdaleno Xitumul (violin), Feliciano Chen (adufe). Recorded in Rabinal, Baja Verapaz, 1995. Time: 3:17.

Track 15. Son San Juan: Q'eqchi' zarabanda ensemble. Francisco Xii Cau (gourd guitar), Domingo Ramos Xii Ba (harp), Santiago Xii Ba (violin), Ana Laura Cau Xii (percussion on harp box). Recorded in Paapa Chamelco, Alta Verapaz, 2004. Time: 1:41.

Appendix 1
Orthography

THE ORTHOGRAPHY of the Achi language used in this book is that suggested by Antonio López, a lingüistic authority in Rabinal. Except for the signs (aa, ee, ii, oo, uu), this alphabet coincides with that used by Alain Breton (1994) in his major work on the Rabinal Achi dance-drama text. Breton simplified the signs used in the most important historical vocabularies, dictionaries, and grammars of K'i and K'qchikel' languages.

The alphabet has thirty-two signs or phonemes:

'(apostroph or glottal stop), **a, aa, b, ch,** ch', e, ee, i, ii, j, k, k', l, **m, n, o, oo, p, q, q',** r, s, t, t', tz, tz', **u, uu, w,** x, y.

Most signs have the same pronunciation as in Spanish. Double vowels are slight prolongations of the vowel sound. In lingüistic terminology, the following signs are considered:

ch'	Glottal palatal fricative
k'	Glottal velar
q'	Glottal uvular
t'	Glottal alveolar
tz'	Glottal fricative alveolar
x	Fricative (sounds like "sh" in English)

All Achi words in this book are underlined.

Appendix 2
Cofradías

	Cofradías in Descending Order of Importance	Paired with Image/ Cofradía of:	Celebration Dates of "Big Days"	Comments
1	Divinio Sacramento del altar, also known as Ajaw (lord, sun)	Virgen del Sacramento, also known as Ixoc Ajaw (female lord)	Corpus Cristi, a Thursday between 23 May and 25 June	Corpus Cristi marks the start of the ritual year and is its most important festival. The third general wake of the year and procession of the saints
2	Virgen del Rosario	San José	7 October	
3	San Pablo, the patron saint of Rabinal—resides in the center of town in the church	His "older" brother, San Pedro Apostol, patron of the SE quarter of Rabinal	25 January (the Conversion of St Paul)	The burden of this cofradía rotates through the four quarters. Cattle fair
4	Virgen de la Natividad	The image of the child Jesus (the cofradía of the Dulce Nombre de Jesus)	8 September	
5	Santa Cruz	Ixoc (woman) Elena (the cofradía of Elena de la Cruz)	3 May	This is the only image with cofradías with mayordomos in each hamlet.
6	San Pedro Apostol, patron of the SE quarter of Rabinal	His "younger" brother, San Pablo, the patron saint of Rabinal	29 June (the Festival of San Pedro and San Pablo)	The second-most important of Rabinal's cofradías. As the older brother of San Pablo he is considered very important.

(continued)

	Cofradías in Descending Order of Importance	Paired with Image/ Cofradía of:	Celebration Dates of "Big Days"	Comments
7	Santo Domingo, patron of the SW quarter of Rabinal	A smaller image of Santo Domingo, which is kept in the cofradía house	4 August	
8	San Sebastian, patron of the NW quarter of Rabinal	A smaller image of San Sebastian, which is kept in the cofradía house	17 January	The first of the year's general wakes and saints' processions (the second is at Easter, involving all four quarters' cofradías).
9	San Pedro Martires, patron of Rabinal's NE quarter	A smaller image of San Pedro Martires, kept in the cofradía house	29 April	
10	San Miguel Arcángel	Mythically paired with the fallen angel Satanas	29 September	The largest of the "small" cofradías
11	San José	The Virgin of the Rosario	19 March	
12	San Jacinto	The image of the Virgen del Tránsito	15 August (the Assumption of the Virgin Mary) and 17 August	San Jacinto is the local name for the Polish St. Hyacinth.
13	San Francisco, also known as the cofradía de las Ánimas		1 November	San Francisco is also known as the King of the Ánimas (souls). Fourth and last general wake and saints' procession
14	Elena de la Santa Cruz, also known as Ixoc Elena	The Image of the Santa Cruz	3 May	Only celebrated with Santa Cruz. See above.
15	The Virgen del Sacramento, also known as Ixoc Ajaw (female lord)	The image of Corpus Cristi or the Sacramento del altar; Ajaw (lord)	Corpus Cristi, a Thursday between 23 May and 25 June	Only celebrated with the Sacramento del Altar on Corpus Cristi.
16	Dulce nombre de Jesus or Child of the Nativity.	Cofradía of the Virgen de la Natividad	15 January	

Appendix 3
Musical Ensembles, Repertoires, and Occasions

Musical Ensemble	Repertoire	Occasion
Violin and adufe (square drum or <u>tupe</u>)	Sones of cofradía	Up to the first decades of the twentieth century, the sones de cofradía for the violin and adufe were played for prayers and zara-bandas in cofradías and life-crisis rituals. Today these sones are played only for anniversaries of the dead.
	Sones of the Chicomudo (mute person's dance)— sones for the beginning and the ending of the dance and sones for each character are included in all dances.	Mainly played and danced for the cofradías of Corpus Cristi and Santa Cruz.
	Sones of the <u>Ixim Kiej</u> (corn-deer) dance	Mainly in the cofradía of Corpus Cristi and San Pedro Apostol. It has not been performed lately.
Little flute and big drum	Sones of cofradía where the toques de procesión (beats for processions) called <u>sepiya</u> are included.	These are played during all cele-brations of cofradías.
	Sones of the San Jorge dance	Performed during the cofradías of Corpus Cristi, Santa Cruz, and Virgen del Carmen in Xococ.
	Sones of La Princesa dance	Performed during the cofradías of Corpus Cristi and Santa Cruz.
	Sones of the Moros Tamorlán dance	Performed for the dance during the cofradía of San Sebastían, San Pablo and San Pedro Apostol. These sones are also performed for other ritual activities during all the celebrations of cofradías.
	Sones of the Moros Conversión	This has not been performed lately.

(continued)

Musical Ensemble	Repertoire	Occasion
Shawm and big drum	Sones of La Conquista dance	Performed in the central square during the Ladino cofradía of the Virgen del Patrocinio.
	Sones of the Cortés dance	Performed during the cofradía of San Pablo. It has not been per formed lately.
	Sones of the San Pablo dance, also called <u>Nima Xajoj</u> (big dance)	Performed during the cofradía of San Pedro Apostol. It has not been performed lately.
Shawm and <u>tum</u> (slit drum)	Sones of the <u>Charamiyex</u> (deaf elder dance)	Performed during Carnival, at the beginning of Lent. It has not been performed lately.
Little flute and <u>tum</u>	Sones of the <u>Kiej</u> (deer) dance	Performed during the cofradía of San Pablo, San Pedro Apostol, and Corpus Cristi.
	Sones of the <u>Balam Kiej</u> (jaguar-deer) dance	Performed during the cofradía of San Pedro Apostol.
Little flute, little tum, and singing	Sones of the <u>Patzca</u> (humble elders) dance-drama, also called <u>Ueuechos</u> (old men with goitres) dance	Performed during the cofradía of Corpus Cristi, in front of the four chapels of the four quarters of the town, located in the central square.
Pregonero (town crier) drum	Toque (beats) of the <u>Patzca</u> dance	Played during the procession of Corpus Cristi.
Pipe and tabor	Sones of the Negritos (Black Men or Four Wise Kings) dance, including the sones to collect contributions and to ask permission for shelter (Mary at the inn)	Performed during Christmas par ties in private houses until Christ mas Eve. Also played in the streets to collect contributions for the celebration of the Three Wise Kings and during the cofradias of the Virgen de la Natividad, and the Virgen del Rosario.
	Sones of the Corrido del niño (the visit of baby Jesus)	Performed during Christmas in the streets and private houses.
Two trumpets and big <u>tum</u>	Sones of the Rabinal Achi dance, also called <u>Xajoj Tum</u> (dance of the drum)	Performed during the cofradía of San Pablo.
Two trumpets	*Toques* (fanfares) of proces-sion, annunciation, and courtesy	Played during the processions every Friday of Lent and Holy Week.
Marimba sencilla de sones (diatonic marimba)	Sones of cofradía	Played during all celebrations of cofradías and on most musical occasions.

Musical Ensemble	Repertoire	Occasion
Pieza marimba (diatonic marimba)	Piezas. All the pieza repertoire, from the old danza and contradanza to popular pieces introduced by recordings and radio such as cumbias, boleros, corridos, guarachas, merengues, pasos dobles, pasillos, and foxtrot.	Piezas may be played on any occasion. Dancers from some stage dances pick the piezas the like to dance when they have their turn to dance individually.
	Piezas and sones for the Costeño dance. It includes the old pieza contradanza, which is performed at the beginning and ending of the dance, and the favorite sones chosen individually by the dancers.	The Costeño dance is the most popular dance and has displaced other dances. This dance can be performed at any cofradía celebration and on other religious occasions.
Pieza marimba, double bass and drum set	Piezas: It includes all the popular music repertoires adapted to the diatonic pieza marimba.	Performed at any festivity, and particularly at the groom's house in weddings.
	Piezas for the Animalitos (little animals) dance. Includes a very old *danza de la muerte*.	Mainly performed during the cofradías of San Pedro Apostol, Corpus Cristi, and Santa Cruz.
	Piezas for the Diablitos (devils) dance. Includes an old danza (the same as that played in the Animalitos dance).	Performed during the cofradía of the Virgen de la Concepción and Santa Cruz. It has not been performed in years.
	Piezas for the Marinero (sailors) dance. Includes the same contredanse.	For various occasions. It has not been performed in years.
	Piezas for Las Flores (the flowers) dance	Performed during the cofradía of the Virgin of Patrocinio.
	Piezas for the <u>Patzca</u> moderno, also called Dance of the Towns (Ordoñez family version)	Can be performed for any of the celebrations of the 16 cofradías, and other occasions.
	Piezas for the Dance of the Towns (Valdizón family version)	Performed on Christmas Eve.
	Piezas. All the pieza repertoire.	For any occasion, but especially for wedding parties.
	Sones of the Costeño dance. It includes a very old dance piece.	The Costeño dance is the most popular dance and it is performed on celebrations of cofradías and other occasions.

(continued)

Musical Ensemble	Repertoire	Occasion
Pieza marimba, double bass and drum set (*continued*)	Piezas for the Moro Español (Spanish Moor) dance	Performed in the cofradía of San Pedro Apostol. It has not been performed lately.
	Piezas for the Sotomayor dance (a modified Spanish version of the <u>Charamiyex</u> dance)	For different occasions
	Sones and piezas	For any musical occasion
Chromatic marimba, double bass and choir	Sones and piezas for the hymns and sung praises in either Achi or Spanish	For Catholic Sunday mass
Guitar, accordion, double bass and choir	Piezas for the hymns and sung praises	Played during evangelical religious services.
Guitar, concertina, double bass, and voices	Sones and piezas such as corridos and polkas	Ensemble of Ladino musicians from <u>Chirrum</u> village. They perform at any musical occasion.
Duo singing, violin and adufe	Son Costa Cobán or <u>rebix</u> son	Performed to bid farewell the souls of the dead at the end of the festivities commanding them to dance.
Choir	Chant Santo Dios	Chanted at the end of the mystery prayers whenever these are performed.

Appendix 4
Synopses of Dance-Dramas

DANCE-DRAMAS in Guatemala are ritual plays (with or without dialogue, produced from memory or written texts) with dance and musical interludes. They are organized by Indians and Ladinos to celebrate the main festivities dedicated to Jesus, the saints, and virgins of towns throughout Guatemala.

Boys and old people wear masks and costumes to represent a story or farce. Each character is identified by its costume, mask, and dramatic role, and is accompanied by a particular *son* or *pieza*. The stories represent historical or mythical Rabinalense stories. Or they can be mockeries of Rabinalense myths and legends in which common sense is turned on its head, resulting in absurd actions and dialogues and provoking great laughter from the spectators.

I registered twenty-four different dance-dramas in Rabinal, of which only fifteen have been performed in the past decade. Each dance-drama is performed at a particular cofradía festivity. Most dance-dramas may be performed during the festivities of Corpus Christi, Santa Cruz, San Pedro Apostol, San Pablo, and on Christmas.

The following are synopses of three of the important popular dance-dramas mentioned in the text. The first is a sixteenth-century Indian account of the pre-Hispanic Achi history. The other two are very popular nineteenth-century *loa* plays (short religious theatrical pieces praising the Virgin Mary; see Correa y Cannon 1958) written in Spanish. The dancing in both of the <u>loa</u> plays is organized in two *cuadrillas* (quadrilles, or groups of dancers) of six dancers each, making six couples all together. Musically speaking, these dance-dramas are important because they preserve contradanza and danza musical pieces from the eighteenth and early nineteenth centuries, revealing the influence of ballroom dances on the Indian and Ladino dance-drama traditions.

SYNOPSIS OF THE <u>XAJOJ TUM</u> OR RABINAL ACHI DANCE-DRAMA

The Rabinal Achi is considered the only early colonial dance-drama in Guatemala that has survived in both written and oral traditions. The written text of the dance-drama was discovered in late 1855 by the French abbot Charles E. Brasseur de Bourbourg. He transcribed it from the Achi-language oral dictation by Bartolo Sis, an Achi elder who was in charge of keeping the text of the dance-drama.

The music of the dance-drama are *sones* and *altos* (fanfares) played by an ensemble of two trumpet players called "alto" (treble) or first and a "bajo" (bass) or second, and a percussionist with a big idiophone or "slit-drum" called tum.

The oral text is faithful to the written text of the Rabinal Achi dance-drama, which is a local literary version of the political and military interethnic conflicts in the Baja Verapaz region that occurred at the end of the fifteenth and beginning of the sixteenth centuries, shortly before the arrival of the Spanish. The story relates how the great warrior of the K'iche' empire attacked the Rabinalense fortress of Cajyup, destroying several towns and kidnapping Job Toj, the sovereign of the Rabinalense. The great warrior Rabinal Achi rescued his sovereign and caught the K'iche' Achi warrior. The two warriors have a long, repetitive dialogue in which they exchange words of admiration for each other's deeds and explicate the motives behind the conflict between the two parties. The Rabinal Achi warrior presents the captive before his sovereign. During a trial the captive is offered his life on the condition of subordination to the Rabinal sovereign. The K'iche' Achi warrior opts to be sacrificed but makes a series of requests first. He requests that he may fight against the Rabinalense Eagle and Jaguar warriors, eat and drink the best of the wares of the Rabinal people, and dance to the music of the tum with a young woman, the mother of the green birds. This woman represents a political alliance of the Rabinalense court and the Q'eqchi' people of Carcha and Cobán, who controlled access to the Maya lowland and its resources. His final wish was to bid farewell his own K'iche' land. After the captive's requests are granted, he is sacrificed.

Synopsis of the Costeño (Coastal Man) Dance-Drama

The Costeño dance-drama is an early nineteenth-century representation of a "bull type" dance-drama composed by Felipe Galiego (Mace 1981). The story tells of the encounter of two groups of merchants who meet in an inn (*posada*) during the festivities of one of the saints of the town. The Ladinos bring cattle to sell and the Indians from the Pacific Coast sell cacao seeds, from which cocoa and chocolate are prepared. The owner of the inn and his wife receive them and invite them to join the celebration. Both groups exchange their products, pay their respects to the Virgin, and then organize a *toreada* (bullfight).

The story relates a common commercial practice between merchants of the highlands and the Pacific Coast that began during colonial times and lasted from the eighteenth century until the early twentieth. Indians from the coast grew cacao trees and even hired highland Indians to work on their plantations. During this long period, Indians traded cacao for other commodities sold by Ladino merchants in the highlands (Alejos 1992). The encounter at the inn, the organization of a bullfight, and the participation of all the merchants, including the owner of the inn and, especially, his wife, have important parallels with the organization of *zarabandas*. Here merchants arriving from outside towns participated in the religious festivities of the towns, drinking and dancing with local women.

The Costeño, the musical ensemble of which comprises the pieza marimba, played by three musicians, is the favorite dance-drama of contemporary Rabinal. Its popularity is due to its short duration and ease of performance, its being in Spanish, and its brisk-tempo marimba son and contradanza theme (track 8 on CD and musical transcription in Chapter 4). In addition, it allows dancers to display their abilities as good dancers and has a bullfight scene where the bull actually chases each of the dancers. The chase of the woman carries sexual connotations that delight the public, and it is this above all that ensures its popularity.

Synopsis of the Animalitos (Little Animals) Dance-Drama

The Animalitos loa is another very popular dance-drama. The story tells how the lion, king of the animals, discovers that the bull is organizing an army against him. When the lion confronts the bull, the bull claims that the object of his army is not to fight the lion but to celebrate the Virgin Mary. Both the lion's and the bull's groups then join to celebrate the Virgin.

The musical ensemble is a *conjunto* marimba that includes a pieza marimba, with four players, a double bass, and a drum set. The music played in this dance-drama is primarily popular *cumbias* and *corridos* (track 3 on CD). It also includes a slow dance piece called *danza de la muerte* (track 9 on CD), which the squirrel dances with its particular slow dance step. The marimba musician Celestino defined the dance as slow, *bolero*-like music (see musical transcriptions in Chapter 4). This dance piece and the contradanza piece are valuable examples of the early nineteenth-century musical influence of the ballroom dance on the popular dance-dramas of rural Indian and Ladino populations.

Notes

1. Throughout this book, Spanish words appear in italics and K'iche' Achi words are underlined.

2. My master's thesis is based on a comparison of a transcription of the dance-drama music published in the middle of the nineteenth century (Brasseur de Bourbourg 1862) and my own transcription of its music from a recording made by Henrietta Yurchenco in Rabinal in 1945. The work suggests a musical continuity of certain rhythmical formulas and melodic designs and, based on this, I hypothe-sized that the written and oral forms of this dance-drama are complementary.

3. The term Ladino (in Guatemala) and Mestizo (in Mexico) refer to the non-Indian population. See Chapter 1 on the process of ladinoization.

CHAPTER ONE

1. A K'iche' lineage speaking a linguistic variant of the K'iche' language, called K'iche' Achi. The word "achi" simply means "man."

2. Under this system, the Spanish Crown granted conquerors the tribute of certain towns as a reward for their service. The encomiendas did not include rights over labor, which were controlled by the Crown under the repartimiento system (see below).

3. Franciscans were the first friars to arrive in New Spain following the con-quest of 1521. In 1536 they established the first secondary school for Indian nobles at their convent of Tlatelolco, which became the most important center for the religious indoctrination and musical training of the indigenous nobility. The syllabus included reading, writing, Latin, rhetoric, logic, philosophy, and indigenous medicine (Ricard 1992, 336).

4. On pre-Hispanic dances, see Mace (1966, 1967); Tedlock (1985, 45, 149–50); Acuña (1978); Breton (1994).

5. For the theater of evangelization in Guatemala, see Correa and Cannon (1958).

6. My investigations revealed that Rabinal has twenty-six distinct dance-dramas, some of which are still performed as an offering and entertainment for the saints and the public during cofradía festivities. Teletor (1955) describes eight-een dances that existed during the first half of the twentieth century.

7. Under this system the colonial government granted private entrepreneurs a fixed amount of Indian labor for their plantations and factories.

8. See Chapter 6 for a discussion of pre-Hispanic religious beliefs.

9. The new cofradías developed from family cults dedicated to particular saints. Both Indian and Ladino families had these saint images, called uachibales.

10. Hermandades are religious communities whose purpose is to spread the expense of masses and funerals incurred by their members' families.

11. I conducted archival research in the parish archive of Rabinal, in the Archbishopric Historical Archive, and in the General Archive of Central America in Guatemala City in 1995.

12. The term "Ladino" was first used in the sixteenth century to describe acculturated or Spanish-speaking Indians (cf. Tax 1941, 21; Sherman 1979, 187); it is in this sense that I use the term here. Historically, the word also designates people of mixed European and Indian ancestry and poor Spanish peasants. By the early twentieth century, the term had disappeared in the rest of Central America (to be replaced by Mestizo) but to Guatemalan Indians Ladino has come to mean "oppressor in the western highlands, and homeless (and therefore permanent) worker in the cities and lowlands" (Smith 1990, 86). In Rabinal the term applies to anyone who is not considered to have an Indian heritage and is therefore labeled an outsider.

13. During the colonial period, the Royal Audience of Guatemala issued royal letters ordering diverse preparations for schools in Indian towns; in places where it was impossible to have a school, the church sacristan was to be responsible for the instruction of classes. The creation of schools was also recommended in 1781, but parish records indicate that these schools were only for boys (AGCA, A1.23, file 1514, p. 68; A1.23, file 1515, p. 1; A1.23, file 1529, p. 499; A1.23, file 4632, p. 44v; A1.23, file 1531, p. 4; AHA, Visitas pastorales, vol. 41). Today, although girls account for 51 percent of the school-age population, 60 percent of pupils enrolled in schools are boys.

14. In the anthropological literature—beginning with Adams (1959)—the concept of *ladinización* bequeathed by humanistic liberals involved the transformation of their moral connotations into a natural process evocative of modern capitalism. This suggests a process of linear progressive transition from Indian "traditionalism" to Ladino "modernization." Later Adams (1994) recognized that the process of acculturation does not necessarily imply the loss of indigenous identity.

15. In order of importance, El Chol, Salamá, and Rabinal were the three towns with the largest Ladino populations. Between 1767–69 and 1812–16, the Ladino population of Chol increased from 102 to 1,150; Salamá from 300 to 1,785; and Rabinal from 128 to 451. During the same period, Rabinal's Indian population increased from an estimated 4,500 to 6,118 (Bertrand 1987, 274, table 7).

16. This was the Crown's and, later, the state's practice of acquiring land and giving it new titles before re-allocating or selling it. Existing titles had to be re-registered to remain valid. The practice was introduced in the second half of the eighteenth century and was intended to incorporate peasants' land into the market. The procedure was repeated after the liberal revolution of Barrios, starting in 1871.

17. Bertrand (1987, 272, 274) does not specify the ethnic and racial characteristics of this Ladino population in Rabinal; he only refers to them as an increasingly Mestizo and undifferentiated population.

18. See Chapter 2 for an explanation of the cofradía hierarchy.

19. Father Avella was also responsible for the silver cofradía staffs, each decorated with the appropriate saint, and other silver church ornaments. Today these treasures are believed to have been left by the Maya Wise Men before they buried themselves under the church at the beginning of the World of Light (see Chapter 2).

20. Ejidal land refers to all land granted by the Spanish Crown and later by the Guatemalan government as common land for Indian towns.

21. Ubico chose villagers from Xococ to carry out police duties in Rabinal municipality. During la violencia (1981–83), Xococ's civil patrols were selected to carry out several massacres in Rabinal (EAFG 1995, 53, 147–53, 174–80).

22. Ubico established the post of military commissioner in 1939; despite their title, these were civilians whose main role was to ensure that all peasants completed their obligatory labor. In 1976 they became directly subordinated to the nearest military base and their role in army recruitment and the provision of "military intelligence" intensified: "They were the eyes and ears of the army" (EAFG 1995, 118).

23. The national popular movement of rural workers over the past few decades led to the politicization of Rabinalense peasants (Le Bot 1995). Rabinal has had several indigenous municipal mayors whose ethnic origins were exploited by Ladinos in order to manipulate the municipality's most reactionary groups.

24. Apostolic Catholicism arose during the anticommunist campaign and accompanying evangelization movement initiated by Castillo Armas, who ousted Arbenz's democratic government in 1954. Rabinalense Apostolics today are concentrated in the village of Vegas Santo Domingo, home to several of the most active local PACs that carried out massacres in Rabinal.

25. The army manipulated local religious concepts, such as the idea that illness is caused by sin, in order to blame the population for the devastating destruction of its own villages (Wilson 1995, 231; cf. Zur 1998).

26. Guatemala's Protestant sects, many financed by their U.S. headquarters, have been identified with an anticommunist and patriotic ideology supported by their affiliation with sectors of the power elite.

27. Conversion increased dramatically in the decade after 1975. Although it stabilized in the 1990s, 40 to 50 percent of Guatemalans are thought to be evangelical (Barry 1992).

28. This gave rise to the concept of *desarrollo excluyente* (economic growth that does not benefit the majority).

29. In English, the Agency for International Development (AID) and Center for Family Integration (CIF).

30. The exploitation of inter- and intraethnic conflicts has a long and ignominious history dating to Spanish conquest. In Rabinal, the conflict with the most far-reaching consequences is that between the Indian authorities living in town and the northern population, living in a vast area called Xococ. Originally owned by the Spanish Crown and much larger than the area known as Xococ today, the

land was divided in 1758 between a private trader, the people of Cubulco (a neighboring municipality), and the people of Rabinal; no Xocoqueños were present during these proceedings. Xococ is Rabinal's largest and most traditional village, and its leaders are strongly allied with local Ladinos and the army.

31. Rabinalense peasants' involvement was limited to providing refuge and replacements for the EGP (Guerrilla Army of the Poor) combatants who fought in El Quiché and Alta Verapaz. For details of CUC and EGP activities in Rabinal, see EAFG (1995, 82–103).

32. For example, there are at least 4,000 people from Cubulco and Rabinal in Chisec municipality, Alta Verapaz, and a similar number have settled on the Concepción finca on the Pacific Coast in Escuintla.

33. For information about military operations in combination with paramilitary forces (including PACs), see EAFG (1995).

34. For an analysis of the civil patrols and their legacy, see America's Watch (1986), EAFG (1995), and Popkin (1996).

35. These include up to 500 people killed in the town market on 15 September 1981; 268 in Plan de Sanchez in July 1982; 100 in Chichupac. In February 1982, 82 Rio Negro men were lured to Xococ and slaughtered; a month later, men from Xococ went to Rio Negro and murdered 70 women and 107 children (EAFG 1995, 127)

36. Las masacres en Rabinal, researched by the Equipo de Antropologia Forense de Guatemala (Forensic Anthropology Team of Guatemala) (EAFG 1995) contains abundant testimony on the ways in which people denounced and murdered each other. The analysis of the Rio Negro, Chichupac, and Plan de Sanchez massacres reveals how the army used local conflicts to facilitate the destruction of entire villages by neighboring communities' patrols.

37. Geographic and statistical information for Rabinal municipality were obtained from Usselmann (1979); Instituto Nacional de Estadística (1991, 1993); Arnauld (1993); EAFG (1995).

38. An alternative, ancient route to Guatemala City passes through Chol municipality; it is more direct but remains unpaved. The modernization of the road network gave priority to routes connecting the national and provincial capitals. This has forced Rabinal's regional market to reorient its business toward Salamá, the capital of Baja Verapaz.

39. From 1950 to 1981, the annual demographic growth rate was 2.8 percent (Le Bot 1995, 39). The rate of growth in Baja Verapaz in 1991 was 3.15 percent (SEGEPLAN 1994, 123).

40. According to Leopoldo Tzian (1994), Guatemala's population in 1993 was 10,029,714, of whom 60 percent spoke one of the twenty Maya languages; 1 percent spoke Garífona (Caribe or Arawako) and Xinka; and 39 percent spoke Spanish as their mother language. K'iche' Achi is a linguistic variant of K'iche', which is the predominant Maya language in Guatemala, spoken by 31 percent of all Maya speakers (about 2 million people). Most Maya women are functionally monolingual, while Maya men are mostly bilingual. In Rabinal only a few Ladino merchants learn K'iche' Achi as a second language.

41. It is no coincidence that all the Rabinalense peasants affiliated with the CUC in 1979 were migrant workers. That the CUC later became the political

branch of the Guerrilla Army of the Poor (EAFG 1995, 90) is a separate issue of which many peasants remain unaware.

42. Smith (1984) on the contrary maintains that the introduction of fertilizers and cash crops reinforced the peasant economy, making them less dependent on wage work. This book coincides with the emergence of an indigenous commercial class that overthrew the power of local Ladinos in certain towns of the western highlands, as shown by Falla (1980). This is not the experience of peripheral Indian towns like Rabinal.

43. Built by INDE, the state-owned electricity company, Pacux was designed to house villagers who were displaced by the construction of the Chixoy dam on the Rio Negro. Villagers were forced to move to Pacux in 1981 after government forces decimated the village.

44. Rabinal health technician, personal communication. In 1995 Rabinal town also had a couple of private medical practices, pharmacies, and an important health project financed by Christian organizations. Most Achi who seek allopathic medical treatment take the advice of the retail pharmacists, who are often unqualified.

CHAPTER TWO

1. The ancient Nahua comprise all the Nahua-speaking groups who lived mainly in the Mexican highlands. They included the Aztecs, who settled in the valley of Mexico during the fourteenth century and a century later controlled all Nahua groups who had settled there before them.

2. For Nahua commemoration practices, see the chronicles of the sixteenth century. Two main chronicles are Sahagún (1979) and friar Motolinia (Nuttini 1988, 64–65).

3. The conversion of Christ, the saints, and virgins into ancestors as a means of incorporating Christian myths into a Maya Achi vision of continuous history results in the surprising idea that the congregation of the indigenous population into new settlements, and the creation of cofradías to celebrate the liturgical calendar (actually enforced by the Spanish in the early colonial era) are the deeds of the ancestors.

4. Similarly, the pagan religions of the classical world reemerged in the early Christian cult of the saints (Brown 1981).

5. The root ajaw (sun) also means señor (lord), patron, and owner, and as such the word is used to refer to religious, political, and social authority. Ajaw is also the root of words such as rajawales and kajawxeles (principal bearers of the cofradía).

6. Cf. Mendelson's (1957) investigation into the "owners of the world" in Santiago Atitlán, which reveals that the owners of all the manifestations of nature are thus "lords of the world."

7. Literally, advocates. Abogados are the advocates of the living in their dealings with God and the dead.

8. *Popul Vuh* (Tedlock 1985) is the most complete record of the Maya creation myths; it is also a history of the origins of and struggles between the K'iche's and their neighbors.

9. Kajyup, Chwitinamit, and Saqkijel are the most important postclassical archaeological sites in the Rabinal basin (Arnauld 1993, 98). Rabinalenses say that Kajyup hill is the residence of the rajawales or spirits of the kings, princesses, and warriors represented by the masks worn by performers of the Rabinal Achi dance-drama, which reenacts the Achi defeat of the K'iche'. Oral history also tells that Chwitinamit was the place of the Poq'omchis, who were expelled toward Cobán by the Rabinalense.

10. Sajorines, also known as ajq' iij (healers, diviners), are the most powerful prayer makers (abogados). They are believed to be descendants of the Maya Wise Men who kept the day count and could predict the future (Colby and Colby 1986). As healers, they cure with prayers and plants; as diviners, they identify the source of witchcraft. People say Rabinal no longer has any diviners, but stories persist about practices performed on nearby Kamba hill to forecast the coming year's rainfall. Prior to the political violence of 1982, the Ixils were well known for their numerous healers and diviners. The word *sajorin* or *sahori* (greeter) is traditionally used in Spain to refer to people who are born with the gift to heal (Foster 1985).

11. Cf. Luke 2:42–52.

12. Also known as *curanderos*, these healers work with prayers and medicinal plants.

13. The Black Men are usually identified with the Three Kings in the Bible story (Matt. 2), though only one is black according to Catholic legend (see Chapter 3).

14. Literally, the umbilical cord of the earth, the umbilical cord of the sky.

15. Today the Divine Sacrament is the largest of Rabinal's sixteen Indian cofradías, whereas the cofradía of the Virgin of the Sacrament is the second-smallest.

16. These actually date from the 1840s.

17. This is another name for the Wise Men. It expresses their junior relationship in relation to Jesus/God. They are also known as ueuechos or "goitre men."

18. The most common cause of goitre is iodine deficiency, which is still a recognizable health problem in Guatemala (Barry 1987, 15). The celebration of this deficiency could be a form of normative behavior, representing conditions of the past. I was told that there are still cases in Xococ, the most traditional of Rabinal's villages.

19. Here the sacrifice of the patzka, who represent rain and the fertilization of land, may be taken as an act that regenerates life (cf. Bloch and Parry 1982, 1–40; Harris 1982, 45–73).

20. The annual calendar of festivities is made up primarily of cofradía celebrations.

21. This slit-drum is known in the Nahautl language as teponaztle. It is not actually a proper drum but an idiophone (an instrument that produces sound by the vibration of its own primary material). See pre-Hispanic drums in the Maya area in Hammond 1972a.

22. The first stage is marriage, which transforms the couple into adult men and women (achi and ixoc, respectively) capable of procreation. The second stage

is that of biological reproduction, when the couple assumes the roles of father (qaw) and mother (chu). The third stage is the role of grandparents, called ati (grandmother) and mam (grandfather). The word mam is applied to older people in general, including established and respected musicians; it also means "ancestor." The common element is knowledge.

23. Farris (1987, 566–93) presents a similar analysis of cyclical and linear concepts of time among the Maya during pre-Hispanic and colonial times.

24. The union of all souls conforms to the Achi idea that regardless of people's behavior or religious belief on earth, after death they all live together under the earth and then, after a time, in heaven. This is a different concept from the Christian idea that the virtuous are rewarded with eternal life in heaven and the unrepentant punished by eternity in hell.

25. For the historical development of the cofradías and their status today, see Chapter 1. For descriptions of the traditional cargo system, see Wagley (1941), Bunzel (1952), Cancian (1965), Reina (1966), and Rojas Lima (1988). For an analysis of the structure and ritual procedures of cofradía festivities in Rabinal, see Breton (1979, 159–78; 1980, 1171–225).

26. The use of the term "mayordomo" can be confusing, as it is often applied to *cargueros* (office holders) in grades 2–7; the use of the word for all but the top position stems from colonial practice. Cargueros are also referred to as "seventh man" (achi) or "seventh woman" (ixoc) or "septimo mayordomo" and "septimo ixoc," and so on.

27. The fourth achi and ixoc have the additional title of *capitan* and *capitana*, respectively, because they are the leaders of the lower group of cargo holders.

28. Kajawxeles (and rajaweles) are "lords of the town" because the ancestors held cargos. For the relationship between civil and religious authorities, see Chapter 1.

29. During colonial times the person substituting as priest in a given parish was called *teniente de cura* (an assistant who stood in for a priest in his absence).

30. Cancian's (1965) analysis of the Zinacantan cargo system reveals that it reflected social stratification. Twenty years later this was no longer the case: The community had been opened to the market economy and alternative economic and political interests had emerged. Nevertheless, those who held the more prestigious cargos were wealthy people (Cancian 1992).

31. These are the cofradías of the Virgin of Patrocinio and the Virgin of the Conception, in which Indians have taken cargos because of Ladinos' growing disinclination to do so.

32. Santo Domingo, San Pedro Martires, and San Sebastián are the cofradías of three of Rabinal's four quarters.

33. Musical ensembles, their repertoires, and the occasions on which they play are shown in Appendix 3.

34. For example, the spirits represented in the ritual dance-dramas. Performers require the permission and protection of the rajawal spirits whose masks they wear in order to avoid failure during the reenactment of the myths.

35. The likely origin of this practice can be found in the rules and statutes of the choir of the metropolitan church of Santiago de Goahtemala, drawn up circa 1770 by its archbishop, Cortés y Larras. The choir's duties included singing the

mass for the dead for the souls in purgatory on the first Monday of each month (see Lemmon 1990).

36. The archaic language of the prayers and the abogado's mumbling chant (not to mention the noise of the marimba) make these prayers virtually unintelligible and so I was unable to make a full translation. What follows is an abogado's explanation of the content of the prayer in a recording I made.

37. A possible explanation for the association between north and zenith, south and nadir, may be that during the period of the year when the days are longer and hotter, the sun changes its position, moving toward the northeast. During the time of year when the days get colder and shorter, the sun appears first in the southeast. See Gossen (1979, 55–57).

38. Cf. Revelations 3:5: "He who is victorious . . . his name I will never strike off the roll of the role of the living, for in the presence of my father and his angels I will acknowledge him as mine."

39. In this instance, kajawxeles refers to the head of the cofradía and his deputies, the second and third mayordomos.

40. In anniversaries of the dead there is only one abogado, but he repeats the prayers twice, once in front of the grave at the cemetery and again in front of the altar in the Calvario cemetery chapel (see Chapter 6).

41. Immortality lies in remembrance and this is prolonged into the personal eternal life granted by God. Where there is no remembrance, there is no hope for immortality. The origins of this belief can be found in Revelations, a very popular text in late medieval Europe: "Wake up, and put some strength into what is left, which must otherwise die. For I have not found any work of yours completed in the eyes of my God. So remember the teaching you received, observe it, and repent" (Rev. 2–7).

42. See López Austin (1996, 207–8) for a similar concept among the ancient Nahua. For a discussion of memory and emotions in relation to music, see Chapters 6 and 7.

43. Among the Maya Tzotzil of Chiapas, Mexico, an individual's strength depends on the "heat" produced by his or her ch'ulel (soul, in the Tzotzil language). This energy varies according to age, sex, and the individual's participation in civil and religious positions (Guiteras 1986, 229–36). López Austin (1996, 223–57) analyzes the animic entities known to Nahua-speaking Aztecs as tonalli (shadow) and teyolia (soul), which are related to the concepts of ch'ulel and ánima among the Tztozil and Achi, respectively.

44. According to abogado Pedro Morales K'ojom, the recent dead become ancestors (mam) when some generations have passed and they are considered to have been judged and to be rightfully with God in heaven.

45. Among the Maya Jacaltec of Huehuetenango, the dead are considered to be chained and suffering because they are separated from their living kin. The living therefore invite the souls to join them, temporarily releasing them from bondage out of fear of harmful retribution from them (McArthur 1977).

46. Cf. Rev. 3:4.

47. In the Catholic belief of the Maya Trixanos, the town is God's realm; the rest of the world—cities, valleys, mountains—is the domain of the devil. Their guardians are his armies and may penetrate and influence the town. This opposition

embodies other concepts concerning the subordination of the Indian world to the Ladino sphere (Warren 1992, 46–48). For other descriptions, see Siegel (1941, 67), Oakes (1951, 93), and Adams (1952, 31).

48. Cf. Colby and Colby (1986) on Ixil diviners' interpretations of dreams.

49. Envy and revenge are included under the rubric of illness rather than conflict.

50. Among the K'iche' of Momostenango, a visit by a soul during a dream is a positive experience (Tedlock 1981; 1990).

Chapter Three

1. Compare the binary categories of the Maya Zinacantecos of Chiapas, Mexico, analyzed by Vogt (1976, 31–34). To Vogt, the most important "binary discriminations" (which he calls "general operators") are rising sun/setting sun, right/left, senior/junior, hot/cold. Gossen (1979) presents a similar analysis of the Maya Chamula worldview.

2. As "Black Men," the biblical Magi are transformed into ancient Maya Wise Men who, needless to say, brought their wives in their retinues.

3. Tedlock (1986) does not mention that the first four men possessed both female and male qualities.

4. Musicians say that the sound effect produced when the musician articulates with his tongue while blowing through the tube of the wind instruments is the sound "su." In effect, when Victor Tum, the first or treble trumpet player, whistled (in fact, more like whispered) the melodies of the first son of the Rabinal Achi dance, he blew the five musical phrases or fanfares without the instruments, producing the following sounds: shiuuuuu, shiiiiiiii, shiiiiii, shiuuuu, uuiii, shiuuuu uuiiii.

5. Some of the names of the percussion instruments are also considered onomatopoeias. An example is the adufe, which is called tupe in Achi. Whenever I asked about the tupe, people smiled and moved their hands as though they were playing the instrument and repeated, "tupe, tupe." The onomatopoeia clearly amused them. Victor Tum told me that the idiophone called tum got its name "because that is the way they sound." He added, "the beat of the first son [in the Rabinal Achi dance] starts like this: *tulum tum, tulum tum, tum; tulum tum, tulum tum, tum.*"

6. This way of presenting themselves sidesteps the fact that they had to conquer the area's previous inhabitants before settling in the Rabinal basin, an event they celebrate annually in the Rabinal Achi dance-drama.

7. The term pieza means "piece." In seventeenth- and eighteenth-century Europe, the term referred to a small, often instrumental, composition. In German the term *stuck* (piece) implies a composition that forms part of a set of compositions (Randel 1986) similar to a set of dances. Although sones are used for social dancing in zarabandas and for dance-dramas, all piezas are considered dance music. In fact, the oldest piezas are dances.

8. Smith (1987, 197–217) has emphasized that this opposition implies a class struggle expressed in ethnic terms. In my opinion this empirical social classification may be useful so long as it is accompanied by explanations of the context

and conditions in which these musical types are practiced; it is necessary to subordinate musical analysis to historical and ethnographic analysis of context.

9. For myths about the origins of music, see Chapter 2; for a history of the son, see Chapter 4.

10. During certain cofradía fiestas, dance-dramas are performed four times a day by up to twenty-five different dance groups, each with its own musical accompaniment. On particularly important and popular festivals, such as Corpus Cristi, two or three dance troupes can perform at the cofradía house at once, while the musicians contracted to play for the fiesta continue to play as if nothing were happening on the other side of the courtyard.

11. In theory, from a local Catholic perspective, a person may serve God and the souls only by taking on religious obligations in a cofradía after he or she marries.

12. The son marimbistas at the bride's house are hired for twenty-four hours, whereas the marimba conjunto ensemble at the groom's house is hired for only four to six hours.

13. Mam is one of the images of the Atitecos. The twelve Nahuals, the ancestral heroes, created Mam to watch over their wives and to prevent them from running off with other men (O'Brien 1975, 152–61).

14. There is a similar relationship between the sacred earth, which is female and the provider of sustenance, and men, who traditionally plant the main corn crop. Here, the act of making the hole in earth with the hoe and planting the seed carries sexual connotations (see Wilson 1995).

15. These features of music structure are common in the son music of other ensembles (except for the marimba, where the voices or parts are harmonically related in the Western sense).

Chapter Four

1. A similar claim was made by Mexican musicologists regarding the marimba tradition in Chiapas (Kaptain 1992, 10–12).

2. These newspaper articles were collected and published in book form by López Mayorical (1978).

3. To satisfy the expectations of tourists, marimba musicians are hired to play in luxury city hotels wearing traditional Indian costumes. Much of twentieth-century cultural nationalism was motivated by the need to construct an external image of a colorful and attractively distinctive indigenous Guatemala to attract tourists.

4. See Kubik (1984).

5. Yves Monino (personal correspondence), based on Guthrie (1967), argues that the root or nominal theme *rimba* or *dimba* with the prefix *ma-* takes the meaning "xylophon" from the proto-Bantu.

6. See the entries "xylophon" and "balo" in the *New groves dictionary of musical instruments* (1984).

7. The General Archive of Central America in Guatemala City contains several seventeenth- and eighteenth-century documents referring to the importation of large numbers of African slaves to the Audience of Guatemala to provide the

labor for indigo production. Some documents indicate the need to divide these slaves between small towns in Nicaragua province and contain resolutions and information on their organization and behavior (Central America General Archive, AGCA, A1.23, file 1527, p. 439; A1.2.4, file 2199, record 15755, p. 50; A1.24, file 2197, record 15751, p. 313; A1.23, file 1540, p. 54; A1.23, file 1513, p. 676; A1.23, file 1514, pp. 22, 37; A1.1, record 25, file 1, pp 1, 13; A1.23, file 1516, p. 57; A1.23, file 1517, p. 108; A1.23, file 1518, p. 211).

8. This would have been the diatonic gourd marimba with an arc to hold the keyboard against the sitting musician, separating him from the keyboard; this instrument is the African prototype of the Guatemalan marimba (Chenoweth 1964, 26, 75). Garfias (1983) gives illustrations of American and African arc marimbas with gourd resonators.

9. For sixteenth- and seventeenth-century decrees forbidding the settlement of Africans, mulattoes, and Mestizos (Ladinos) in Indian towns, see AGCA, A1.23, file, 4575, p. 433v; A1.23, file 1513, 557r; A1.24, file 1558, p. 198v.

10. See Hudson (1980) on "sarabande."

11. Fernando Ortíz (1965, 314; 1993, 216–18) describes the dances of Ogun and the zarabanda. A variety of web sites refer to the zarabanda in the Santería religion in Cuba. Those sources consider the zarabanda an equivalent of the warrior god Ogun.

12. The same applies to the term *fandango*, which has been used since the eighteenth century to refer to a social gathering where dance music is played (Pérez Montfort 1994, 31–43).

13. For a description and interpretation of this dance, see Chapter 5.

14. The musical ensemble identified by Saenz Poggio also includes the adufe, which is no longer part of the instrumental group of Alta Verapaz but is extant in the violin-and-adufe group of Rabinal, Baja Verapaz.

15. AGCA, A1.23, file 1515, p. 3.

16. The "barreño" son by Laureano Mazariegos (Godínez 2002, 207n21, 212) is surely one of the numerous written versions of this ancient son.

17. At the end of the nineteenth century, art and artisan schools were created that included carpentry workshops; this suggests that the production and sale of marimbas probably already existed in these areas (Dary 1991). These provinces are the main centers of production today (Camposeco 1992).

18. Groups of guitar, harp, and violin are still very popular among different Maya groups (Tzotzil, Tzeltal, Kanjobal, K'iche', and Q'eqchi).

19. The civil and religious authorities were also concerned about the economic consequences of Indian celebrations (see Chapter 5).

20. However, it is possible to infer from an earlier document that the groups of women described as visiting different houses were dancers. See the 1669 prohibition of zarabandas in Ladino cofradías in Zapotitlán province, which describes groups of mulatto and Mestizo women dancing in cofradías (Ordoñez 1989).

21. Carlos Fernández (1998a, 694) describes Costa Rica's musical bow or *quijongo* and notes that in Guanacaste during colonial times this instrument accompanied a marimba or guitar, which were played at dances. The author adds that nowadays this instrument can be found in Nicaragua, El Salvador, and Honduras, where it is called a caramba. This data jibes with information about the

music and instruments played at wakes in Apastepeque, El Salvador, during the eighteenth century and suggests that the marimba ensemble, together with caramba or guitar, was a musical ensemble found throughout Latin America. Saenz Poggio (1997, 81) has also found evidence of the caramba in Guatemala during the eighteenth century.

22. AGCA, A1, record 39868, file 4659.

23. A similar tradition exists in Ecuador, where contemporary Quichua play the harp at children's wakes (Schechter 1992). Apart from a comment that "one of the goals of the runa harpist's performance during the vigil is precisely to draw the [child's] mother into the dancing, out of her grief—even momentarily" (155), Schechter makes no comment on the emotions of the participants or about what harp music means to the Quichua.

24. AGCA, A1, file 2815, record 24823. Zarabandas are still held every Saturday night in Cubulco, Baja Verapaz.

25. The *Diccionario de autoridades* (1990) defines the seguidilla as a literary composition or stanza of four verses, where the second and fourth verses are assonant and have five syllables, whereas the first and third verses have seven syllables.

26. Aurelio Tello (2001) published the first volume of the songbook by Gaspar Fernández, with a very comprehensive introductory article about the life and works of this composer. Music from this cancionero can be heard on the CD *Mexican Colonial Music from the Sixteenth and Seventeenth Centuries*, performed by the Ars Nova ensemble (copyright Claudio Valdéz Kuri, 1993).

27. In Guatemala the dramatic representation of dances—dance-dramas—are simply called bailes. Mace (1981, 83) asserts that there are at least seventy different dance-dramas in Guatemala.

28. Rabinalenses call small marimbas tenor. There are two types of tenor marimba; One is chromatic and forms part of the double marimba ensemble, and the other is a smaller, one-player diatonic marimba.

29. This type of marimba can also be found forming an ensemble with a flute and accompanying the Mexicanos dance-drama in Totonicapán (Arrivillaga 1993, 86).

30. Small numbers of arc marimbas with gourd resonators and marimbas with bamboo resonators were still being made for the tourist market in Escuintla municipality in 1960 (Chenoweth 1964). These instruments can be found today in Guatemala City's craft stores.

31. Kaptain (1992, 14–15) presents a chronology of the history of the Chiapan marimba, where marimbas with wooden resonators were made in the 1840–50s. Information provided by Saenz Poggio suggests that this improvement had already been made by the eighteenth century.

32. Other marimba-music families from Quezaltenango during this time were the Ovalle and the Bethancourt families (Godínez 2002, 157–76; Sánchez Castillo 2001, 125–91).

33. Lester Godínez (2002, 126–31) rightly defends the popular origin of the marimba, although I don't understand his difficulty in accepting that the hegemonic nationalistic discourse of the petite bourgeoisie consists precisely in appropriating popular symbols in order to legitimize itself as a ruling class.

34. Wax actually allows the lowering of the tonality of the keys and not their raising, as suggested by Paniagua and by Godínez (2002, 121–26).

35. Julio Sánchez Castillo (2001) gives a list of 2,153 pieces that make up a large part of the national marimba production of dance music registered in the Guatemalan Association of Authors and Composers (AGAYC); 12 percent of these compositions pertain to those deemed folklore son or típico son.

36. Recent publications by Tánchez Coutiño (1998), Sánchez Castillo (2001), and Godínez (2002) are invaluable sources on the history of Guatemalan music, particularly the marimba and its players and composers.

37. Lester Godínez (2002, 214–16) confirms that the guarimba rhythm was created by the composer Victor Wotzbeli Aguilar (1897–1940) and was originally a foxtrot in 6/8 beat, that is, a fusion of a simple binary meter of 2/2 but written in a 6/8 meter. According to Tánchez Coutiño (1998, 98), this is a rhythm derived from the son written in a rapid 6/8 meter. This rhythm is still considered the best of Guatemalan popular dance music.

38. In the past decade, the cost of hiring a son marimba for one hour is the same as the cost of a flute-and-big drum ensemble for a full day.

39. Dance-drama costumes are made for hire in shops in Totonicapán. See García Escobar (1992, 37) for a historical overview of these shops (morerias), which date to the eighteenth century.

40. That is, the family had just celebrated the fourteenth anniversary of his death.

41. The capitals of the provinces of Baja Verapaz and Alta Verapaz, respectively.

42. This is not strictly true; some piezas can be adapted for the son marimba.

43. Temporary cantinas were set up on chinamas (long wooden planks) around the plaza.

44. Paulino Jerónimo boasted that his grandfather and great-grandfather developed this practice: "They alone transposed it," he claimed. "They had the ability to change its voice, applying wax quickly and thus modifying it. The double marimba came later."

45. For detailed descriptions of marimba craftsmanship, see Chenoweth (1964); for photographs of the construction process, see Camposeco (1992).

46. Vibrating membranes that modify a sound produced in some other way, adding a nasal or buzzing quality (Randel 1986).

47. There are two chromatic tenor marimbas in Rabinal dedicated solely to playing hymns and prayers for the Catholic parish services.

48. For more technical information about the double marimba, see Chenoweth (1964).

49. The Caballero family has produced several generations of musicians. Fifty years ago they formed a brass band and an ensemble of string instruments (violin and counter-bass).

50. As mentioned in Chapter 3, the Rabinalense tradition distinguished sones according to context: dance son and cofradía son. In musical terms this distinction implies that the sones are played in a different order.

51. A wide variety of instrumental groupings is possible in the Indian son.

52. The words of the farewell son are: <u>xaja uala nana, xaja uala tata,</u> which means: dance mother ancestor, dance father ancestor.

53. For a discussion of processes of change and the relationship between soundscape and social meaning, see Leyshon, Matless, and Revill (1998).

54. Loudspeakers were installed to announce lottery and sports results during fairs, a practice that continues today.

55. Many homes now have radio-cassette recorders, although batteries and tapes are economically restricted for most people.

CHAPTER FIVE

1. Some of the prohibitions of the colonial era (sixteenth to early nineteenth centuries) can be found in the General Archive of Central America and in the Archbishopric Historical Archive in Guatemala City. Those that refer to Indian dances and celebrations by name are published—e.g., "Decree prohibiting the Tum dance, year 1593," A1.39.1751, p. 46; A1.68.3, record 48127, file 5555; "Se prohibe el baile de la zarabanda en los pueblos de la provincia de Zapotitlan año 1669" (Ordoñez Jonama 1989, 97–104); "Decree prohibiting dances and zarabandas in the Guatemala valley, year 1749," A1.22.1508, p. 221. Other bans on dances in Guatemala include A1.68-3, file 2589, record 21110, p. 1; "Royal provision to the Verapaz mayor on the excesses ensuing from celebrations, year 1799," A1, file 4659, record 39868; "Prohibition of zarabandas in Suchitepequez, year 1802", A1.68.24.823–.2815. Acuña (1975) offers an analysis of church decrees and prohibitions against the <u>Tum</u> dance-drama, which he identifies as the predecessor to the Rabinal Achi dance-drama.

2. As early as 1617 provincial civil authorities were running taverns in Indian towns (AGCA, A1.23, file 1515, p. 3). Several centuries later, roughly between 1850 and 1930, the alcohol business was formally recognized in the *habilitación* system (Chapter 1).

3. "Captains" were cargo holders of cofradias (see Chapter 2).

4. Another version survives among Ladinos of Retauhuleu province. Known as the zarabanda de lazo, this is a social dance in which a lazo (ribbon) is tied across the dance hall to separate couples who make a donation for each pieza they dance.

5. See Warren's (1992) discussion of mythology as the separatist ideology of a bi-ethnic society.

6. Strictly speaking, Achi discourse does not assign a gender to alcohol (sugar cane spirits), although it is not uncommon for alcohol to be personified.

7. My personal experience with alcohol among the Maya Tzeltales of Chanal, Chiapas, led me to conclude that surrendering completely to drunkenness is a means of expressing trust. The minute I started drinking in the same manner as the Chanaleros, falling into a stupor with them in the places where we drank, people began to have a friendlier attitude toward me (Navarrete Pellicer 1988).

8. Participants give musicians alcohol and cigarettes in thanks for the music.

9. Many celebrations of the Catholic calendar also relate to the fertility of the earth and include prayers and dances performed for the mountain spirits so

that they will send rain (Percheron 1979, 74–75). Examples include Rabinal's two main Christian celebrations, the festival of the Holy Cross (3 May) and Corpus Christi (June–July).

10. A "good" husband buys his wife a full outfit, including all of these items, for a fiesta such as that in honor of the municipio's patron saint.

11. I did not realize that he was putting his work "on top" of the marimba, which later allowed him to claim rights over it (her), when I sold it.

12. Zur (1998, 145) describes the harsh criticism of a young woman widowed in the political violence who remarried quickly because her peer group believed she enjoyed sexual relations.

13. Harvey (1994, 73–78) discusses the conflicting nature of kinship in the indigenous societies of the Peruvian Andes, where the balance in the husband/wife relationship depends on the man's ability to show his maleness and wield dominance and control over his woman.

14. Guatemala's counterinsurgency war separated men from their women, as they became either fighters or civilian victims. Many men formed liaisons in their place of refuge; sometimes when a man failed to return after the war, his wife was unsure if her husband was dead or had abandoned her for another woman (Zur 1998).

15. PAC chiefs who raped women in their husbands' absence secured their victims' silence through threats (Zur 1995).

16. Cf. Esteban Uanché's reaction to the "rape" of his marimba (see Chapter 9).

17. Women were blamed even for the rapes committed by the army and PACs during the 1980s (Zur 1998).

18. Some young Rabinalense widows who had formed a widows' group supported by the National Coordination of Widows in Guatemala (CONAVIGUA) stated that they were constantly accused of prostitution, particularly by men who had colluded with the army's repression of their own people or participated in one way or another in local massacres. The local practice of controlling women through sexual harassment and threats results from the men's fears concerning Guatemala's new political openness and the widows' political activism.

19. This idea seems to be a direct descendant of the early colonial judicial authorities' views mentioned above.

20. Achi mythology is rich in interpretations of Scripture, particularly of Genesis, where Eve's disobedience to God makes her a sinner or transgressor of the human's finite freedom (Ricoeur 1969, 252–60), a vehicle of lust, and the creator of human misfortune and mortality.

21. Social pressures make staying single an unattractive alternative for women that becomes even less appealing as they get older and questions of character failure arise.

22. What follows is my recollection of his story.

23. A Maya-Q'eq'chi woman from Cobán, Alta Verapaz. Q'eq'chi women are considered beautiful and desirable partners, just like the princess mother of the character Greenfeathers in the sixteenth-century Rabinal Achi dance-drama. This categorizes the woman not only as an outsider but as someone out of place and time.

CHAPTER SIX

1. During election campaigns, the various political parties try to win support by simulating alegrías, contracting marimba de sones, and distributing free drinks and small gifts to attract voters.

2. Some feelings and actions are classified as both sentimientos and/or emociones, depending on the context. Examples include sik'inik (shout), which can be an expression of happiness or sorrow; rajb'al uk'u'x (a heart's desire, enthusiasm for work, expression of love); kak'un chu k'u'x (to remember, longing) with joy or sadness.

3. Cf. Vogt (1976) on percussive sounds as signaling devices in Zinacanteco ritual of the Tzotzil Maya of Chiapas, Mexico.

4. Goffman's theory of daily life performance is used to demonstrate that music, as a process of communication, depends on social interaction during both musical performance and daily life (see Chapter 9).

5. On this matter Schieffelin (1995) analyzes the creation of spiritual presences in the séances of Kaluli society and suggests that the emergent quality and success of these sessions depend on the medium's ability to convince audience members of the presence of spirits during the séance (for a discussion of the emergent quality of performance, see Bauman 1984, 37–45).

6. Unlike all other prayers, novenas are said in Spanish. The novena practice is also observed by the Ladino population.

7. Some families hire a marimba for the fortieth-day celebration. Choices of music (and, in the first place, whether to have music at all) and of different groups of musicians represent distinct attitudes toward the deceased.

8. Families who lost kin at the height of la violencia were unable to celebrate the first anniversary because alegrías were banned for three years beginning in 1981; in the case of "the disappeared," celebrations did not take place because relatives were uncertain whether death had occurred.

9. First-, seventh-, and fourteenth-anniversary celebrations currently cost between $150 and $200, or more than 1,000 quetzales each. This is equivalent to three or four months' wages on the plantations.

10. The massacres were committed by the army, Ladinos from Rabinal town, and the villages of Pachalum and Pichec, who were acting as "judicial police," and civil defense patrols from the village of Xococ.

11. For the spirits called in these prayers, see Chapter 2.

12. These are titles given to all elder abogados (prayer makers) for having served God in cofradía cargos in the past and for having served the community in higher municipal positions.

13. This is the common way of entering an altar during any fiesta. Breton (1980) describes it in detail as part of the entrance rite during cofradía celebrations.

14. This is the only time I saw a young person express an interest in this most ancient instrumental ensemble. Youngsters say that the music of the violin is "little music" and not as exciting as the marimba music.

15. There were six quetzales to the U.S. dollar in 1995.

16. Despite this belief I did see evangelists remembering their dead during the general celebration of all saints and all souls on 1 and 2 November at the cemetery. This spoke to me of the ambiguous religious position of some evangelists.

17. The mysterio includes several repetitions of the Lord's Prayer and Hail Mary, the Confession of Faith, and the Glory Be, and concludes with a hymn to the Holy Father.

CHAPTER SEVEN

1. The pre-Hispanic idea that a person's destiny is determined according to the day on which he or she is born persists. Each day has its <u>nahual</u> (day owner) or saint, who helps people born on their day, orienting them and giving them knowledge. Unlike some indigenous groups, such as the Momosteco and the Ixil, the Achi are generally unaware of the Maya calendar.

2. It is a "toy" because, for a child, no responsibilities are attached to playing the marimba.

3. I did see fathers marking keys with pieces of paper in order to help apprentices memorize mallet positions. However, their sons found this superfluous and it seems to me that this simple technique is better suited to adult apprentices such as myself, as it provides a means of remembering the keys in the teacher's absence.

4. Theories of a folk-urban continuum suggest unilinear cultural development. Although these theories have been proved erroneous, they can be used to illustrate cultural oppositions and influences between folk and urban traditions (see Singer 1958).

5. Many homes now have radio-cassette recorders, although use is restricted by the owner's ability to purchase tapes and batteries, which are luxury items.

6. The expression of an opinion (even as the result of persistent enquiry by an outsider) is a direct and personal communication and, as such, exposes the person to vengeance through witchcraft (Chapter 9).

7. The marimba they chose for me was named Marim Balam, which is a contraction of marimba Balam (jaguar marimba) or Maria Balam (jaguar woman).

8. This comparison has an important symbolic connotation (see Chapter 5).

9. Santiago (St. James) was the patron saint of Spanish soldiers even before the conquest; known as the "killer of Moors" (*Matamoros*) during the long war to expel Muslims from Spain, the saint became known as the "killer of Indians" (*mata-indios*) in the New World (Wright 1985, 201).

10. Juan Ordoñez has a more conciliatory attitude: "They did not hear them when they were living here but nevertheless they appreciate them if the alegría celebration is for them."

11. Society seems to impose limits on stylistic innovations that become too abstruse and complicated. Cf. Herndon and McLeod's (1990) description of a traditional folk guitarist in Malta who was rejected by his musical colleagues for these reasons.

12. That Esteban failed to conform in other ways also affected attitudes toward his music. See Chapters 8 and 9.

CHAPTER EIGHT

1. <u>Ki'koteem</u> or <u>jorob'eem</u> refers to positive pride related to happiness and admiration.

2. Someone described as <u>ku' an nim che riib'</u> only wants things for himself (negative self-pride).

3. During the boom of cantina zarabandas in the 1950s, a son marimba ensemble charged $3 for a twenty-four-hour gig. The same gig today costs between $26 and $40, depending on the prestige of the marimba ensemble.

4. Many evangelicals confess that one reason for their conversion was to avoid the expense of participating in the cofradía cargo system.

5. The FRG (Republican Front of Guatemala) is the political party of Rios Montt, the dictator who presided over the height of la violencia.

6. Indian voters tend to be cynical about democracy, saying that local candidates want personal power and a chance to plunder the municipal budget.

7. In Malawi the market economy is already a given and people see nothing wrong with looking for prosperity through involvement in it. However, arguments about how that prosperity is achieved are expressed through reference to witchcraft (Englund 1996).

8. As the Achi believe that one person's gain is another's loss, this implies that an individual who accumulates money, goods, or land "in God's name" has been given God's blessing to do so.

9. These themes are closely related to envy, social conflict, and witchcraft as mechanisms of social responsibility.

10. The choice of marimba ensemble can increase a cofradía's annual music expenditure by 10 to 15 percent. If there is an obligation to perform a dance-drama, where the major expense is the marimba ensemble, then costs climb another 5 to 7 percent or more.

11. Rabinalenses believe that all things have a spirit or *dueño* (keeper) who has control over them.

CHAPTER NINE

1. I am referring here to communication as defined by Feld, that is, as "a socially interactive and intersubjective process of reality construction through message production and interpretation" (1984, 15).

2. I consider the process of musical communication to be synonymous with the process of the production and consumption of music.

3. I heard of two cases in which this happened, both among conjunto marimba ensembles created outside the family, whose members had bought the instruments together.

4. I found that their count fell far short and that they tended to repeat the same sones. They explained that there were more that they could not bring to mind, that some are sones sin nombre (without names), and that some were simply named after their place of origin (there are four Cubulero sones, for example). There were also other sones whose names they did not know, which is a great disadvantage for marimbistas.

5. Bauman (1984) says that competence among performers is a central criterion for eligibility and access to performance; this criterion varies from culture to culture.

6. Here I use the term "gossip" to mean conversation about absent third parties. Haviland (1977) discusses gossip among the Maya people of Zinacantan as an indirect way of evaluating people's behavior.

7. Rabinal's recent history is a testament to the army's effective use of gossip and rumor to divide society, pitting neighbors and even family members against each other.

8. Mal hecho differs from other forms of witchcraft in that it is neither deliberate nor directional.

9. Ajq" mes cure through prayers, which may be combined with the use of medicinal plants. Ajq" iij also heal with prayers and plants and are also diviners who can identify witchcraft.

10. What follows is a brief reconstruction of Esteban's account of the affair.

11. For the treatment of female family members, see Chapter 5.

12. Children under the age of twelve are not believed to be able to think for themselves, so parents hit them to make them learn.

13. Two years later, in 1953, Mario Valdizon put his observations to personal use and opened what became Rabinal's most famous cantina, El Motagua, just off the plaza. Until 1981, he regularly hired two marimbas for zarabandas.

Chapter Ten

1. In Rabinal, Catholic Action never directly opposed the cofradía system.

2. For a historical perspective on Ladino-Indian identities as inverse images, see Hawkins (1984).

Glossary

Abogado. Advocate, surrogate agent mediating between people and the supernatural; prayer maker. Also called *cabezante* or *devocionista* (head or leader and devotion maker). When a prayer maker leads a *cofradía* ritual he is called *teniente* (lieutenant); when praying at weddings and anniversaries of the dead he is called *padrino* (godfather) or tz'onowel' (petition maker).

Adufe. Square drum, called tupe in the Achi language.

Alegría. A Rabinalense social musical occasion.

Ánimas. Souls or spirits of the dead.

Bolero. A popular music piece of the *pieza* genre. Originally a Spanish dance music form in triple meter.

Cabo de año (**end of year**). Anniversary of the dead. Achi people commemorate the death of their family members. A series of commemorations that help the souls of deceased family members rest in peace take place seven or nine days and forty days after death has occurred. Subsequent commemorations occur on the first, seventh, and fourteenth anniversaries of the death. After the fourteenth anniversary, relatives' obligations to the dead cease.

Calvario (**Calvary**). Chapel of the Lord of mercy built at the entrance of the main cemetery situated at the west end of town and facing east toward the entrance of the main church in town. It is mainly used by abogados on Mondays, when they pray for the souls of the dead.

Canción ranchera. Mexican country songs.

Chromatic marimba. A marimba built with a chromatic-scale keyboard.

Cofradía. In Latin America the cofradías are sodalities or brotherhoods that take care of the saints, including the organization of their festivities. There are sixteen indigenous cofradías in Rabinal.

Colear. To follow; in marimba music the harmony or center player and the bass player follow the leading part of the treble player.

Conjunto marimba. An ensemble formed by a pieza marimba for four players, a double bass, and a drum set. The conjunto marimba plays all the urban popular repertoire. A few conjunto marimba ensembles have a chromatic marimba instead of a diatonic pieza marimba.

Contradanza (**contredanse**). A ballroom dance of the late eighteenth century and first half of the nineteenth. The structure has two parts, both of which have an eight-measure theme that repeats with variations, including different endings. The dancers form two lines, one in front of the other. Each dancer takes his turn, and turns alternate between the two lines. Each dancer makes the same figures in crossing to the other line. This piece is the theme played in the Costeño dance-drama.

Corrido. (1) A popular musical piece of the pieza genre derived from the polka dance music of the border between Mexico and the United States; (2) a style of playing the bass voice of the marimba, consisting of playing a chord simultaneously with both hands.

Costeño. The favorite traditional dance-drama of Rabinal. It is danced to marimba music.

Cuchubal. Partnership in a task or business.

Cumbia. A popular Afro-Caribbean dance-music piece considered a pieza in Rabinal. It originated in Colombia.

Danza. An eighteenth-century dance piece called *danza de la muerte* (death dance) played in the Animalitos dance-drama. It is a bolero dance in triple meter, with an A-B-A-B-B-A structure. The piece is danced by a couple of animal characters holding arms, side by side, in a slow walking motion.

Double Marimba. A set of two marimbas, a large one called the *marimba grande* for four players and a smaller one called *tenor* for three players. Both marimbas have chromatic-scale keyboards and can therefore be used to play any musical piece composed in more than one key or tonality.

Dueño. Spirit owner of the world, and of all things on earth.

Encadenarse. An error in musical performance that happens when the bass and/or harmony marimba musicians play behind and not simultaneously with the treble player.

Guaracha. A popular type of dance music considered part of the pieza genre in Rabinal, originating in Puerto Rica and Cuba.

Interval. The distance between two pitches or the sound frequency difference between two pitches, which may be measured in a number of whole tones and semitones.

Jalar. To pull; as a musical term this refers to the treble player's leading a marimba ensemble; the complementary response to this is the *colear* or following by the remaining two players.

Ladino. Non-Indian, or person who does not follow the Indian tradition.

Marcado. A style of playing the bass part of the marimba as an *arpeggio* or as a melodic formula.

Merengue. A popular dance-music piece considered a pieza in Rabinal. This originated in the Dominican Republic.

Mestizo. Person of mixed race. Equivalent to Ladino.

Mozo. A contract worker. A marimba mozo is an individual with experience and knowledge of the musical repertory who offers his services for an event to marimba owners who are missing a player.

Pasillo. A popular dance-music piece of the pieza genre.

Pieza. A term used by Achi Rabinalenses to refer to all popular urban music as a genre.

Pieza marimba. A diatonic marimba used for the repertoire of piezas. It has forty-two keys arranged in a diatonic scale and is played by four musicians.

Simple marimba. A diatonic marimba with forty keys for three players in the case of the son marimba, or forty-two keys, for three or four players, in the case of the pieza marimba, which is also used for the conjunto marimba ensembles.

Siuanaba. A female evil spirit who appears before drunken men, especially young men, who have a strong sexual desire for women other than their wives or girlfriends. She is the devil, or death, disguised as a beautiful woman and lures men to their death.

Son. A traditional dance-music genre that is believed to be the music of the ancestors. It may be played by different types of musical ensembles, but the largest repertoire of sones is played on the diatonic marimba at a moderate to rapid tempo, combining elements of compound duple and simple triple metres. The form has two to four eight-measure sections that repeat in different order.

Son con cera (**son with wax**). A type of son played in the key adjacent to the original key of the diatonic marimba. Musicians place little balls of wax under the keys of the seventh degree of the diatonic scale keyboard of the diatonic marimba. The wax lowers the pitch of the keys by approximately half a tone, thereby changing the keyboard scale to a neighboring tonality (e.g., C to F major). Sones *sin cera* (without wax) are all those sones played in the original key of the diatonic marimba.

Son de dos baquetas (**two-mallet son**). A type of son classified according to the number of mallets used by the middle player, who carries the harmony on the son marimba. The middle player may use two, three, or four mallets, depending on the complexity of the harmony; accordingly there are two-, three-, and four-mallet sones.

Son marimba. A diatonic marimba used for the repertoire of sones. It has forty keys arranged in a diatonic scale and is played by three musicians.

Tiple. Marimba treble player or position.

Tupe. Square drum, called adufe in Spanish. The tupe and violin form an ensemble.

Vuelta. Musical term with multiple meanings. It may refer to the ornamentation of a melody, to a section, strophe, or part of the piece, to a variation, chorus, or repetition of a section, or to an improvisatory style.

Zarabanda. Sarabande; in contemporary Rabinal this refers to a social gathering where people drink and dance to the son marimba.

Discography

Antologìa del maestro Marco Antonio Castillo. N.d. Compact Disc. Guatemala: Difosa.

Ars Nova. 1993. *Mexican Colonial Music from the Sixteenth and Seventeenth Centuries*. Compact Disc. Copyright: Claudio Valdéz Kuri.

Casa Kójom. 1987. *Música indígena de Guatemala*. Cassette. Guatemala: K'ojom.

Marimba Hurtado Hermanos. 1992. *Sixteen Grandes Exitos*. Discos de centroamérica.

Marimba Maderas Chapinas. N.d. *Alegría chapina*. Vol. 33. Compact Disc. Guatemala: Difosa.

Marimba Mayalandia. 1983. One 45 RPM record. Fonica Records.

Marimba Reina del ejercito. N.d. *Naranjales de Rabinal*. Guatemala: Estudios AGAYC.

Marimba Teclas Morenas de Oliverio Navarro. N.d. *Recordando a Rafael Ibarra*. Guatemala: IM Records.

Taller de sonido Tezulutlán. 1998. *Sones de mi tierra. Música de la etnia Achi*. Vol. 1. Cassette. Guatemala: Producciones Tezulutlán.

References

Acroyd, Peter. 1998. *The life of Sir Thomas More*. London: Chatto and Windus.

Acuña, René. 1975. *Introducción al estudio del Rabinal Achi*. Mexico City: Universidad Nacional Autónoma de México.

———. 1978. *Farsas y representaciones escénicas de los mayas antiguos*. Mexico City: Universidad Nacional Autónoma de México.

Adams, Richard N. 1952. *Creencias y prácticas del indígena*. Guatemala City: Instituto Indigenista Nacional.

———. 1959. La ladinización en Guatemala. *Integración social en Guatemala* 2 (9): 123–37.

———. 1994 Guatemalan ladinization and history. *The Americas* 50 (4): 527–43.

AGCA (Central America General Archive, Guatemala City). A1, file 183, record 3747; A1.23, file 1527, p. 439; A1.2.4, file 2199, record 15755, p. 50; A1.24, file 2197, record 15751, p. 313; A1.23, file 1540, p. 54; A1.23, file 1513, p. 676; A1.23, file 1514, pp. 22, 37; A1.1, record 25, file 1, pp. 1, 13; A1.23, file 1516, p. 57; A1.23, file 1517, p. 108; A1.23, file 1518, p. 211; A1.39, file 1751, p. 46; A1.68-3, record 48127, file 5555; A1.22, file 1508l, p. 221; A1.68-3, file 2589, record 21110, p. 1; A1, file 4659, record 39868; A1.68.24.823.2815.

AHA (Archdiocesan Historical Archive, Guatemala City). Visitas pastorales, vol. 41; Vicaría de Verapaz, 1844–54, 68, vol. 7.

Alejos, José. 1992. Los Guatemaltecos de 1770 en la descripción de Pedro Cortés y Larraz. *Estudios de Cultura Maya* 19: 215–68.

Almorza Alpírez, Antonio. 1994. *Historia de la radiodifusion Guatemalteca*. Guatemala City: San Antonio.

Alvarez-Pereyre, Frank, and Simha Arom. 1993. Ethnomusicology and the emic/etic issue. *World of Music* 35 (1): 7–33.

America's Watch. 1986. *Civil patrols in Guatemala*. New York: America's Watch Committee.

Anderson, Benedict. 1991. *Imagined communities: Reflections on the origins and spread of nationalism*. London: Verso.

Apel, Willi. 1961. *The notation of polyphonic music, 900–1600*. Cambridge, Mass.: Medieval Academy of America.

App, Lawrence J. 1998. Afro-Colombian traditions. In *The Garland encyclopedia of world music*. Vol. 2, *South America, Mexico, Central America, and the Caribbean*, ed. Dale A. Olsen and Daniel E. Sheehy, 400–412. New York: Garland Publishing.

Arias, Arturo. 1990. Changing Indian identity: Guatemala's violent transition to modernity. In *Guatemala Indians and the state, 1540–1988*, ed. Carol Smith, 230–57. Austin: University of Texas Press.

Armas, Lara Marcial. 1970. *Origen de la marimba, su desenvolvimiento y otros instrumentos músicos.* Guatemala City: Folklore Guatemalteco.

Arnauld, Marie-Charlotte. 1993. Los territorios políticos de las cuencas de Salamá, Rabinal y Cubulco en el posclásico. In *Representaciones del espacio político en las tierras altas de Guatemala*, coord. Alain Breton, 43–110. Guatemala City y Mexico City: Centro de Estudios Mexicanos y Centroamericanos.

Arrivillaga Cortés, Alfonso. 1990. La música tradicional garífuna en Guatemala. *Latin American Music Review* 11 (2): 251–80.

———. 1993 Del "xul" a los "Xacalcojes": La música Maya Quiché de Totonicapán." *Tradiciones de Guatemala* 39: 83–89.

Baily, John. 1990. John Blacking and his place in ethnomusicology. *Yearbook for Traditional Music* 22: xii–xxi.

Barry, Tom. 1987. *The roots of rebellion: Land and hunger in Central America.* Boston: South End Press.

———. 1992. *Inside Guatemala.* Albuquerque: Interhemispheric Education Resource Center.

Bartók, Béla. 1987. *Escritos sobre música popular.* Mexico City: Siglo Veintiuno.

Barz, Gregory F., and Timothy J. Cooley, eds. 1997. *Shadows in the field: New perspectives for fieldwork in ethnomusicology.* New York: Oxford University Press.

Basso, Ellen B. 1981. A "musical view of the universe": Kalapalo myth and ritual as religious performance. *Journal of American Folklore Society* 94 (July–Sept): 273–91.

Bateson, Gregory. 1972. *Steps to an ecology of mind.* New York: Ballantine Books.

Bauman, Max. 1993. Listening as an emic/etic process in the context of observation and enquiry. *World of Music* 35 (1): 34–62.

Bauman, Richard. 1984. *Verbal art as performance.* Prospect Heights, Ill.: Waveland Press.

———. 1992. Performance. In *Folklore, cultural performances, and popular entertainment: A communications-centered handbook*, ed. Richard Bauman, 41–49. Oxford: Oxford University Press.

Béhague, Gerard. 1980. Guatemala I: Art music. In *New groves dictionary of music and musicians*, ed. Stanley Sadie, 7:775–76. London: Macmillan.

———. 1991. Reflections on the ideological history of Latin American ethnomusicology. In *Comparative musicology and anthropology of music: Essays on the history of ethnomusicology*, ed. Bruno Nettl and Philip V. Bohlman, 56–68. Chicago: University of Chicago Press.

Berger, Peter. 1967. *The sacred canopy: Elements of a sociological theory of religion.* New York: Anchor Books.

Bertrand, Michel. 1987. *Terre et societe coloniale: Les communautés Maya-Quiché de la région de Rabinal du XVIe au XIXe siècle.* Collection Etudes Mésoaméricaines 1–14. Mexico City: Centre d'Etudes Méxicaines et Centraméricaines.

Bierhorst, John. 1985. *Cantares mexicanos: Songs of the Aztecs.* California: Stanford University Press.

Blacking, John. 1971. Deep and surface structures in Venda music. *Yearbook of the International Folk Music Council* 3: 91–108.

———. 1977. Some problems of theory and method in the study of musical change. *Yearbook of the International Folk Music Council* 9: 1–26.

———. 1977. On the question of universals. *World of Music* 19 (1–2): 2–13.

———. 1985. The context of Venda possession music: Reflections on the effectiveness of symbols. *Yearbook for Traditional Music* 17: 64–87.

———. 1986. Identifying processes of musical change. *World of Music* 21 (1): 3–15.

Bloch, Maurice. 1989. *Ritual, history and power: Selected papers in anthropology.* London: Atholone Press.

Bloch, Maurice, and Jonathan Parry. 1982. *Death and the regeneration of life.* Cambridge: Cambridge University Press.

Bode, Barbara. 1961. The dance of the conquest of Guatemala. In *The native theater in middle America.* Middle American Research Institute no. 27: 203–98. New Orleans: Tulane University Press.

Bourdieu, Pierre. 1986. *Outline of a theory of practice.* Cambridge: Cambridge University Press.

Brading, D. A. 1990. Images and prophets: Indian religion and the Spanish conquest." In *The Indian community of colonial Mexico*, ed. Arij Ouweneel and Simon Miller, 184–204. CEDLA no. 58. Amsterdam: Rozenberg Publishers.

Brasseur de Bourbourg, Charles E. 1862. *Rabinal Achi ou le drame-ballet du Tun.* Vol. 2 of *Collection de documents dans les langues indigenes pour servir a l'etude de l'histoire et de la philologie de l'Amerique ancienne.* Paris: Arthus Bertrand.

Breton, Alain. 1979. De saints et des hommes: Les confréries de culte à Rabinal. In *Cahiers de la R. C. P. 500 No. 1: Rabinal et la vallée moyenne du rio Chixoy, Baja Verapaz–Guatemala*, 159–88. Paris: Centre National de la Recherche Scientifique, Institut d'Ethnologie.

———. 1980. Etude d'un fete de confrérie a Rabinal: L'exemple de Saint Pierre Apôtre. In *Cahiers de la R. C. P. 500 No. 2: Rabinal et la vallée moyenne du rio Chixoy, Baja Verapaz–Guatemala*, 171–22. Paris: Centre National de la Recherche Scientifique, Institut d'Ethnologie.

———. 1987. El "complejo ajaw" y el "complejo mam": Actores rituales y heroes miticos entre los Quiche-Achi de Rabinal. Inaugural Conference, Coloquio Internacional de Mayistas, Campeche, Mexico, 17–27 August. Mexico City: Universidad Nacional Autónoma de México.

———. 1993. Territorio, alianzas y guerra en el "Rabinal-Achi": La continuación de un mito, un viraje decisivo de la historia. In *Representaciones del espacio político en las tierras altas de Guatemala*, coord. Alain Breton, 29–41. Cuadernos de Estudios Guatemaltecos 2. Guatemala City: Centro de Estudios Mexicanos y Centroamericanos.

———. 1994. *Rabinal Achi: Un rame dynastique Maya du quinzième siècle.* Nanterre: Sociéte des Américanistes et Société d'ethnologie.

Brintnall, Douglas E. 1979. *Revolt against the dead: The modernization of a Maya community in the highlands of Guatemala.* New York: Gordon and Breach.

Brocheux, Pierre. 1983. Moral economy or political economy? The peasants are always rational. *Journal of Asian Studies* 42 (4): 791–803.

Brown, Peter. 1981. *The cult of the saints: Its rise and function in Latin Christianity.* Chicago: University of Chicago Press.

Bunzel, Ruth. 1952. *Chichicastenango, a Guatemalan village.* New York: J. J. Austin.

Burke, Peter. 1997. *Varieties of cultural history.* Cambridge: Polity Press.

Cabarrus, Carlos. 1979. *La cosmovisión K'eckchi' en proceso de cambio.* San Salvador: Universidad Centroamericana.

Camposeco, José Balvino. 1992. *Te' Chinab' o K'ojom: La marimba de Guatemala.* Guatemala City: Ministerio de Cultural y Deportes, Subcentro Regional de Artesanías y Artes Populares.

Cancian, Frank. 1965. *Economics and prestige in a Maya community: The religious cargo system in Zinacantán.* Stanford: Stanford University Press.

———. 1992 *The decline of community in Zinacantán: Economy, public life, and social stratification, 1960–1987.* Stanford: Stanford University Press.

Carlsen, Robert S., and Martin Prechtel. 1991. The flowering of the dead: An interpretation of highland Maya culture. *Man* 26 (1): 23–42.

Carmona, Gloria. 1984. La música en México al iniciarse la independencia (1810–1821). In *La música de México I, Historia.* Vol. 3, *Periodo de la independencia a la revolución (1810–1910),* ed. Julio Estrada, 11–15. Mexico City: Universidad Nacional Autónoma de México.

Carrasco Pirard, Eduardo. 1999. Canción popular y política. In *Música popular en América Latina,* ed. Rodrigo Torres, 63–70. Santiago, Chile: Fondart.

Castillo, Jesus. 1977. *La música Maya Quiché.* Guatemala City: Editorial Piedra Santa.

Cervantes, Fernando. 1994. *The devil in the new world: The impact of diabolism in new Spain.* New Haven: Yale University Press.

Chaclán, José, trans. 1993. Sobre averiguar la forma en que se celebran los velorios de los párvulos en el pueblo de Apastepeque. Año de 1769. *Boletín del Archivo Histórico Arquidiocesano "Francisco de Paula García Peláez"* 2 (2): 83–86.

Chance, John K., and William B. Taylor. 1985. Cofradías and cargos: A historical perspective on MesoAmerican civil–religious hierarchy. *American Ethnologist* 1 (1): 1–26.

Chenoweth, Vida. 1964. *The marimbas of Guatemala.* Lexington: University Press of Kentucky.

Clifford, James, and George E. Marcus, eds. 1986. *Writing culture: The poetics and politics of ethnography.* Berkeley and Los Angeles: University of California Press.

Colby, Benjamin, and Lore Colby. 1986. *El contador de los dias: Vida y discurso de un adivino Ixil.* Mexico City: Fondo de Cultural Económica.

Connerton, Paul. 1992. *How societies remember.* Cambridge: Cambridge University Press.

Cornell-Drury, Diane. 1999. Significar el compromiso político: La música de la peña chilena. *Música popular en América Latina,* ed. Rodrigo Torres, 76–83. Santiago, Chile: Fondart.

Correa, Gustavo, and Calvin Cannon. 1958. *La loa en Guatemala: Contribución al estudio del teatro popular hispanoamericano.* New Orleans: Tulane University Press.

Csordas, Thomas J., ed. 1994. *Embodiment and experience: The existential ground of culture and self.* Cambridge: Cambridge University Press.

Dary, Claudia. 1991. Escuelas y sociedades de artesanos en la ciudad de Guatemala (1871–1898). *Tradiciones de Guatemala* 35–36: 7–38.

Diccionario de autoridades. 1990. Madrid: Editorial Gredos.

Diocesis del Quiché. 1994. *El Quiché, el pueblo y su iglesia, 1960–1980.* Guatemala City: Diocesis del Quiché.

EAFG (Equipo de Antropológia Forense de Guatemala). 1995. *Las masacres en Rabinal: Estudio histórico antropológico de las masacres de Plan de Sanchez, Chicupac y Rio Negro.* Guatemala City: EAFG.

Eliade, Mircea. 1987. *Shamanism: Archaic techniques of ecstasy.* Princeton: Princeton University Press.

Englund, Harri. 1996. Witchcraft, modernity, and the person: The morality of accumulation in central Malawi. *Critique of Anthropology* 16 (3): 257–80.

Evans-Pritchard, E. E. 1976. *Witchcraft, oracles, and magic among the Azande.* Oxford: Clarendon Press.

Eyler, David P. 1993. The Hurtado brothers' royal marimba band of Guatemala. *Percussive Notes* 31 (Feb.): 48–54.

Falla, Ricardo. 1980. *Quiché rebelde: Estudio de un movimiento de conversión religiosa, rebelde a las creencias tradicionales, en San Antonio Ilotenango Quiché (1948–1970).* Vol. 7 of Editorial Universitaria Colección "Realidad Nuestra." Guatemala City: Universidad de San Carlos.

———. 1986. *Esa muerte que nos hace vivir: Estudio de la religión popular de Esquintla (Guatemala).* San Salvador: UCA.

Farriss, Nancy. 1984. *Maya society under colonial rule: The collective enterprise of survival.* Princeton: Princeton University Press.

———. 1987. Remembering the future, anticipating the past: History, time, and cosmology among the Maya of Yucatan. *Comparative Studies in Society and History* 29 (3): 566–93.

Feld, Steven. 1984. Communication, music, and speech about music. *Yearbook for Traditional Music* 16: 1–18.

———. 1990. *Sound and sentiment: Birds, weeping, poetics, and song in Kaluli expression.* 2d ed. Philadelphia: University of Pennsylvania Press.

Fernández, Carlos. 1998a. Costa Rica. In *The Garland encyclopedia of world music.* Vol. 2, *South America, Mexico, Central America, and the Caribbean,* ed. Dale A. Olsen and Daniel E. Sheehy, 680–705. New York: Garland Publishing.

———. 1998b. Bribri and Cabecar. In *The Garland encyclopedia of world music.* Vol. 2, *South America, Mexico, Central America, and the Caribbean,* ed. Dale A. Olsen and Daniel E. Sheehy, 631–36. New York: Garland Publishing.

Fernández, Nohema. 1989. La contradanza Cubana y Manuel Saumell. *Latin American Music Review* 10 (1): 116–34.

Foster, George M. 1965. Peasant society and the image of the limited good. *American Anthropologist* 67 (2): 293–315.

———. 1985. *Cultura y conquista: La herencia española de América*, trans. Carlo Antonio Castro. Mexico City: Universidad Veracruzana Editorial.

Friso, Alfonso, M. 1981. La música y el canto religioso entre los Kekchis de Guatemala, ayer y hoy. *Estudios Teológicos* 8 (15): 113–92.

Furst, Jill, and Leslie McKeever. 1995. *The natural history of the soul in ancient Mexico.* New Haven: Yale University Press.

García Escobar, Carlos René. 1992. *Talleres, trajes y danzas tradicionales de Guatemala: El caso de San Cristóbal Totonicapán.* Guatemala City: Universidad de San Carlos.

Garfias, Robert. 1983. The marimba of Mexico and Central America. *Latin American Music Review* 4 (2): 203–13.

Geertz, Clifford. 1984. From the native point of view: On the nature of anthropological understanding. In *Culture theory: Essays on mind, self, and emotion,* ed. Richard Shweder and Robert Le Vine, 123–36. Cambridge: Cambridge University Press.

Godínez, Lester. 2002. *La marimba Guatemalteca.* Mexico City: Fondo de Cultura Económica.

Goffman, Erving. 1959. *The presentation of self in everyday life.* London: Penguin Books.

———. 1974. *Frame analysis: An essay on the organization of experience.* Cambridge: Harvard University Press.

———. 1976. Performances. In *Ritual, play, and performance,* ed. Richard Schechner and Mady Schuman, 89–96. New York: Seabury Press.

Gossen, Gary H. 1979. *Los Chamulas en el mundo del sol.* Mexico City: Instituto Nacional Indigenista.

Gourlay, K. A., and Lucy Durán. 1984. Balo. In *New groves dictionary of musical instruments,* ed. Stanley Sadie, 1:117. New York: Macmillan.

Greene, Oliver. 1998. Belize. In *The Garland encyclopedia of world music.* Vol. 2, *South America, Mexico, Central America, and the Caribbean,* ed. Dale A. Olsen and Daniel E. Sheehy, 666–79. New York: Garland Publishing.

Guiteras, Calixta. 1986. *Los peligros del alma: visión del mundo de un Tzotzil.* Mexico City: Fondo de Cultura Económica.

Guthrie, Malcolm. 1967. *Comparative Bantu: An introduction to the comparative linguistics and prehistory of the Bantu languages.* London: Greggs.

Halbwachs, Maurice. 1980. *The collective memory.* New York: Harper Colophon Books.

Hale, Charles. 1997. Consciousness, violence, and the politics of memory in Guatemala. *Current Anthropology* 38 (5): 817–38.

Hamilton, Malcolm B. 1995. *The sociology of religion: Theoretical and comparative perspectives.* London: Routledge.

Hammond, Norman. 1972a. Classic Maya music. Part I: Maya drums. *Archaeology* 25 (2): 125–31.

———. 1972b. Classic Maya music. Part II: Rattles, shakers, raspers, wind and string instruments. *Archaeology* 25 (3): 222–28.

Harris, Olivia. 1982. The dead and the devils among the Bolivian Laymi. In *Death and the regeneration of life,* ed. Maurice Bloch and Jonathan Parry, 45–73. Cambridge: Cambridge University Press.

_____. 1995. The sources and meaning of money: Beyond the market paradigm in an *Ayllu* of northern Potosí. In *Ethnicity, markets, and migration in the Andes: At the crossroads of history and anthropology*, ed. Brooke Larson and Olivia Harris, 296–328. Durham: Duke University Press.

Harrison, Frank, and Joan Harrison. 1968. Spanish elements in the music of the two Maya groups in Chiapas. *Selected Reports Los Angeles: Institute of Ethnomusicology* 1 (2): 1–44.

Harvey, Penelope. 1994. Domestic violence in the Peruvian Andes. In *Sex and violence: Issues of representation and experience*, ed. Penelope Harvey and Peter Gow, 66–89. London: Routledge.

Harvey, Penelope, and Peter Gow, eds. 1994. *Sex and violence: Issues of representation and experience*. London: Routledge.

Harwood, Dane L. 1979. Contributions from psychology to musical universals. *World of Music* 21 (1): 48–64.

Haviland, John Beard. 1977. *Gossip, reputation, and knowledge in Zinacantan*. Chicago: University of Chicago Press.

Hawkins, John. 1984. *Inverse images: The meaning of culture, ethnicity, and family in postcolonial Guatemala*. Albuquerque: University of New Mexico Press.

Hernández, Jose Jesus. 1974. *El aguardiente de caña en México (1724–1810)*. Sevilla: Escuela de Estudios Hispano-Americanas de Sevilla.

Herndon, Marcia. 1971. The Cherokee ballgame cycle: An ethnomusicologist's view. *Ethnomusicology* 15 (3): 339–52.

_____. 1974. Analysis: The herding of sacred cows? *Ethnomusicology* 18 (2): 219–62.

_____. 1993. Insiders, outsiders: Knowing our limits, limiting our knowing. *World of Music* 35 (1): 63–80.

Herndon, Marcia, and Norma McLeod. 1990. *Music as culture*. Darby, Pa.: Norwood Editions.

Herskovits, Melville J. 1974. *El hombre y sus obras: La ciencia de la antropología cultural*. Mexico City: Fondo de Cultura Económica.

Hill, Robert M., and John Monaghan. 1987. *Continuities in highland Maya social organization: Ethnicity in Sacapulas, Guatemala*. Philadelphia: University of Pennsylvania Press.

Hobsbawm, Eric, and Terence Ranger. 1993. *The invention of tradition*. Cambridge: Cambridge University Press.

Hood, Mantle. 1971. *The ethnomusicologist*. New York: McGraw Hill.

Horspool, Glen A. 1982. The music of the Quiche-Maya of Momostenango in its cultural setting. Ph.D. diss., University of California at Los Angeles.

Horton, Donald. 1943. The functions of alcohol in primitive societies: A cross-cultural study. *Quarterly Journal of Studies on Alcohol* 4: 199–320.

Hudson, Richard. 1980. Sarabande. In *New groves dictionary of music and musicians*, ed. Stanley Sadie, 16:489–93. London: Macmillan.

Ingham, John M. 1986. *Mary, Michael, and Lucifer: Folk Catholicism in central Mexico*. Austin: University of Texas Press.

Instituto Nacional de Estadística. 1991. *Estimaciones de población urbana y rural por departamento y municipio 1990–95.* Guatemala City: Instituto Nacional de Estadística.

———. 1993. *X Censo nacional de población y vivienda de habitación, 1992–93.* Guatemala City: Instituto Nacional de Estadística.

———. 1995. *X Censo nacional de población y vivienda de habitación, 1994.* Guatemala City: Instituto Nacional de Estadística.

Jopling, Carol F., comp. 1994. *Indios y negros en Panamá en los siglos XVI y XVII.* Guatemala City: Centro de Investigaciones Regionales de Mesoamérica, Antigua, Guatemala, and S. Woodstock, Vt.: Plumsock Mesoamerican Studies.

Kaptain, Lawrence. 1992. *The Wood That Sings: The Marimba in Chiapas, Mexico.* Everett: Honeyrock.

Koskoff, Ellen. 1988. Cognitive strategies in rehearsal. In vol. 7 of *Selected reports in ethnomusicology: Issues in the conceptualization of music,* ed. James Porter and Ali Jihad Racy, 59–68. Los Angeles: University of California, Department of Ethnomusicology.

Kubik, Gerhard. 1984. Marimba 1: Africa and Latin America. In *New groves dictionary of musical instruments,* ed. Stanley Sadie 2:614–16. New York: Macmillan.

La Farge, Oliver. 1994. *La costumbre en Santa Eulalia, Huehuetenango en 1932.* Guatemala City: Cholsamaj.

Leavitt, John. 1996. Meaning and feeling in the anthropology of emotions. *American Ethnologist* 23 (3): 514–39.

Le Bot, Yvon. 1995. *La guerra en tierras mayas: Comunidad violencia y modernidad en Guatemala (1970–1992).* Mexico City: Fondo de Cultura Económica.

Lehnhoff, Dieter. 1986. *Espada y pentagrama: La música polifónica en la Guatemala del siglo XVI.* Guatemala City: Universidad Rafael Landivar.

———. 1994. *Rafael Antonio Castellanos: Vida y obra de un músico guatemalteco.* Guatemala City: Universidad Rafael Landivar.

Lemmon, Alfred E. 1990. Reglas y estatutos del coro de la santa metropolitana iglesia de Santiago de Goathemala. *Mesoamerica* 11 (Dec. 1990): 299–314.

Lévi-Strauss, Claude. 1995. *The story of lynx.* Chicago: University of Chicago Press.

Leyshon, Andrew, David Matless, and George Revill, eds. 1998. *The place of music.* New York: Guilford Press.

López Austin, Alfredo. 1996. Cuerpo humano e ideología. Mexico City: University Nacional Autónoma México.

López Mayorical, Mariano. 1978. *La polémica de "la marimba."* Guatemala City: Jose de Pineda Ibarra.

López Mena, Sergio. 1996. *Pedro Trejo, cancionero.* Mexico City: Universidad Nacional Autónoma de México.

Lovell, W. George, and Christopher H. Lutz. 2000. *Demografía e imperio: Guia para la historia de la población de la América Central Española, 1500–1821.* Guatemala City: Plumsock Mesoamerican Studies, Editorial Universitaria, Universidad de San Carlos de Guatemala.

Lutz, Catherine A., and Lila Abu-Lughud. 1990. *Language and the politics of emotion.* Cambridge: Cambridge University Press.

Mace, Carroll E. 1966. Three Quiche dance-dramas of Rabinal, Guatemala. Ph.D. diss., Tulane University.

_____. 1967. Nueva y mas reciente información sobre los bailes-drama de Rabinal y del descubrimiento de Rabinal-Achi. In *Anthropologia e historia de Guatemala*, 19:20–37. Guatemala City: Ministerio de Educación Publicación.

_____. 1981. Some aspects of native dances from Guatemala and Rabinal. *Mesoamérica* 1 (2): 83–136.

Manuel, Peter. 1991. The cassette industry and popular music in North India. *Popular Music* 10 (2): 189–204.

Marcus, George E., and Michael M. J. Fischer. 1986. *Anthropology as cultural critique: An experimental moment in the human sciences*. Chicago: University of Chicago Press.

Marroquin, Salvador. 1998. El Salvador. In *The Garland encyclopedia of world music*. Vol. 2, *South America, Mexico, Central America, and the Caribbean*, ed. Dale A. Olsen and Daniel E. Sheehy, 706–20. New York: Garland Publishing.

McArthur, Harry. 1962. Origenes y motivos del baile del Tzunum. *Folklore de Guatemala* 2: 139–52.

_____. 1977. Releasing the dead: Ritual and motivation in Aguacatec dancers. In *Cognitive studies of southern MesoAmerica*, ed. Helen Neuenswander and Dean Arnold, 3–34. Dallas: SIL Museum of Anthropology.

McCreery, David. 1994. *Rural Guatemala, 1760–1940*. Stanford: Stanford University Press.

McLeod, Norma, and Marcia Herndon, eds. 1980. *The ethnography of musical performance*. Darby, Pa.: Norwood Editions.

Mendelson, Michael E. 1957. Religion and world-view in Santiago Atitlan. Ph.D. diss., University of Chicago.

Merriam, Alan P. 1964. *The anthropology of music*. Evanston: Northwestern University Press.

Meyer, Leonard B. 1956. *Emotion and meaning in music*. Chicago: University of Chicago Press.

_____. 1993. Cognitive study of music as culture: Basic premises for "cognitive ethnomusicology." *Proceedings of the First International Conference on Cognitive Musicology, 26–29 August 1993*, ed. Jouko Laaksamo and Jukka Louhivuori. Jyväskylä, Finland: Jyväskylä yliopiston monistuskeskus.

Monsanto, Carlos. 1982. Guatemala a través de su marimba. *Latin American Music Review* 3 (1): 60–71.

Montoya, Matilde. 1970. *Estudio sobre el baile de la conquista*. Guatemala City: Editorial Universitaria.

Morales Hidalgo, Italo. 1983. Los pueblos indígenas de Cahabón y Lanquín en el departamento de Verapaz año de 1847. *Anales de la Academia de Geografía e Historia de Guatemala* 57: 57–79.

Moreno Rivas, Yolanda. 1989. *Historia de la música popular mexicana*. Mexico City: Editorial Patria.

Nash, June. 1970. *In the eyes of the ancestors: Beliefs and behavior in a Mayan community*. New Haven: Yale University Press.

Navarrete Pellicer, Sergio. 1988. *La flor del aguardiente*. Mexico City: Instituto Nacional de Antropología e Historia.

———. 1994. The Maya music of the Rabinal Achi. Master's thesis, University of Maryland at College Park.

———. 1999. The meanings of marimba music in rural Guatemala. Ph.D. diss., University of London.

———. 2001. El bien y el mal: Música, alcohol y mujeres. *Latin American Music Review* 22 (1) (2001): 63–82.

Nettl, Bruno. 1977. On the question of universals. *World of Music* 19 (1–2): 2–13.

Nettl, Bruno, and Philip V. Bohlman, eds. 1991. *Comparative musicology and anthropology of music: Essays on the history of ethnomusicology*. Chicago: University of Chicago Press.

Neuenswander, Helen. 1986. *Dualism: A linguistic and cultural phenomenon among the Cubulco Achi Mayan*. Guatemala City: Summer Institute of Linguistics of Central America.

Nordstrom, Carolyn, and Antonius C.G.M. Robben, eds. 1995. *Fieldwork under fire: Contemporary studies of violence and survival*. Berkeley and Los Angeles: University of California Press.

Nuttini, Hugo G. 1988. Pre-Hispanic component of the syncretic Cult of the Dead in MesoAmerica. *Ethnology* 27 (1): 57–78.

Oakes, Maud. 1951. *The two crosses of todos santos, survivals of Mayan religious ritual*. New York: Pantheon Books.

O'Brien, Linda. 1975. Songs of the face of the earth: Ancestor songs of the Tzutuhil-Maya of Santiago Atitlan, Guatemala. Ph.D. diss., University of California, Los Angeles.

———. 1980. Guatemala II: Folk Music. In *The new groves dictionary of music and musicians*, ed. Stanley Sadie, 7:776–80. London: Macmillan.

Olsen, Dale A., and Daniel E. Sheehy, eds. 1998. *The Garland encyclopedia of world music*. Vol. 2, *South America, Mexico, Central America, and the Caribbean*. New York: Garland Publishing.

Ordóñez, Ramiro, transcriber. 1989. Se prohibe el baile de la sarabanda en los pueblos de la provincia de Zapotitlán año de 1669. *Boletín del Archivo Histórico Arquidiocesano "Francisco de Paula García Peláez"* 1 (3): 97–104.

Ortíz, Fernando. 1965. *La africanía de la música folklórica de Cuba*. Havana: Editora Universitaria.

Ortner, Sherry B., and Harriet Whitehead. 1981. *Sexual meanings: The cultural construction of gender sexuality*. Cambridge: Cambridge University Press.

Pacini Hernández, Deborah. 1998. Popular music of the Spanish-speaking regions. In *The Garland encyclopedia of world music*. Vol. 2, *South America, Mexico, Central America, and the Caribbean*, ed. Dale A. Olsen and Daniel E. Sheehy, 100–106. New York: Garland Publishing.

Pages Larraya, F. 1976. Modos culturales de beber en los aborígenes de Chaco. *Acta Psiquiátrica Psicológica de América Latina* 21–22: 21–45.

Paret-Limardo de Vela, Lise. 1962. *Folklore musical de Guatemala*. Guatemala City: Talleres de la Tipografía Nacional.

———. 1963. *La danza del venado en Guatemala.* Guatemala City: Ministerio de Educación Publica.

Parish Archive of Rabinal, Baja Verapaz, Guatemala. Cofradía books without classification.

Parker, Barbara. 1988. Moral economy, political economy, and the culture of entrepreneurship in highland Nepal. *Ethnology* 27 (2): 181–94.

Parry, Jonathan, and Maurice Bloch. 1989. *Money and the morality of exchange.* Cambridge: Cambridge University Press.

Percheron, Nicole. 1979. Les cofréries religieuses de Rabinal a l'epoque coloniale. In *Cahiers de la R. C. P. 500 No. 1: Rabinal et la vallée moyenne du rio Chixoy, Baja Verapaz–Guatemala,* 59–107. Paris: Centre National de la Recherche Scientifique, Institut d'Ethnologie.

———. 1981. Le Pouvoir et les hommes: Les caciques de Rabinal au 16ème siecle. In *Cahiers de la R. C. P. 500 No. 3: Rabinal et la vallée moyenne du rio Chixoy, Baja Verapaz–Guatemala,* 5–47. Paris: Centre National de la Recherche Scientifique, Institut d'Ethnologie.

Pérez Fernández, Rolando. 1990. *La música Afromestiza Mexicana.* Mexico City: Universidad Veracruzana.

Pérez Montfort, Ricardo. 1994. *Estampas de nacionalismo popular Mexicano: Ensayos sobre cultura popular y nacionalismo.* Mexico City: CIESAS.

Piel, Jean. 1989. *Sajcabajá: Muerte y resurrección de un pueblo de Guatemala, 1500–1970.* Mexico City: Centre d'Etudes Mexicaines et Centramericaines.

Popkin, L. Margaret. 1996. *Civil patrols and their legacy: Overcoming militarization and polarization in the Guatemalan countryside.* Washington, D.C.: Robert F. Kennedy Memorial Center for Human Rights.

Pozas, R. 1977. *Chamula.* Vols. 1–2. Mexico City: Instituto Nacional Indigenista.

Qureshi, Regula Burckhardt. 1982. Qawwali: Making the music happen in the Sufi assembly. In *Performing arts in India: Essays of music, dance, and drama,* ed. Bonnie C. Wade, 121–60. Berkeley: University Press of America.

———. 1986. *Sufi music of India and Pakistan: Sound, context, and meaning in Qawwali.* Cambridge: Cambridge University Press.

Randel, Don, ed. 1986. *The new Harvard dictionary of music.* Cambridge: Belknap Press of Harvard University Press.

Recinos, Adrian, Delia Goetz, and Dionisio Chonay, trans. 1967. *The annals of the Cakchiquels: Title of the lords of Totonicapan.* Norman: University of Oklahoma Press.

Reina, Ruben E. 1966. *The law of the saints: A Pokoman community culture.* New York: Pantheon Books.

Ricard, Robert. 1992. *La conquista espiritual de México: Ensayo sobre el apostolado y los métodos misioneros de las órdenes en la Nueva España de 1523–1524 a 1572.* Mexico City: Fondo de Cultura Económica.

Ricoeur, Paul. 1969. *The symbolism of evil.* Boston: Beacon Press.

Rojas Lima, Flavio. 1988. *La cofradía: Reducto cultural indígena.* Guatemala City: Litografías Modernas.

Rosaldo, Michelle Z. 1984. Toward an anthropology of self and feeling. In *Culture theory: Essays on mind, self, and emotion,* ed. Richard Shweder and Robert Le Vine, 137–57. Cambridge: Cambridge University Press.

Sacor, Hugo, Silvia Alvarez, and Enrique Anleu. 1991. *Rabinal Achi o danza del tun*. Guatemala City: Dirección General de Investigación, Universidad de San Carlos de Guatemala.

Sadie, Stanley, ed. 1984. *New groves dictionary of music and musicians*. London: Macmillan.

Saenz Poggio, José. 1997. *Historia de la música guatemalteca: Desde la monarquía española, hasta fines del año 1877*. Guatemala City: Editorial Cultura.

Sahagún, Bernardino de. 1979. *Historia general de las cosas de Nueva España*. Mexico City: Editorial Porrúa.

Sahlins, Marshall. 1977. *Economía de la edad de piedra*. Madrid: Akal.

———. 1993. Goodbye to *tristes tropes*: Ethnography in the context of modern world history." *Journal of Modern History* 65 (March): 1–25.

———. 1999. Two or three things that I know about culture. *Journal of the Royal Anthropological Institute* 5 (3): 399–421.

Saint-Lu, A. 1968. La Verapaz, espirit évangélique et colonisation: Centre de recherches Hispaniques. Thèsis, Mémoires at Travaux 10. Institut d'Etudes Hispaniques, Paris.

Salazar, Adolfo. 1949. Música, instrumentos y danzas en las obras de Cervantes. *Nuestra Música* 4 (16): 293–361.

Saldívar, Gabriel. 1987. *Historia de la música en México*. Mexico City: Gobierno del Estado de México.

Sánchez Castillo, Julio César. 2001. *Producción marimbística de Guatemala*. Serie Comunicación Cultural, Guatemala. Guatemala City: Guatemaltecade Autores y Compositores.

Schechter, John M. 1992. *The indispensable harp: Historical development, modern roles, configurations, and performance practices in Ecuador and Latin America*. Kent: Kent State University Press.

———. 1998. Ecuador. In *The Garland encyclopedia of world music*. Vol. 2, *South America, Mexico, Central America, and the Caribbean*, ed. Dale A. Olsen and Daniel E. Sheehy, 413–33. New York: Garland Publishing.

———. 1999. Beyond region: Transnational and transcultural traditions. In *Music in Latin American culture: Regional traditions*, ed. John M. Schechter, 425–57. New York: Schirmer Books.

Schieffelin, Edward. 1976. *The sorrow of the lonely and the burning of the dancers*. New York: St. Martin's Press.

———. 1985. The cultural analysis of depression affect: An example from Papua New Guinea. In *Culture and depression*, ed. A. Kleinman and B. Good, 168–82. Berkeley and Los Angeles: University of California Press.

———. 1995. On failure and performance: Throwing the medium out of the séance. In *The performance of healing*, ed. C. Laderman and M. Roseman, 59–90. New York: Routledge.

Schneider, Albrecht. 1991. Psychological theory and comparative musicology. In *Comparative musicology and anthropology of music: Essays on the history of ethnomusicology*, ed. Bruno Nettl and Philip V. Bohlman, 293–317. Chicago: University of Chicago Press.

Schultze, Jena. 1954. La vida y las creencias de los indios Quichés de Guatemala. *Anales de la Sociedad de Geografía e Historia de Guatemala* 20 (1): 145–60.

Scott, James C. 1976. *The moral economy: Rebellion and subsistence in southeast Asia.* New Haven: Yale University Press.

Scruggs, T. M. 1998a. Nicaragua. In *The Garland encyclopedia of world music.* Vol. 2, *South America, Mexico, Central America, and the Caribbean,* ed. Dale A. Olsen and Daniel E. Sheehy, 747–69. New York: Garland Publishing.

———. 1998b. Honduras. In *The Garland encyclopedia of world music.* Vol. 2, *South America, Mexico, Central America, and the Caribbean,* ed. Dale A. Olsen and Daniel E. Sheehy, 738–46. New York: Garland Publishing.

———. 1998c. Miskitu. In *The Garland encyclopedia of world music.* Vol. 2, *South America, Mexico, Central America, and the Caribbean,* ed. Dale A. Olsen and Daniel E. Sheehy, 659–65. New York: Garland Publishing.

———. 1998d. Cultural capital, appropriate transformations, and transfer by appropriation in western Nicaragua: *El baile de la marimba. Latin American Music Review* 19 (1): 1–30.

———. 1999a. Let's enjoy as Nicaraguans: The use of music in the construction of a Nicaraguan national consciousness. *Ethnomusicology* 43 (2): 297–321.

———. 1999b. Central America: Marimba and other musics of Guatemala and Nicaragua. In *Music in Latin American culture: Regional traditions,* ed. John M. Schechter, 80–125. New York: Schirmer Books.

Seeger, Anthony. 1987. *Why Suyá sing: A musical anthropology of an Amazonian people.* Cambridge: Cambridge University Press.

———. 1992. Ethnomusicology and music law. *Ethnomusicology* 36 (3): 345–60.

Seeger, Charles. 1977. *Studies in musicology, 1935–1975.* Berkeley and Los Angeles: University of California Press.

SEGEPLAN. 1994. *Plan marco de desarrollo del departamento de Baja Verapaz.* Guatemala City: SEGEPLAN/GTZ.

Sherman, William L. 1979. *Forced native labor in sixteenth-century Central America.* Lincoln: University of Nebraska Press.

Siegel, Morris. 1941. Religion in western Guatemala: A product of acculturation. *American Anthropologist,* n.s. 43: 62–76.

Singer, Milton. 1958. The great tradition in a metropolitan center: Madras. *Journal of American Folklore* 71: 347–88.

Smith, Carol A. 1984. Local history in global context: Social and economic transitions in western Guatemala. *Comparative Studies in Society and History* 26 (2): 193–228.

———. 1987. Culture and community: The language of class in Guatemala. In *The year left 2: An American socialist yearbook,* ed. Mike Davis, Manning Marable, Fred Pfeil, and Michael Sprinker, 197–217. London: Verso.

———, ed. 1990. *Guatemalan Indians and the state, 1540 to 1988.* Austin: University of Texas Press.

Smith, Ronald. 1998. Panama. In *The Garland encyclopedia of world music.* Vol. 2, *South America, Mexico, Central America, and the Caribbean,* ed. Dale A. Olsen and Daniel E. Sheehy, 770–85. New York: Garland Publishing.

Smith, Sandra. 1998. Kuna. In *The Garland encyclopedia of world music.* Vol. 2, *South America, Mexico, Central America, and the Caribbean,* ed. Dale A. Olsen and Daniel E. Sheehy, 637–49. New York: Garland Publishing.

Stanford, Thomas. 1984a. *El son Mexicano*. Mexico City: Fondo de Cultura Económica.

———. 1984b. La música popular de México. In *La música de México I, Historia*. Vol. 5, *Periodo Contemporáneo (1958–1980)*, ed. Julio Estrada, 7–78. Mexico City: Universidad Nacional Autónoma de México.

Stevenson, Robert. 1986. La música en el México de los siglos XVI a XVII. In *La música de México I, Historia*. Vol. 2, *Periodo Virreinal (1530–1810)*, ed. Julio Estrada, 7–74. Mexico City: Universidad Nacional Autónoma de México.

Stigberg, Daniel. 1986. Son chapin. In *The new Harvard dictionary of music*, ed. Don Randel, 767. Cambridge: Belknap Press of Harvard University Press.

Stokes, Martin. 1994. Place, exchange, and meaning: Black Sea musicians in the west of Ireland. In *Ethnicity, identity, and music: The musical construction of place*, ed. Martin Stokes, 97–115. Oxford: BERG.

Stoll, David. 1990. *Is Latin America turning Protestant? The politics of evangelical growth*. Berkeley and Los Angeles: University of California Press.

———. 1993. *Between two armies in the Ixil towns of Guatemala*. New York: Columbia University Press.

Stone, Ruth M. 1981. Toward a Kpelle conceptualization of music performance. *Journal of American Folklore* 94 (2): 188–206.

Stone, Ruth M., and Verlon L. Stone. 1981. Event, feedback, and analysis: Research media in the study of music events. *Ethnomusicology* 25 (2): 215–26.

Tánchez Coutiño, Jesus Eduardo. 1998. *La música en Guatemala: Algunos músicos y compositores*. Guatemala City, by author.

Tarn, Nathaniel, and Martin Prechtel. 1986. Constant inconstancy: The feminine principle in Atiteco mythology. In *Symbol and meaning beyond the closed community: Essays in Mesoamerican ideas*, ed. Gary Gossen, 173–84. New York: Institute for Mesoamerican Studies.

Taussig, Michael. 1980. *The devil and commodity fetishism in South America*. Chapel Hill: University of North Carolina Press.

Tax, Sol. 1941. World view and social relations in Guatemala. *American Anthropologist* 43 (1): 27–42.

———. 1953. *Penny capitalism: A Guatemala Indian economy*. Washington, D.C.: U.S. Government Printing Office.

Taylor, B. William. 1979. *Drinking, homicide, and rebellion in colonial Mexican villages*. Stanford: Stanford University Press.

Tedlock, Barbara. 1981. Quiché Maya dream interpretation. *Ethos* 9 (4): 313–30.

———. 1990. *Time and the highland Maya*. Albuquerque: University of New Mexico Press.

———. 1991. From participant observation to the observation of participation: The emergence of narrative ethnography. *Journal of Anthropological Research* 47 (spring): 69–93.

Tedlock, Dennis, trans. 1985. *Popul Vuh: The definitive edition of the Mayan book of the dawn of life and the glories of gods and kings*. New York: Simon and Schuster.

_____. 1986. Creation in the Popol Vuh: A hermeneutical approach. In *Symbol and meaning beyond the closed community: Essays in Mesoamerican ideas*, ed. Gary Gossen, 77–82. New York: Institute for Mesoamerican Studies.

Teletor, Celso Narciso. 1945. Bailes que representan los indígenas en la Baja Verapaz. *Anales de la Sociedad de Geografía e Historia* 20 (1): 51–52.

_____. 1955. *Apuntes para una monografía de Rabinal y algo de nuestro folclor*. Guatemala City: Editorial del ministerio de educación pública.

Tello, Aurelio. 1990. *Archivo musical de la catedral de Oaxaca: Catálogo*. Mexico City: Cenidim.

_____. 2001. *Cancionero musical de Gaspar Fernández*. Mexico City: Cenidim.

Thompson, Paul. 1991. *The voice of the past: Oral history*. Oxford: Oxford University Press.

Tolbert, Elizabeth. 1992. Theories of meaning and music cognition: An ethnomusicological approach. *World of Music* 34 (3): 7–21.

Trouillot, Michel-Rolph. 1986. The price of indulgence. *Social Analysis* 19 (Aug.): 85–89.

Tumin, Melvin M. 1952. *Caste in a peasant society: A case study in the dynamics of caste*. Princeton: Princeton University Press.

Turino, Thomas. 1991. The history of a Peruvian panpipe style and the politics of interpretation. In *Ethnomusicology and modern music history*, ed. Stephen Blum, Philip V. Bohlman, and Daniel M. Neuman, 121–38. Urbana: University of Illinois Press.

_____. 1999. Signs of imagination, identity, and experience: A Peircian semiotic theory for music. *Ethnomusicology* 43 (2): 221–55.

_____. 2003. Nationalism and Latin American music: Selected case studies and theoretical considerations. *Latin American Music Review* 24 (2): 169–209.

Turner, Terence. 1986. Production, exploitation, and social consciousness in the "Peripheral Situation." *Social Analysis* 19 (Aug.): 91–115.

Turner, Victor. 1979. *Process, performance, and pilgrimage: A study in comparative symbology*. New Delhi: Concept Publishing.

_____. 1984. Liminality and the performance genres. In *Rite, drama, festival, spectacle: Rehearsals toward a theory of cultural performance*, ed. John J. MacAloon, 19–41. Philadelphia: Institute for the Study of Human Issues.

_____. 1986. *The anthropology of performance*. New York: PAJ Publications.

Tzian, Leopoldo. 1994. *Mayas y ladinos en cifras: El caso de Guatemala*. Guatemala City: Cholsamaj.

United Nations. 1995. *Acuerdo sobre identidad y derechos de los pueblos indígenas*. Guatemala City: Cholsamaj.

Usselmann, Pierre. 1979. Les milieux physiques des environs de Rabinal. In *Cahiers de la R. C. P. 500 No. 1: Rabinal et la vallée moyenne du rio Chixoy, Baja Verapaz–Guatemala*, 9–16. Paris: Centre National de la Recherche Scientifique, Institut d'Ethnologie.

Van der Lee, Pedro. 1995. Zarabanda: Esquemas rítmicos de acompañamiento en 6/8. *Latin American Music Review* 16 (2): 199–220.

Van Gennep, A. 1960. *The rites of passage*. Chicago: University of Chicago Press.

Vansina, Jan. 1973. *Oral tradition*. Harmondsworth: Penguin Books.

_____. 1985. *Oral tradition as history*. Madison: University of Wisconsin Press.

Vela, David. 1958. *Information on the marimba*, trans. and ed. Vida Chenoweth. Auckland: Institute Press.

Vogt, Evon Z. 1976. *Tortillas for the gods: A symbolic analysis of Zinacanteco rituals*. Cambridge: Harvard University Press.

Wade, Peter. 1994. Man the hunter: Gender and violence in music and drinking contexts in Colombia. In *Sex and violence: Issues of representation and experience*, ed. Penelope Harvey and Peter Gow, 115–37. London: Routledge.

Wagley, Charles. 1941. *Economics of a Guatemalan village*. Menasha, Wisc.: American Anthropological Association.

———. 1949. *The social and religious life of a Guatemalan village*. Menasha, Wisc.: American Anthropological Association.

Wallis, Roy, and Steve Bruce. 1992. Secularization: The orthodox model. In *Religion and modernization: Sociologists and historians debate the secularization thesis*, ed. Steve Bruce, 9–30. Oxford: Clarendon Press.

Warren, B. Kay. 1992. *The symbolism of subordination: Indian identity in a Guatemalan town*. Austin: University of Texas Press.

Watanabe, John B. 1994. *Mayan saints and souls in a changing world*. Austin: University of Texas Press.

Waterman, Christopher A. 1991. Jùjú history: Toward a theory of sociomusical practice. In *Ethnomusicology and modern music history*, ed. Stephen Blum, Philip V. Bohlman, and Daniel M. Neuman, 49–67. Chicago: University of Chicago Press.

Wilson, Richard. 1995. *Maya resurgence in Guatemala: Q'eqchi' experiences*. Norman: University of Oklahoma Press.

Woolf, Rosemary. 1972. *The English mystery plays*. Berkeley and Los Angeles: University of California Press.

Wright, Ronald. 1985. *Time among the Maya: Travels in Belize, Guatemala, and Mexico*. London: Bodley Head.

Yurchenco, Henrietta. 1980. Review of *Information on the marimba*, by David Vela, *Ethnomusicology* 24 (1): 125–26.

Zemp, Hugo. 1978. "Are" are classification of musical types and instruments. *Ethnomusicology* 22 (1): 37–68.

———. 1979. Aspects of "are" are musical theory. *Ethnomusicology* 23 (1).

Zur, Judith. 1995. The psychological effect of impunity: The language of denial." In *Impunity in Latin America*, ed. Rachel Sieder, 57–72. London: Institute of Latin American Studies.

———. 1998. *Violent memories: Mayan war widows of Guatemala*. Boulder: Westview Press.

Index

Sergio Navarrete Pellicer is Professor and Researcher at the Centro de Investigaciones y Estudios Superiores en Antropología Social (CIESAS) in Oaxaca, Mexico.